Mozambique

Mozambique

The Tortuous Road to Democracy

João M. Cabrita

First published 2000 by
PALGRAVE
Houndmills, Basingstoke, Hampshire RG21 6XS and
175 Fifth Avenue, New York, N. Y. 10010
Companies and representatives throughout the world

PALGRAVE is the new global academic imprint of
St. Martin's Press LLC Scholarly and Reference Division and
Palgrave Publishers Ltd (formerly Macmillan Press Ltd).

ISBN 0–333–92001–5

This book is printed on paper suitable for recycling and made from fully managed and sustained forest sources.

A catalogue record for this book is available from the British Library.

Library of Congress Cataloging-in-Publication Data
Cabrita, Joao M., 1953–
    Mozambique : the tortuous road to democracy / Joao M. Cabrita.
       p. cm.
    Includes bibliographical references (p.) and index.
    ISBN 0–333–92001–5 (cloth)
    1. Mozambique—History—Revolution, 1964–1975. 2. Mozambique–
–History—Independence and Civil War, 1975–1994. 3. Democracy–
–Mozambique. 4. FRELIMO. 5. RENAMO (Organization) I. Title.
    DT3387 .C33 2000
    967.9—dc21
                                                          00–040457

10   9   8   7   6   5   4   3   2   1
09   08   07   06   05   04   03   02   01   00

Printed and bound in Great Britain by
Antony Rowe Ltd, Chippenham, Wiltshire

Contents

Part III   Resistance

Part IV   The Turning Point

Part V   Rumours of Peace

Part VI   Foreign Intervention

List of Tables

List of Maps

Acknowledgements

In researching for this book, I counted on the support of a great many people. Listing them in a sequence similar to the book's chronological order, I would like to thank Armando Khembo dos Santos for introducing me to several members of the exiled Mozambican community in Kenya, notably Fanuel Mahluza, Manuel Lisboa Tristão and Afonso Kantelu, who, like Santos, gave me a valuable insight into the founding of Frelimo and developments leading to Mozambique's independence. Lawe Laweki, Francisco Nota Moisés and Joaquim Njanje provided more information on Frelimo's 1967–68 student crisis.

Barnabé Ngauze Lucas introduced me to a number of sources in Maputo, and on my behalf researched for data and facts. Also in Maputo,Renamo chief whip Raúl Manuel Domingos referred me to Adriano Faustino, through whom I met Hermínio Morais, Vareia Manje, Filipe Augusto, John Kupenga, Chinagana Celestino, Amade Viajem, Olímpio Cambona, Francisco Manuel, Henrique Damião, Manuel Mussindo, Manuel Rudolfo, Virgílio Tomo, Martins Gamito Wizimane, Manuel da Maia and Anselmo Víctor who went out of their way in helping me to reconstruct specific events in the country's civil war.

I would also like to thank Frank M Machak, Casey Dowell and Karla M Kaplan of the Office of Freedom of Information at the State Department in Washington for handling the request submitted on my behalf by Hilary Andersson for the release of classified documentation relating to Eduardo Mondlane and Frelimo; Suzanne K Forbes and Stuart Culy of the John Fitzgerald Kennedy Library, and Andrew Walker and John E Haynes of the Manuscript Division of the Library of Congress in Washington for additional documentation on Mondlane and Frelimo; Moore Crossey and William R Massa, Jr of the African Collection and Manuscripts and Archives of the Yale University Library for photocopies of the Immanuel Wallerstein Collection of Political Ephemera on Mondlane and Frelimo; Lesbia O Varona, Cuban Bibliographer, Cuban Heritage Collection at the University of Miami Library, for materials on Che Guevara's stay in the Congo and how it impacted on Frelimo and its then leader; and the staff members of the Arquivo Histórico de Moçambique and Centro de Estudos Africanos libraries in Maputo for their varied assistance.

A special thanks to Joele and Carla and others who reviewed the manuscript and advised on ways of enhancing its style and format.

The views and interpretation of events expressed in this book are mine and do not reflect any other position, official or otherwise.

List of Abbreviations

AMM	Associação Académia de Moçambique
ADEV	Associação Desportiva Estrela Vermelha
AIM	Agência de Informação de Moçambique
Amodeg	Associação Moçambicana de Desmobilizados de Guerra
ANC	African National Congress
BMATT	British Military Advisory and Training Team
BO	Brigada de Operações
BOSS	Bureau of State Security
BTI	Brigada Técnica de Investigações
CAIL	Complexo Agro-Industrial do Limpopo
CIM	Contra-Inteligência Militar
CIO	Central Intelligence Organization
CONCP	Conferência das Organizações Nacionalistas das Colónias Portuguesas
Coremo	Comité Revolucionário de Moçambique
DGS	Direcção Geral de Segurança
DIP	Departamento de Informação e Propaganda
DMI	Department of Military Intelligence
DPCCN	Departamento de Prevenção e Combate às Calamidades Naturais
DSL	Defense Systems Limited
DTIP	Departamento do Trabalho Ideológico do Partido
GD	Grupo Dinamizador
GE	Grupos Especiais
GEP	Grupos Especiais Pára-quedistas
GLCB	Grupo de Luta Contra Bandidos
GVP	Grupos de Vigilância Popular
FAM	Forças Armadas de Moçambique
FLNA	Frente de Libertação Nacional de Angola
Frelimo	Frente de Libertação de Moçambique
Fumo	Frente Unida Democrática de Moçambique
Funipamo	Frente Unida Anti-imperialista Popular Africana de Moçambique
ICS	Instituto de Comunicação Social
IM	Instituto Moçambicano
INLD	Instituto Nacional do Livro e do Disco

MAA	Makonde African Association
MANC	Mozambique African National Congress
MANU	Mozambique African National Union
MFA	Movimento das Forças Armadas
MML	Movimento Moçambique Livre
MPLA	Movimento Popular de Libertação de Angola
ONJ	Organização Nacional de Jornalistas
PAIGC	Partido Africano para a Independência da Guiné e Cabo Verde
PCN	Partido de Coligação Nacional
PIC	Polícia de Investigação Criminal
PIDE	Polícia Internacional e de Defesa do Estado
PRM	Partido Revolucionário de Moçambique
Remo	Resistência Moçambicana
Renamo	Resistência Nacional Moçambicana
SADF	South African Defense Force
SAPA	South African Press Association
SARDC	Southern Africa Research and Documentation Centre
SAS	Special Air Service
SIIP	Serviço de Informação Interna do Partido
SMO	Serviço Militar Obrigatório
Snasp	Serviço Nacional de Segurança Popular
Socimo	Sociedade Comercial e Industrial de Moçambique
TANU	Tanganyika African National Union
TIS	Tanzania Intelligence Service
TPDF	Tanzania People's Defense Force
Udenamo	União Democrática Nacional de Moçambique
Unami	União Nacional Africana de Moçambique Independente
UNAR	União Nacional Africana de Rumbézia
UNHCR	United Nations High Commissioner for Refugees
UNITA	União Nacional para a Independência Total de Angola
UPA	União dos Povos de Angola
ZANU	Zimbabwe African National Union
ZNA	Zimbabwe National Army

Map 1 — Mozambique
Designed by Haider-Soft

Introduction

In October 1992, the Frelimo government of Mozambique and the Renamo guerrilla movement signed a peace accord that ended a 16-year civil war. At the root of the conflict, which broke out not long after the country gained independence from Portugal in 1975, lay the totalitarian regime imposed by Frelimo and the nature of its political, economic and social program. The war was inevitable, given Frelimo's conflictual past.

Ever since its founding, Frelimo has been at odds with itself and those it seeks to rule. The pattern of internal dissent, persecution and physical elimination of members and opponents that characterized the liberation movement during the years of exile continued after independence, except now in far larger proportions as Frelimo became the ruling party. The government's foreign policy, notably its decision to challenge some of its neighbours militarily, paved the way for foreign intervention in Mozambique, thus at the same time providing a channel for the frustrations of dissatisfied nationals.

A clear understanding of the causes of the 1976–92 civil war requires an exploration of events preceding and following independence. Reading between the lines of the often cryptic Frelimo papers and interviewing some of its founders and former members has been an invaluable aspect of reconstructing events and, indeed, reinterpreting the official view. Of priceless importance in this regard is a set of about 150 documents obtained from the United States under the Freedom of Information Act. In these, Frelimo's early history is at times narrated in the first person by Eduardo Mondlane, a Mozambican academic living in the United States who wished to control a revolution started in his absence, only to find himself in conflict with not only his colonial enemies, but his own people.

New light is shed on Mozambique's post-independence period, particularly the circumstances in which resistance to the established order arose. Those who organized resistance against the Frelimo government give an account of their movement's formation and how it evolved politically and militarily.

The dynamics of the war, the government's efforts to resolve the conflict militarily, and how the government eventually opted for a political settlement are reappraised.

Part I
A Tradition of Conflict

1
Marriage of Convenience

In the relatively short existence of Portugal as a Republic, the Armed Forces intervened in the country's political affairs twice. After the monarchy fell in 1910, Portugal entered a period of political instability, which over the next 16 years saw 44 changes of government (an average of three governments every year), eight presidents and 20 uprisings.[1] This prompted the Armed Forces to stage a coup in May 1926. Ultimately, the coup led to a Fascist dictatorship, which ruled Portugal for nearly 50 years, first under António Salazar, and then, upon his departure for health reasons in 1968, by Marcello Caetano.

The Armed Forces support for the regime which stemmed from the 1926 coup was unquestionable, save the occasional signs of dissatisfaction, which the loyalists suppressed. The situation changed when the Portuguese government, faced with a war in three of its African colonies, called upon the Armed Forces to play a more active role in the defense of what the regime saw as a 'multicontinental nation', stretching from Minho in northern Portugal, to Timor in Asia. Rather than being confined to barracks or used in extraneous governmental tasks, the Armed Forces were suddenly faced with a new reality altogether. Owing to their direct contact with the colonial wars, the Armed Forces began to change their perception of nationhood.

As the wars gained momentum, it became clear that the Armed Forces were heading for a collapse. Portugal's position had become critical in Guinea-Bissau where Amílcar Cabral's PAIGC guerrillas had made great inroads. Yet, the Portuguese government refused to consider a political settlement because it believed that that would inevitably pave the way to the crumbling of its empire. As Prime Minister Caetano told General António de Spínola, then Guinea-Bissau's governor general and commander-in-chief of the Armed Forces stationed there, he would prefer a

3

withdrawal through an honorable military defeat than an agreement with terrorists.[2]

For the Armed Forces, the longer they stayed in Africa, the greater the chance of being caught in a quagmire, with humiliating consequences. This they were not prepared to let happen, especially after the 1961 events in Portuguese India. The Salazar regime preferred to sacrifice Portugal's military presence in Goa, Damão and Diu than to submit to the sovereignty demands of India. In their view, the Portuguese Armed Forces, as an elite institution, were being threatened by the stubbornness of the country's politicians. The regime's continuation, which the Armed Forces had propped up for the last 48 years, was no longer a viable proposition. Thus, the Armed Forces Movement (MFA) brought down the Caetano government on 25 April 1974.

Initially, the new Portugal was divided into three factions. One was embodied in General Spínola's call for a Lusophone federation. The second was for the colonies' immediate independence so as to permit Portugal's integration into the European Union. The third, Marxist-oriented MFA officers, merely wanted power transferred to the nationalist organizations of Guinea-Bissau, Angola and Mozambique. In the ensuing power struggle, a younger generation of officers gained the upper hand, thwarting Spínola's neocolonial alternative.

The colonial crisis was settled in the traditionally undemocratic manner of Portuguese institutions, of which the apparently progressive MFA was an integral part. After all, the genesis of the MFA had not been ideological, but classist in the sense that its leaders were brought together by a dispute over promotions. Without a sufficient officer corps to lead the colonial wars, the Caetano government decided to promote non-career officers over professional soldiers, causing unrest and dissatisfaction within the military establishment.

No arrangements were made to ensure a democratic basis for the future African countries. Power was transferred to the nationalists, who were regarded as the authentic representatives of the people, a claim based on their years of fighting for independence.

In Mozambique's case, power was transferred to the Frente de Libertação de Moçambique (Frelimo), under the terms of the Lusaka Accord of 7 September 1974. The accord had been partially negotiated between MFA and Frelimo officials without the knowledge of the Portuguese president, and the foreign minister, Mário Soares. Spínola was unaware that the MFA issued orders to the Portuguese Armed Forces in Mozambique to disengage from operations against Frelimo and withdraw. Other groups were excluded from independence negotiations because the MFA regarded them as either puppets or last-minute opportunists, although no political opposition had been allowed in Portugal and in the colonies during the deposed regime. Coremo, or Comité Revolucionário de Moçambique, a Frelimo dissident guerrilla movement, was not invited to the peace talks. On 25 June 1975, the colony became the People's Republic of Mozambique. No provisions were made for elections.

The formation of Frelimo was announced for the first time in Accra on 29 May 1962 by the União Democrática Nacional de Moçambique (Udenamo) and the Mozambique African National Union (MANU).[3] For several months, the two organizations of exiled Mozambicans had been holding unity talks in their Tanzania base. A third organization, the União Nacional Democrática de Moçambique Independente (Unami), joined before Frelimo's official debut in Dar es Salaam in June 1962. It was more a marriage of convenience imposed on the Mozambicans than a genuine united front against Portuguese colonialism, ultimately contributing to divisions within the colony's independence movement. Interference by African governments with different agendas for continental issues had been a determining factor in the marriage.

Formed in Rhodesia in November 1960, Udenamo was the first of the three Mozambican independence movements to advocate violence to bring about independence. Udenamo was influenced by Zimbabwean politics, and its members had a history of involvement with Joshua Nkomo's National Democratic Party. Adelino Gwambe, a 20-year-old Mozambican from Inhambane, led the organization. As a campaign for the independence of Mozambique could not be waged from white-ruled Rhodesia, Gwambe and his followers left for Tanzania, where, in view of its forthcoming independence, Udenamo would be better positioned to wage an armed campaign against the Portuguese.

Once based in Dar es Salaam, Udenamo continued to attract Mozambicans. In April 1961, Udenamo's vice-president, Fanuel Mahluza, wrote to Eduardo Mondlane, a US educated Mozambican anthropologist working for the UN Trusteeship Council in New York, inviting him to join the organization. Mondlane did not accept the invitation. He had his own agenda, which did not conform to Udenamo's. Mondlane, who had established close links with the Kennedy administration, had just completed a tour of Mozambique, where, in addition to the red-carpet treatment accorded to him by a Portuguese government eager to win him over, he saw that nationalist sentiment was strong.

During a two-day meeting at the State Department in Washington, DC in May, Mondlane gave a full account of his February-March 1961 stay in Mozambique.[4] Although Mondlane had successfully applied in 1960 to be transferred from the UN Trusteeship Council to the Addis Ababa-based Economic Commission for Africa, he now wanted the United States to locate a non-UN position for him, which would permit him to support his family while carrying on nationalist activities, and to give him funds to operate a nationalist organization that would seek a non-violent solution in Mozambique. Mondlane was concerned over the possibility of a war being waged from Tanzania because, as he put it in a report on his Mozambique tour given to US Undersecretary of State Chester Bowles, 'one shudders at the consequences of such an eventuality, judging by Portugal's reaction to a similar situation in Angola'. Mondlane suggested in his report that the

> United States should be in a position to encourage Portugal to accept the principle of self-determination for the African peoples under her control; set target dates and take steps towards self-government and independence by 1965; and help formulate and finance policies of economic, educational, and political development for the people of Portuguese Africa and to prepare them for an independence with responsibility.[5]

Mondlane struck a favourable chord in the State Department. In a note to National Security Adviser McGeorge Bundy at the White House, Bowles described Mondlane as 'a moderate person with the potential for top leadership in Mozambique'.[6] Reporting on the May meeting at the State Department, William Wight, Jr, the deputy director of the East African Division in the Department, noted that Mondlane 'seemed genuinely friendly to the United States and genuinely desirous of seeking a non-violent solution in Mozambique if such a thing were possible'.[7]

Mondlane not only saw himself as leader of Mozambique's independence cause, but also the unifying force of all anti-Portuguese liberation movements, although an organization seeking that goal had already been established in Casablanca in April 1961 as the Conferência das Organizações Nacionalistas das Colónias Portuguesas, CONCP.

During another meeting at the State Department in February 1962, Mondlane said he did not regard the ideological schisms within the various nationalist movements opposed to Portugal as a stumbling block for his overall plan. He knew Mário de Andrade, a leading member of Angola's MPLA movement, from his student days in Portugal as a non-communist. The other MPLA members as well as the PAIGC were, as he put it, 'salvageable' from their communist stance.[8]

This view differed from that of Marcelino dos Santos who had joined Udenamo in April 1961. A 32–year-old Mozambican mulatto,[9] Marcelino dos Santos studied electronic engineering in Lisbon. There he came into contact with students from other Portuguese colonies, notably Lúcio Lara and Agostinho Neto of Angola, as well as Rui Nazaré and Orlando Costa, two intellectuals from India, who, he admits, had a profound influence on his political thinking. His stay in Portugal was cut short after quarrelling with a Portuguese lecturer during a test. Marcelino dos Santos left for France in 1951 to continue his studies, but then changed to political science. He moved not only in French leftist circles, but in Eastern bloc countries as well. In 1953 he attended the Bucharest youth festival, and in the following year visited China where he met Chou En Lai. In 1955 he traveled to Warsaw for another youth festival. He was in Moscow for the 1957 World Youth Festival, causing a row with the Portuguese Communist Party delegation whom he accused of consisting of agents of the Portuguese political police, the PIDE.[10] Marcelino dos Santos was expelled from France in January 1960, claiming the French had acted at the request of PIDE. He moved to Morocco, becoming involved in the preparations for the founding of CONCP. In that capacity, he invited Gwambe to represent Udenamo at the CONCP's founding conference.

Gwambe's decision to appoint Marcelino dos Santos there and then as Udenamo's deputy secretary general undoubtedly provided the organization with its most capable intellectual and organizer, but also with a dedicated Stalinist. His appointment was to have far-reaching consequences not only in the subsequent armed struggle against the Portuguese, but also in independent Mozambique. It was Marcelino dos Santos who drafted Udenamo's constitution, structuring it under the principles of 'democratic centralism'.

As Udenamo expanded its links further afield, its leaders saw signs of uneasiness on the part of their hosts. Tanzania's Julius Nyerere government was concerned over the organization's links with Ghana, established through the Ghanaian Bureau of African Affairs when Udenamo operated from Rhodesia. Ghana, the first country to assist Udenamo financially, extended regular invitations for the organization's senior officials to visit Accra. It funded Gwambe's visits to Conakry and Helsinki, and provided an office for the Udenamo representative in Accra. The Tanzanians viewed Ghana's Kwame Nkrumah as too radical a leader for their taste. They resented what they believed to be Nkrumah's blatant effort to bring the Mozambican nationalists under his sphere of influence. Fearing that he could in fact pose a threat to Nyerere's desire to become the champion of southern Africa's nationalist cause, the Tanzanians took action.

The Nyerere government opted for MANU, essentially an organization of Makonde people with roots in Mozambique's Cabo Delgado province, bordering Tanzania. Some of its members had been born and reared in Tanzania, others in Zanzibar and Kenya. In the early 1960s, there were an estimated 250 000 Mozambicans, notably Makonde, living in Tanzania. They worked primarily in plantations, but were also involved in trade union and political activities. Rashidi Kawawa, who became secretary general of the ruling Tanzanian party, TANU, was a Makonde from Mozambique. Oscar Kambona, the Tanzania home affairs and foreign minister, was another Mozambican. A Mozambican Makonde was the president of the Tanganyika Territory African Civil Service Association. Mozambican Makonde in the three countries were affiliated with the Makonde African Association (MAA). In Cabo Delgado itself, the Makonde campaigned politically as the Sociedade dos Africanos de Moçambique, and were behind the events that preceded the Mueda massacre of June 1960.

In January 1961, the MAA branches in Dar es Salaam, Mombasa and Zanzibar, led respectively by Matthew Mmole, Samuly Diankali and Ali Madebe, merged as MANU. The presidency and vice-presidency of the new party were given to Mmole and Lawrence Malinga Millinga, both born in Tanzania. The similarities between MANU and TANU were not only in the name. Some in MANU aimed at the unification of Cabo Delgado with Tanzania for a greater Makonde homeland.

Udenamo felt that the prospect of an armed struggle looked unlikely. The Tanzanian government discontinued food supplies and other assistance that it had been giving Udenamo. Tanzania declared Adelino Gwambe *persona non grata* for stating in a news conference on the eve of that country's independence that arrangements had been made for Udenamo to start the armed struggle in Mozambique. He had to leave for Accra, but was allowed to return to Tanzania soon afterwards. When Ghana invited Udenamo to attend the May–June 1962 African Freedom Fighters Conference in Accra, the Tanzanians refused to issue travel documents to the Udenamo delegation. These had to be organized by the Ghanaian High Commission in Dar es Salaam.

It was not only the Tanzanian government that had grown distrustful of Nkrumah. Marcelino dos Santos was not at all impressed with Nkrumah for regarding him as not truly representative of the black people of Mozambique since he was a mulatto. To prevent a worsening of relations with Tanzania, and bearing in mind the strategic importance of that country for the attainment of Mozambique's independence, Marcelino dos Santos advised his fellow leaders to merge with MANU. Gwambe rejected the idea outright; Marcelino dos Santos reacted by threatening to leave Udenamo and join MANU. But at several meetings of Udenamo's Executive Committee held throughout October 1961, it was decided that, in order to overcome the prevailing situation, Udenamo and MANU should unite. In order to gain MANU's sympathy, Udenamo officials made use of their financial resources to virtually bribe members of the Makonde organization to join them. In another move, Udenamo included MANU leaders in its delegation to the African Freedom Fighters Conference in Accra.

At a ceremony held under the auspices of the Tanzanian government in Dar es Salaam on 24 May 1962, Udenamo and MANU finally 'decided to bring unity of all patriotic forces of Mozambique by means of forming a common front', pending the return of the respective leaders from Accra.[11] Much to the irritation of the Tanzanians, Gwambe told a news conference in Accra five days later that the decision to merge was in response to Nkrumah's call for the closing of ranks for the liberation of Africa.[12] As proposed by Mahluza, the front was to be known as the Frente de Libertação de Moçambique.

With unity talks between Udenamo and MANU under way, José Baltazar da Costa Chagonga, the leader of Unami, arrived in Dar es Salaam. In 1959, Chagonga had founded the Associação Nacional Africana de Moatize, ostensibly a cultural association of Moatize coal mineworkers as well as Mozambican migrants in Zambia, Malawi and Rhodesia. In reality, the association promoted nationalist ideals among its members. An advocate of peaceful change, Chagonga had been petitioning the Portuguese to review unsavoury labor practices in the colony. This resulted in his detention. Upon his release, Chagonga fled to Malawi where in May 1960 he renamed his organization Unami.

The joyful mood of the Mozambican nationalists while in Ghana contrasted sharply with the showdown in store for them in Dar es Salaam in the days preceding the official debut of Frelimo. Mondlane, who had resigned from his UN post to become a professor at New York's University of Syracuse, arrived in Dar es Salaam in the first half of June.

Discussing his planned trip to Tanzania with State Department officials in Washington on 8 February 1962, Mondlane reiterated his intention to lead the Mozambique independence movement, and that he would be willing to negotiate with Portugal, but could only accept 'the negotiations of equals'. Mondlane said he had approached Angola's

UPA guerrilla leader, Holden Roberto, to enlist the support of Tunisian President Habid Bourguiba for the movement he intended to lead. As Mondlane told the State Department officials, Bourguiba was deeply concerned with communist penetration in sub-Saharan Africa, and particularly worried by Soviet arms shipment to the area. Mondlane did not seem to regard Udenamo and MANU as a major obstacle to his plans. He saw Gwambe as a second-rate figure, and MANU a group artificially stimulated by the Tanzanians with no organization within Mozambique. Mondlane noted that any successful MANU-oriented insurrection in Mozambique would be an 'outside job', and might result in the cession of Cabo Delgado and Niassa to Tanzania.[13]

In Dar es Salaam, Mondlane encountered strong resistance to his plan among the Udenamo and MANU leaders. Gwambe was committed to taking upon himself the leadership of Frelimo and soon starting the war of independence with the backing of Ghana where Mozambicans had reportedly undergone military training. For Mondlane, time was running out. He had to be back at Syracuse before the end of June.

On 18 June, a despondent Mondlane called on Thomas Byrne, the acting American chargé d'affaires in Dar es Salaam, to report his dismay at Gwambe's complete commitment to Nkrumah and to communist bloc countries. Mondlane alleged that the Udenamo leader was a regular recipient of substantial funds from Ghana and the USSR, and that he had recently received $14 000 from the Ghanaians. Mondlane was also disturbed to learn that Mmole and his lieutenants were in Gwambe's pay. Mondlane realized that there was a degree of discontent among Udenamo's rank and file over the tight control that Gwambe had over the organization's financial resources. Mondlane informed the chargé d'affaires that he had raised this issue with Kambona, pointing out to him that a continuation of the existing arrangement, whereby Gwambe had ample resources while both the Udenamo and MANU treasuries were empty, meant that the Mozambique nationalist movement belonged to Gwambe and he in turn could deliver it to his Ghanaian and Russian paymasters. Mondlane urged Kambona to consider the advantage of securing funds from Western sources in order to free the Mozambique movement from Gwambe.[14]

Mondlane's recommendations were music to the Tanzanians' ears in view of their reluctance to have an organization based in their country, but under Ghanaian influence. Moreover, by this time the Tanzanians realized that of all the Mozambicans who had flocked to Dar es Salaam, Mondlane was the one who possessed the best qualities to head an independence movement: mature, well-educated, articulate, able to move in diplomatic circles, and committed to a negotiated settlement with Portugal, an option they initially preferred for Tanzania felt impotent to deal with possible Portuguese military retaliation.

To counter Gwambe's financial clout, on his way to Syracuse Mondlane planned to stop over in Cairo, Tunis, Geneva and London and raise funds. 'As soon as he reaches the United States', reported Byrne, 'Mr Mondlane plans to get in touch with Deputy Assistant Secretary [of State for African Affairs] Wayne Fredericks.'[15] Mondlane planned to be back in Dar es Salaam in September when he would make his final bid for the Frelimo leadership.

Subsequent developments enabled Mondlane to secure his position as Frelimo leader on 25 June. With Gwambe away in India between 17 and 23 June, Mondlane was able to rally the support of Mozambicans in Dar es Salaam, virtually unopposed. He reviewed his earlier position, and decided to meet Mozambicans in Dar es Salaam as a Udenamo member. Mondlane, who had always shown concern over the educational elevation of his fellow countrymen, lured Udenamo and MANU members to his side with genuine promises of scholarships in the United States. Until then, Gwambe had discouraged Mozambican refugees from contacting the American Embassy in Dar es Salaam for scholarship requests, claiming that Portuguese agents would kidnap them while en route to the United States. Still according to Byrne, Mondlane had informed him that he had persuaded the Ghanaians, through the Ghana High Commissioner in Dar es Salaam, of Gwambe's unsuitability as Frelimo leader. Mondlane also stated that Gwambe's lieutenants and MANU officials had promised to oppose Gwambe on condition that Mondlane found alternative sources of income to finance their activities.[16]

On 28 June, Mondlane made yet another call on chargé d'affaires Byrne, asking him to inform Fredericks of his desperate need for funds in order to consolidate Frelimo's independence from Ghanaian and Communist bloc countries. Mondlane added that he had spent over $1000 of his personal funds towards that goal.[17]

Mondlane's behind the scenes canvassing was a success. His name was included in the list of candidates to the presidency of Frelimo's Supreme Council due to be elected on 25 June. After Gwambe and Mmole had signed a declaration agreeing to transfer all assets owned and controlled by their organizations to the Supreme Council of Frelimo immediately after the election of this body, a 20-man ad hoc committee composed of an equal number of Udenamo and MANU members nominated Mondlane, Simango and Chagonga as candidates to the post. Gwambe

refused to stand for election as long as Mondlane was part of the organization.

Mondlane received 116 votes from a total of 135 ballots cast. Ethnic
considerations, more than his academic and professional qualifications,
prevailed in Mondlane's election. With Gwambe out of the race, Udenamo members from southern Mozambique preferred to have a southerner as Frelimo leader rather than Reverend Uria Simango, a Ndau from
the central region, despite the latter's long-standing membership of
Udenamo. Simango secured the vice-presidency of Frelimo, and other
Udenamo members gained key positions in the organization. David
Mabunda and Paulo Gumane received the posts of secretary general
and deputy secretary general respectively. The foreign affairs secretariat
was assigned to Marcelino dos Santos, and the defense and security
secretariat to João Munguambe with Filipe Magaia as his deputy. The
administration department was given to Silvério Nungo. Gumane's wife,
Priscilla, was appointed Women's League secretary. Leo Milás became
Frelimo's information and publicity secretary. Milás, who lived in the
United States and had established links with Udenamo shortly after the
organization surfaced in Dar es Salaam, accompanied Mondlane to
Tanzania. Mmole was elected treasurer, and Millinga became Frelimo's
executive secretary of the Scholarship Committee.

After the elections, Mondlane, in a move apparently to have Gwambe
removed from the scene, told Kambona that he and his wife, Janet, were
under surveillance of armed men owing allegiance to Gwambe, claiming
that the latter had informed the Portuguese of Mondlane's travelling
plans so that he could be abducted while in transit in Rome. The
Tanzanians ordered the arrest of Gwambe on 27 June, but fell short of
declaring him *persona non grata* again upon his release. Kambona assured
Mondlane that Gwambe would not be allowed to re-enter the country
once he left on 3 July to attend a World Peace Council meeting in
Moscow.

As for his relations with Ghana, Mondlane felt that they were bound
to improve since he was now the elected Frelimo leader. He told Byrne
that the Ghanaian High Commission in Tanzania had even invited him
to visit Accra, giving him air tickets.[18]

Byrne commented in a cable to the Department of State:

Dr Mondlane's position as leader of the Mozambique Liberation
Front appears at the moment to be strong. His future prospects will
depend to a great extent upon how successful he is in obtaining
money to carry on the party's activities here. Another as yet unclear

factor is the sincerity of Kambona's assurance of support. If Ghana is now shifting its support from Gwambe to Mondlane, the latter's position should be secure.[19]

2
Profile of a Leader

Eduardo Mondlane was born in 1920 of a family who were traditional rulers of the Chope people. He was educated by Calvinist Swiss missionaries who arranged for Mondlane to further his studies in South Africa, Portugal and the United States. Mondlane could not graduate from the Witwatersrand University because the South Africans refused to renew his visa. In 1950, he enrolled at the Lisbon University because the missionaries felt it would be advantageous for Mondlane to acquire the basis of Portuguese culture, which would help in his work once he returned to Mozambique.[20] But he did not stay in Lisbon long, pursuing instead his education in the United States where he obtained a doctorate in anthropology in 1960.

The Portuguese viewed Mondlane's departure for the United States in 1951 as the result of the US policy of wooing undergraduates from their colonies, rather than of Mondlane's anti-colonial stance. In fact, Mondlane took a moderate view of the low educational and health standards Portugal maintained in Mozambique. 'The most important reason' for this state of affairs, wrote Mondlane, was 'a material one: Not enough money', and that 'the Portuguese government (had) done everything in its power to eliminate disease in Mozambique'.[21]

In 1957, Mondlane joined the UN Trusteeship Council. He established cordial links with the Portuguese delegation at the United Nations, Portugal being only too keen to court him. Adriano Moreira, minister of the Portuguese colonies, whom Mondlane regarded as willing to introduce far-reaching changes to Portugal's African policy, recalls having arranged for a gold necklace to be delivered to the Mondlane couple as a birthday present for their son.[22]

Mondlane and his American wife now visited Mozambique after an 11-year absence. The Portuguese made a concerted effort to impress the couple. Mondlane, who arrived in Lourenço Marques in February 1961, attended a number of lavish functions held in his honor, socializing with senior government officials. At a sundowner in Chongoene beach, Mondlane sat next to the local chairman of Salazar's Fascist-styled União Nacional party. The state media covered the visit in a manner true to form, referring to Mondlane as 'the Portuguese professor', quoting him as saying that he was leaving Mozambique 'more Portuguese than he used to be'.[23]

Mondlane hinted to the Portuguese that he would like to be a university lecturer either in Mozambique or in Portugal. In Lisbon, en route to New York, Moreira offered him a position at the Institute of Tropical Medicine. Mondlane told Moreira that he would rather get the post by standard admission procedure. According to Moreira, 'Mondlane did not follow it up because he felt that I would not be able to stay in office longer'.[24]

Portugal's flirtation with Mondlane did not last long. With Mondlane already in the United States, his wife met Moreira in Lisbon to let him know that her husband would not be returning to either Mozambique or Portugal, considering the reforms of the Portuguese too limited. Nevertheless, in the years to come, Mondlane continued to hold Moreira in high esteem.[25]

Although he outmanoeuvred Gwambe in his bid for the Frelimo leadership, Mondlane never succeeded in fully consolidating his position in view of Frelimo's complex ideological and ethnic undercurrents, and different perceptions of how and when independence should be achieved. Mondlane favoured a negotiated settlement with Portugal, and believed that the West would exert pressure on Lisbon to resolve the colonial dispute peacefully. Other Frelimo officials supported immediate military action. Even when Mondlane opted for armed struggle, he preferred Frelimo not to undertake large-scale operations against the Portuguese until Frelimo and Tanzania would be able to contain Portuguese counter-attacks. Mondlane's distaste of violence attracted criticism, giving rise to claims that he was not committed to independence. His association with the United States, traditionally an ally of Portugal, strengthened this view. Certain quarters, which in principle would have backed any nationalist leader, instead openly opposed him. In addition to Ghana, Algeria and Cuba expressed dissatisfaction with Mondlane.

Mondlane's plan of leading Frelimo on a part-time basis soon foundered. Owing to his job, Mondlane wanted Frelimo's first congress, scheduled for September 1962, to be held in December. Given the pace of developments in Dar es Salaam, Mondlane compromised on 23–25

September. He applied for leave from Syracuse between January 1963 and February 1964. As an alternative source of income, Mondlane had suggested, before leaving for the Frelimo Congress, a Tanzanian job offer to Nyerere. He told Nyerere that:

> The alternative to this [...] is for me to resign from my current position, pack up and ask the world to send me and my family to Tanganyika. If by any chance some interested soul or government, which are very difficult to find, donated the required amount for the air fare to Dar, where would I lodge my family, and what would I feed them with, etc.?[26]

In August 1962, Gumane publicly embarrassed Mondlane, by expressing Frelimo's 'disgust (at) the action taken by the United States of America and other colonialist and imperialist countries at the United Nations on the case of Mozambique'. Afterwards, Gumane explained to the US Embassy that his statement was an attempt to deflect Gwambe's claims that Mondlane was an American stooge.[27]

In Cairo in the same month, Mmole and Gwambe issued a statement suggesting dual presidency of Udenamo and MANU leaders for Frelimo.[28] Gwambe denounced Mondlane as a traitor and as 'Mozambique's Tshombé'. In a letter to Frelimo members, Gwambe said he would never be part of Frelimo under Mondlane because he had 'proof that Mondlane (was) selling out Mozambique to the imperialists led by the United States of America'.[29]

Early in September, Millinga wrote an open letter to the American assistant secretary of state for African affairs, Mennen Williams, protesting the inconsistency between the US public stance on Africa and the American vote at the United Nations 'against resolutions calling to free Mozambique Africans from barbaric Portuguese rule'. Once again, Gumane apologized to the American Embassy, promising the censure of Millinga.[30]

Furthermore, Frelimo was facing difficulty in supporting its members financially. Frelimo could not support party officials in Tanzania, let alone delegates arriving for the September Congress. Eventually, money was obtained from the Ghanaian Embassy in Cairo, although the Ghanaians were under the impression that they were financing Gwambe's crusade against Mondlane.[31]

At the Congress, Marcelino dos Santos delivered the most militant speech. The constitution he had drafted for Udenamo was adopted by Frelimo, retaining its Marxist outlook.

Mondlane afterwards left for the United States, leaving the running of the party to Mabunda. He was to return to Tanzania only in March 1963. Meanwhile, internal dissent continued to plague the new organization. Mabunda and Gumane accused Santos of nepotism, a claim that was addressed by a Political Council meeting. Consequently, the two as well as João Munguambe and three other Frelimo members were expelled in January 1963. They left for Cairo, where Fanuel Malhuza, the Frelimo representative, welcomed them in his house. For this, he was expelled in March.[32]

In response to this purge, the former Frelimo members in Cairo decided to revive Udenamo as Udenamo–Moçambique, with Gumane as president. A party branch was opened in Zambia. Links were developed with Angola's UPA. Mondlane explained to an American Embassy official that this was because UPA leader Holden Roberto resented Frelimo for not recognizing his party as the sole Angolan independence movement.[33]

In May 1963, Frelimo expelled Mmole for his association with Gwambe. Based in Uganda, Gwambe had reorganized his party, calling it Udenamo–Monomotapa. Gwambe and Mmole formally announced the withdrawal of Udenamo and MANU from Frelimo and, on 21 May 1963, they constituted the Frente Unida Anti-Imperialista Popular Africana de Moçambique, Funipamo.[34] The coalition included the Mozambique African National Congress (MANC) which Peter Balamanja, a Malawian-born Mozambican, had founded in Rhodesia the year before.[35]

In Funipamo's view, Mondlane was delaying the armed independence struggle, disrupting relations among Mozambicans, and promoting tribalism. Funipamo felt that Frelimo was 'composed mainly of a clique of US-hired stooges', and that there was 'either a US conspiracy with Portugal or a US plot to replace Portugal through the back door'.[36] Funipamo disliked Mondlane's close links with the Kennedy administration, accusing him of having flown secretly to the United States in 1963.

It was clear that Mondlane was being closely monitored. Briefly returning to Tanzania in March 1963, he then returned to the United States. In mid-April, he met Wayne Fredericks and the attorney general, Robert Kennedy. According to Mennen Williams, President Kennedy shifted the responsibility of dealing with representatives of almost independent African states to the attorney general. As Williams noted:

There were some people that had a more revolutionary task that [President Kennedy] could not very well diplomatically see. But

Bobby saw them and Bobby helped him, helped us, helped them through overt and covert means and was sympathetic and helpful.[37]

Mondlane asked Robert Kennedy for assistance under the guise of a refugee program, stressing that others in Frelimo were seeking aid in Ghana, the USSR, and other places not attuned to American interests. Kennedy was impressed with Mondlane and sympathetic to his requests. In addition to referring the matter to National Security Adviser McGeorge Bundy, the attorney-general told Williams that Mondlane's 'program for refugees from his country would seem to merit our attention and help where feasible and I just wanted you to know of my interest'.[38] Williams, who came under criticism from the pro-Salazar element in the administration, felt relieved by Kennedy's action, telling the attorney-general that:

> your interest in Eduardo Mondlane can be an important link in keeping the United States in tune with the progress of American self-determination. For your interest and service, I am most grateful and I believe that when the whole story is written, our country will be too.[39]

According to James Symington, Robert Kennedy's administrative assistant who arranged the meeting, 'Mondlane need[ed] about $50 000 to keep the lid on his people and also stay on top'.[40] Consequently, Mondlane secured a $96 000 grant from the Ford Foundation of which US Defense Secretary Robert McNamara had been president.

Ghana was incensed over Mondlane's acceptance of the grant for the creation of the Instituto Moçambicano (IM), an educational establishment catering for Mozambican refugees in Tanzania. The IM worked closely with the African-American Institute. Betty King, a secretary with the African-American Institute, assisted Mrs Mondlane in the running of the IM. Harvard University volunteers also helped at the IM.[41]

This, coupled with Mondlane's decision to have Frelimo's military personnel trained in Algeria and Israel instead of Ghana, soured relations with Nkrumah. Inevitably, Accra's *Freedom Fighter* newspaper labeled Mondlane an 'imperialist stooge'.

Tanzanian officials were also concerned that Mondlane's *modus operandi* could lead to him losing control of Frelimo. H Bellege, TANU's acting deputy secretary general, told the American Embassy in Dar es Salaam that considerable comment was aroused by Mondlane living in a 'white man's hotel and spending more time with Europeans and Americans than with the Makonde membership of Frelimo'.[42] The Tanzanians were also acutely aware of Makonde apprehensions about Frelimo being led by Mondlane, a southerner. In the Makondes' view, southerners formed part of the colonial administration by virtue of their being assigned governmental and civil posts by the Portuguese in Cabo Delgado. Although the Portuguese could well have been promoting ethnic division, the fact was that southerners benefited more in terms of education and training due to the colonial administration being more strongly felt in the south of Mozambique.

Mondlane dismissed Bellege's criticism as springing from that of Gumane and Mabunda. However, he did check out of the hotel, only to settle in the plush Oyster Bay residential area. And as for allegations of misuse of funds leveled at Frelimo officials by a member of the organization, who even reported the matter to the Dar es Salaam police, Mondlane felt that 'the ordinary Frelimo member in Tanganyika had no right to object or inquire concerning the leadership's use of funds' because he 'contributes only "nickels and dimes"'.[43]

Mondlane's apparent inability to relate to the grass roots remained a cause for concern in the following years. The CIA commented in November 1965, that the Frelimo leader

> is a US-educated intellectual who has only a tenuous relationship with the Makondes, and it will be extremely difficult for him to build up dedication to a political cause among these largely primitive tribesmen...[44]

Mondlane seemed to have overlooked that, for Tanzanians, relations between black and whites were still taboo, even though he had seen how the Nyerere government had handled the case of two Portuguese Air Force officers who had defected to Frelimo in 1963. Like Hélder Martins in 1961, the two – Jacinto Veloso and João Ferreira – had to leave Dar es Salaam because of the colour of their skin. In the case of Ferreira, though, Mondlane had no qualms about his departure. The Frelimo leader told a US Embassy official that he was certain Ferreira was a communist.[45]

In late 1963, Baltazar Chagonga found himself in disagreement with Frelimo over the fate of a group of young Mozambican refugees. He was consequently suspended for three months. Aware of these developments, the Ghanaian high commissioner invited Chagonga, then in charge of Frelimo's department of social affairs, to Accra. Encouraged by him to withdraw his party from the coalition and join Funipamo,

Chagonga did leave the organization, but instead returned to Malawi in December.

Chagonga's complaint against Frelimo was that it was ruled along tribal lines, with southerners having precedence over central and northern Mozambicans, who were perceived as uneducated and fit only for military training. He saw Mondlane as inappropriately conscious of his educational achievements, 'acting like a Portuguese towards the uneducated'.[46]

3
Southerners and Those from Afar

Like Chagonga, most Mozambicans from the central and northern regions of the country have a bias against those from the south. The so-called southerners live south of the Save River and are generally referred to as the Shangaan. In fact different ethnic groups inhabit southern Mozambique, some with a history of hostility towards one another.

Shangaan is a generic term describing the followers of Soshangane, the grandson of Gaza, who stemmed from Zwide's Ndwandwe Kingdom in present-day northern region of KwaZulu-Natal, South Africa. In the late 17th century, Soshangane became chief of the Gaza people, but traditional law barred him from the Ndwandwe kingship. With the collapse of Ndwandwe, as a result of the defeat of Zwide's army at the hands of Zulu warriors in 1818, Soshangane moved eastwards into southern Mozambique.[47]

Pressed by the Zulu expansion, other peoples moved northwards. The *mfecane*, as this migration of the Nguni people came to be known, left a mark still visible today in a vast area of Mozambique, notably the southern region, in the Province of Tete, and to a less extent in Niassa and Cabo Delgado. And beyond Mozambique, the *mfecane* covered areas of Malawi, Tanzania, Kenya and Uganda. Some, led by N'qaba, headed to the coastal region of Inhambane from where they went northwest to establish a foothold in the Espungabera mountainous range of central Mozambique. From here, N'qaba launched incursions against peoples that inhabited the region between the Save and Pungué Rivers, up to the coast. Others, led by Zongendaba, a member of the junior house of the Ndwandwe royal family, first established a foothold in the Incomáti valley. In 1835, Zongendaba crossed the Zambeze River, establishing himself in the northeastern highlands of Tete Province in an area that

21

to date bears the name of the Nguni, but which the Portuguese called Angónia or Nguniland. Zongendaba's warriors continued their conquest eastwards into Malawi where they established yet another foothold, LiZulu becoming the house of the Nguni in the British-administered territory.

Soshangane first subjugated the peoples of southern Mozambique, including the Ronga, the Bitonga, the Cambambe, the Hlengués, the Maluleques, the Valois, the Djongas and the N'cunas. He then crossed the Save River, forcing N'qaba to move towards the Zambeze valley. North of the Save River, Soshangane dominated the Shona people, whom the warriors nicknamed the Ndau in view of their habit of greeting people with *Ndawe!*, while clapping their hands. Soshangane's warriors eventually established the capital of the Kingdom of Gaza in Mossurize, at the source of the Búzi River in central Mozambique.

The uprooting of those who resisted its rule marked the reign of the Gaza. Entire settlements were destroyed and a typical Nguni lifestyle imposed, leading to the emergence of a Creole language rooted on the Zulu, commonly known as Shangaan. Those willing to bow to Gaza's authority were spared and absorbed into its army. The Ndau of Manica and Sofala formed an important element of the Kingdom of Gaza's army.[48] In 1889, some 80 000 Ndau soldiers reportedly engrossed the ranks of the Gaza army when it decided to overrun the regions of southern Mozambique still under the influence of the Chope, in Inhambane and parts of Gaza provinces. The Gaza army was defeated in November 1895 in Coolela in clashes in which the Portuguese fought alongside the Chope. The battle marked the end of the Kingdom of Gaza headed by Gungunyane, a grandson of Soshangane. Gungunyane (the name, some scholars claim, is a corruption of Ngonyama – the Lion – a title given to Zulu paramount rulers) was deported to Portugal.[49] He died in the Azores in 1906.

Even now the animosity between those living to the south and north of the Save River is still felt. Ironically, Portugal played a stabilizing role in southern and thereafter central Mozambique, forcing conflictual ethnic groups to live together, calling all of them Portuguese from a land as artificial as their new identity. The so-called Shangaan derogatorily refer to the Chope as the *tsungu wa ndangani*, literally meaning the native whites. The irreverence has its origins in the early days of Portuguese colonization of Mozambique. After landing near what is today the city of Inhambane, the Portuguese called it the Terra da Boa Gente or The Land of the Good People in view of the warm reception accorded to them by the Chope. Inhambane is a corruption of *bela ku nyumbani*, meaning come on in, an expression the Chope reportedly used when welcoming the first Portuguese during a rainy day. Like several other Mozambican ethnic groups, Chope is a nickname given to them by the Nguni people to describe the speed and accuracy with which the Chope warriors hurled their assegais in the battlefield. As for the peoples living to the north of the Save River, the 'southerners' call them the Chigondo, the outsiders or the people from afar.

Frelimo, after Mondlane, attempted to remedy the dispute by creating another problem. That was the time of 'killing the tribe'.

4
Mondlane's Dilemmas

Although formed in mid-1962, Frelimo only began its independence war more than two years later. The delay not only caused impatience among idle Frelimo forces – some of them had left the Bagamoyo Base to seek employment – but was viewed by Frelimo dissidents as another indication that Mondlane was deliberately forestalling Mozambique's independence. Mondlane's apparent indecisiveness was interpreted as proof of his collusion with Portugal and her allies. Mondlane's pro-Western stance, and in particular his ties to the Kennedy administration, provided the credibility needed for these criticisms. Statements coming from Noureddine Djoudi, the Algerian ambassador to Tanzania who also represented his country on the African Liberation Committee, fueled the criticisms. He labeled Mondlane an American stooge, lacking in militancy and incapable of leading a revolutionary movement.[50]

Frelimo's stance towards the independence war should be seen in light of the international and regional situation prevailing at the time. Mondlane's rise to power coincided with a change in American policy towards Portuguese colonialism. Portugal had become not only an embarrassment, but also an obstacle to its NATO ally. Its refusal to move towards independence jeopardized American interests in Africa. In view of the Eastern Bloc's self-proclaimed status as champion of African self-determination, the United States, as President Kennedy said, had no intention of abdicating leadership in the world-wide independence movement. The process of African self-determination had faltered once Salazar realized that, bereft of her colonies, Portugal would be able neither to join in the new scramble for Africa nor play a role in East-West rivalry over the continent. Without its colonies, the survival of Portugal as a nation was felt to be at stake.

As Richard Mahoney[51] noted, Kennedy had pledged that, if elected, the United States would no longer abstain from voting in colonial issues in the United Nations, nor prevent the expression of subjugated peoples. The Kennedy administration first backed Angola's quest for independence, providing support for Holden Roberto's UPA. In July 1961, the United States earmarked $1 million in medical and nutritional aid for Angolan refugees in the Congo. US missions in Kinshasa and Accra offered scholarships to Angolan refugee students.

In Portugal itself, the Kennedy administration, through dissatisfied members of the Armed Forces, encouraged Salazar's overthrow. Salazar saw the foiled April 1961 coup engineered by Defense Minister General Botelho Moniz as being US-inspired.

The Kennedy administration was forced to reconsider its policy when Salazar threatened that American use of the Azores Air Force Base would be discontinued unless a more lenient policy was adopted towards Portugal's colonies. The United States, which was to negotiate a new lease for the base in June 1962, had no alternative but to backtrack. In January 1962, Portugal forbade refueling in the Azores to US planes carrying UN troops to the Congo, arguing that the flights did not fit within the framework of the NATO treaty. The base had gained importance during the 1961 Berlin crisis as a transit point for American military equipment. During the Cuban missile crisis of 1962, the base would also be crucial.

Despite Wayne Frederick's advice to Kennedy that the United States should, in case of war, simply seize the Azores isles, the US president bowed to Salazar. In December, when the lease on the base was due to expire, the United States walked out on the Afro-Asian bloc at the United Nations, voting with the Portuguese, South Africa, and a few Western-aligned nations in a General Assembly resolution condemning Portugal's colonial policy. In the end the lease was not renewed, but Portugal allowed the United States a day-to-day use of the base.[52]

Early 1961 events in Angola led Mondlane to conclude that Portugal would agree to a negotiated solution for the Mozambican problem, believing that Salazar would be quicker to give up Mozambique than Angola due to the latter's greater importance. Being more of an academic than a revolutionary and his Christian devotion still featuring in his reasoning, Mondlane wanted to avoid a repetition of the Angolan bloodshed of 1961. In March that year, UPA guerrillas gained notoriety for their indiscriminate killing of hundreds of civilians, both Portuguese and Angolan, though failing to seize power.

As Mondlane told a US Embassy official in September 1963, he was reluctant to initiate violence, pointing out the impossibility of controlling Mozambicans in the event of serious disorders.[53] Given UPA's failure to oust the Portuguese from Angola, Mondlane's preference was for a peaceful settlement. It is fair to assume that the Kennedy administration, with the recent Angolan fiasco, would not have wished to worsen relations with Portugal. Instead, it could have well encouraged Mondlane to consider a settlement with Portugal.

In October, Mondlane left for a meeting in New York with Portugal and nine African countries chosen by the OAU to discuss the Portuguese colonies. Before departure, Mondlane told the American ambassador that he hoped the talks would allow for progress towards self-determination. His three-point agenda for an eventual meeting with the Portuguese included the right to self-determination, safeguarded return of Frelimo leaders to Mozambique, and free elections under the auspices of either the United Nations or other international organization. Mondlane rejected a ten-year transition to independence.[54]

In light of Lisbon's multi-continental doctrine, the Portuguese team at the talks sought a redefinition of self-determination. It also pledged to bring more people from the colonies into the decision-making bodies. The possibility of a plebiscite on the colonial issue being held 'throughout the Portuguese nation' was suggested.[55]

The meeting ended inconclusively. The OAU refused to accept that an African territory should be politically linked to a non-African country. As for the plebiscite, the OAU said the results would only be accepted if they were favourable to Africa. In any event, it would have been difficult to accept the results of a plebiscite, given the Lisbon government's record on matters of balloting.

Mondlane was not invited to the talks, which he saw as meaningless. He felt the Portuguese had no intention of making any substantive concessions and were in fact using the talks to avoid uncomfortable UN debates. The Portuguese representative, Mondlane told US officials, believed 'that the principal threat to Africa was the "great powers"', not Portugal, taking issue with the United States for 'wanting to take over the Portuguese territories with its economic imperialism.'[56]

The possibility of further American pressure on Salazar was now unlikely, particularly in view of Kennedy's assassination. Mondlane had no alternative but to take immediate action against the Portuguese. But his military resources were limited, and help from the OAU African Liberation Committee had so far been disappointing. Marcelino dos Santos wanted Mondlane to visit China and accept the Chinese offer of assistance. Although Mondlane had a personal dislike of Santos, both for his 'silly' ideas about socialism and the 'people', and the way he conducted his private life,[57] the visit to China went ahead in November 1963.

The Chinese attached conditions to their offer. To start with, they specified that Mondlane was not to travel via the Soviet Union.[58] During the talks in Beijing, Mondlane told the US Embassy in Tanzania after the visit, 'China made certain demands incompatible with the independence of Frelimo'.[59] He did not elaborate, but according to a Frelimo official these included a severance of ties with the United States and the USSR in exchange for military assistance.[60]

Events in Dar es Salaam shortly after his return from China made Mondlane feel uncertain about the prospects of his independence campaign being waged from Tanzania. In January 1964, the Tanzanian Armed Forces mutinied over salary increases and the presence of British officers in senior positions, which precluded their promotion. With the mutineers threatening to overthrow the government, Nyerere had to ask Britain for assistance.

The instability facing Nyerere, coupled with his fears of Portuguese retaliation at a time when Tanzania's military capabilities were virtually non-existent, forced him to curb Frelimo's activities. A consignment of Algerian weapons destined for Frelimo was impounded. Only in May was Frelimo permitted limited access to the weapons. Mondlane complained that the delay had been damaging to him because both his followers and critics had been pressing for more militant Frelimo activity. Members of the Tanzanian cabinet had paradoxically accused him of being unwilling to fight. According to Mondlane, the Tanzanians wanted him to furnish a list of arms requirements, but would only release some of them for 'familiarization' and then under Tanzanian supervision. The arms consignment could not be turned over to Frelimo until its forces were positioned along the Mozambican border.[61] Mondlane was also bitter about Tanzania's decision to designate Kambona to manage a fund that the Chinese had earmarked for Frelimo.[62]

Aware of Mondlane's China visit, the USSR invited him to Moscow for the May Day celebrations in 1994. The Soviets were uneasy over the growing Chinese involvement in Africa. The USSR, Mondlane told the American Embassy in Dar es Salaam, was prepared to accept his relations with the United States since this was a deterrent to China's presence in Mozambique, thus ultimately serving Moscow's interests. The USSR, he said, was willing to provide increasing support to Frelimo, but preferred Mondlane to diversify his assistance from the United States by seeking aid from private American sources.[63]

In view of Chinese influence in Tanzania, Beijing's assistance to Frelimo prevailed, though preferences for the USSR continued within sectors of the movement's leadership. In May 1965, Frelimo officials left for political training in Nanking.

Mondlane's tolerance of both the USSR and China stemmed from Frelimo's dependence on their military support. Mondlane remained loyal to the West, despite changes in the American attitude towards Portugal. But within Frelimo itself, the influence received from communist countries had a marked impact on many of its members, some of whom would oppose Mondlane in communist-capitalist rivalry.

Meanwhile, disputes within Frelimo continued. In August 1964, Frelimo expelled six of its members, including Leo Milás. Mondlane, who had recently put Milás in charge of the defense portfolio, was at pains to justify his expulsion. In OAU Liberation Committee circles it was suggested that Milás was an American spy. The Frelimo leader accused Milás of associating 'himself with persons known to be involved with Portuguese colonialism and imperialism'. Mondlane later claimed that Milás was not even a Mozambican, but an American from Texas, whose real name was Leo Clinton Aldridge.

Milás, who insists on his Mozambican descent, had grown restless over communist encroachment into Frelimo. Publicly, however, Milás told a news conference that his expulsion had to do with his opposition to 'Mondlane's operation of Frelimo as his own personal petty dictatorship, and his constant violation of the constitution and interests of the party to advance his own personal interests and ambitions'. Milás said he 'opposed Dr Mondlane's policy of doing nothing as regards beginning the armed struggle in Mozambique, while devouring the aid of the OAU and spending his time or the greater part of it in America, where he still owns a house, or in Europe'. He added: 'Less than 1/3 of this supposed leader's time is spent in Africa.'[64]

The other expelled Central Committee members included Amós Sumane and Joseph Chiteje, originally from Niassa Province. After their expulsion, Sumane and Chiteje formed the Mozambique Revolutionary Council, Moreco, in Dar es Salaam on 25 September 1964. With their backs to the wall, Moreco merged with Gumane's Udenamo in early 1965.

5
Independence War

The reverberations of the 1962 split within Frelimo continued to be felt. In August 1964, tired of waiting for Frelimo's initiative, Makonde loyal to MANU decided to spearhead the struggle against Portuguese colonialism. Slipping across the border into Mozambique, a MANU group raided the Nangololo Catholic Mission, killing a Dutch missionary.

On 25 September 1964, Frelimo made its historic declaration of 'general armed insurrection of the Mozambican people against Portuguese colonialism for the total and complete gain of Mozambique's independence'. The attack on the administrative post of Chai in Cabo Delgado is listed as the first military operation. In Niassa, operations were initially reported along the northern shore of Lake Malawi where, the day before the official start of the war, Cóbuè was attacked, and on the following day a Portuguese Navy launch was fired at from the lakeshore.

Mondlane, who was on an European tour when the war started, disclosed afterwards to a US Embassy official in Dar es Salaam that seven raiding parties had entered northern Mozambique, with varied success. Three were captured by the Portuguese, two dispersed after sustaining a number of casualties, while the other two remained intact. Mondlane was critical of Tanzania for having banned a Frelimo news conference, which was intended to publicize the start of the war. The Tanzanian government's restraint on Frelimo, according to Mondlane, suggested that Nyerere still hoped that the Portuguese would negotiate a settlement before the war escalated.[65]

In the first two years of the war,[66] Frelimo attempted to expand southwards. In Cabo Delgado, the guerrillas moved southerly and southwesterly towards the Messalo River, while establishing positions in the Mueda highlands, the home of the Makonde.

In Niassa, Frelimo guerrillas operated in most parts of the province. In 1965, they reached the Nantuego area to the west, and by 1966 were east of the Lugenda River towards Marrupa and bordering Cabo Delgado.

Limited activity was reported in Zambézia where Frelimo had the support of traditional authorities in a region on the Malawi border, notably in Môngoè and Tacuane. Operations were discontinued when the Malawian government, faced with domestic dissent and fearing Portuguese encouragement of it, prohibited Frelimo from operating militarily through Malawi. Frelimo maintained a political presence in Malawi for the rest of the war, channeling Mozambican refugees, including recruits, to Tanzania.[67] Frelimo was not entirely successful in entering the province through Niassa due to ethnic constraints, involving Zambézia's Makua people and the Islamized Yao of the North. Frelimo resumed military operations in Zambézia in July 1974 after the Lisbon coup, as independence talks progressed.

Also active in Zambézia at the time and opposing Frelimo was the Exército de Libertação Nacional do Monomotapa, Elinamo, the armed wing of Udenamo-Monomotapa. In December 1964, the Portuguese reported that Elinamo had raided Chire.[68] There were no subsequent reports of Elinamo activity.

In Tete province attacks were carried out on Mutarara and Zóbuè in November 1964, and on Charre the following month. As in Zambézia, Frelimo discontinued activity in Tete due to restrictions imposed by the Malawian authorities. Frelimo reopened the Tete Front in March 1968, using Zambia as a transit point. But this was short-lived. It was only in 1969 that Frelimo managed to make inroads in the province.

Plans to start guerrilla operations in other areas of the country were even less successful than in Tete and Zambézia. In Nampula, guerrillas were neutralized by the authorities while mobilizing the local population. A similar situation arose in the provinces of Inhambane, Gaza, and Lourenço Marques (currently Maputo) where guerrillas entering through Rhodesia and Swaziland in November 1964 were arrested. Based on information gathered from detained guerrillas, the Portuguese dismantled Frelimo cells in Lourenço Marques.[69] Numerous intellectuals linked to Frelimo, including Luís Bernardo Honwana, José Craveirinha and Domingos Arouca were detained. The Portuguese cracked down on civic organizations perceived to be furthering Frelimo's goals.[70]

Portugal viewed early guerrilla incursions with alarm. Carlos Mesquita, the chief of Portuguese Navy Intelligence in Mozambique, confided to the American consul in Lourenço Marques that Frelimo's sophisticated strategy was paving the way for widespread ethnic subversion.[71] The Portuguese Army General Staff attributed Frelimo's initial success to a lack of effective communication routes, terrain difficulties, and limited administrative and military structures in the remote areas of northern Mozambique.

Frelimo's call for general armed insurrection in 1964 spoke of its confidence in an early victory. Mondlane predicted that Mozambique would be liberated five years after the war's start.[72] He failed to take into account that the Portuguese, who had not only contained Angolan guerrilla incursions but had also reversed the situation there, were confident of similar success in Mozambique. By 1967, the Portuguese prevented Frelimo from moving further south, pushing the guerrillas back in some parts.

In Cabo Delgado the year after the start of hostilities, the construction of strategic hamlets, or *aldeamentos*, curtailed guerrilla contact with the local population, disrupting Frelimo's rapid southward movement.

In Niassa, guerrillas were pushed to the north bank of Lugenda River, with the Portuguese reclaiming Catur and Lichinga regions. The Portuguese combined their military response with ruthless action against civilians, much in line with the behaviour of an army of occupation. Battle-hardened Portuguese commandos were transferred from Angola and conducted a scorched earth campaign in Mozambique.

The Portuguese would later attempt a psychological warfare program, but it proved to be incompatible with the Armed Forces' counter-insurgency tactics. Nonetheless, it became clear that, in view of the Portuguese response, Frelimo would have to review its concept of a rapid military victory and opt instead for a protracted war.

According to a Portuguese assessment,[73] by 1968 Frelimo's strongholds in Cabo Delgado were confined to the Mueda highlands, extending from Miteda and Muidumbe, north to Mocímboa do Rovuma; and the Mape highlands west of the Chai–Macomia road. Independent assessments, however, revealed that Frelimo groups operated along the coastal road linking Porto Amélia to the Tanzanian border. They were active around Mucojo, Quiterajo, Mocímboa da Praia and Palma. Frelimo was also active along the Rovuma River, and its presence felt in the area between the Messalo and Montepuez Rivers.[74]

By Frelimo's own admission, its attempts to militarily activate Nampula proved unsuccessful. Frelimo attributed this to ethnic rivalry between Nampula's Makua villagers and Makonde guerrillas attempting to enter the province. The establishment of *aldeamentos* south of the Messalo River was another factor.

In Niassa, Mozambique's most sparsely populated province, the Portuguese reported guerrilla activity in the highlands between Vila Cabral and Maniamba. Attacks were reported on the railway line near Catur and in areas between Vila Cabral and the Lugenda River. Guerrillas were established within the Jéci mountain range.

In late 1968, it was estimated that half of Niassa's population and a quarter of Cabo Delgado's had been concentrated in *aldeamentos*. The *aldeamento* program, arguably successful from a military standpoint, alienated the rural population from the Portuguese.

With the appointment in March 1970 of General Kaúlza de Arriaga as commander-in-chief of the Portuguese Armed Forces in Mozambique, an effort was made to reverse the military situation. By then, Frelimo had consolidated its positions in the Mueda highlands and isolated numerous Portuguese outposts by mining roads under its 'Operação Estrada'. Arriaga's predecessor, General Augusto dos Santos, noted that he had neither sufficient ground nor air transportation to ensure the mobility of his forces. He had been given only two helicopters for use in the two northern provinces.[75] The helicopters were for daylight-only operations and evacuations.

Arriaga immediately stepped up the *aldeamento* program on the south bank of Messalo River. Minesweeping was launched. Military operations along the south bank of the Rovuma River attempted to destroy Frelimo bases. For the first time, helicopter-borne troops were used in a fashion similar to that of the United States in Vietnam. The Portuguese claimed to have overridden a major Frelimo base at Omar.

In July, Operation Gordian Knot was launched, involving 8000 men. Mechanized engineering units were pioneered to allow ground troops to storm the Gungunhana, Moçambique and Nampula bases. Helicopter gunships ferried commando units and halted retreating guerrillas.[76] As Operation Gordian Knot had not relied on the element of surprise, Frelimo guerrillas could vacate their bases before the actual attack and regroup elsewhere.

Proof that no major clashes occurred during Operation Gordian Knot can be found in statistics Portugal released after the war. In 1970, there was an increase of 41 men killed in action in the whole territory, compared with 1969, and 11 less than in 1971 (see Table I.5.1). According to Arriaga, 26 men were killed and 26 seriously wounded during Operation Gordian Knot. Critics within the Portuguese military viewed the operation as a failure. They perceived Arriaga as unwilling to militarily commit himself for fear that a high casualty figure would have been detrimental to his bid for Portuguese presidency in 1972. Others,

Table I.5.1 Portuguese Armed Forces Personnel Killed in Mozambique, 1964–74

Year	In action	Other causes	Total
1964	3	50	53
1965	3	53	136
1966	121	108	229
1967	92	86	178
1968	111	137	248
1969	147	207	354
1970	188	106	294
1971	199	121	320
1972	218	144	362
1973	202	197	399
1974	117	203	320*
Grand total: 2 893			

* Up to the 25 April 1974 *coup d'état*, 117 troops had been killed, 45 in action. In the five-month period between the coup and the signing of the 7 September cease-fire accord, 203 troops were killed, 72 in action.

Source: Resenha Histórico-Militar das Campanhas de África (1961–1974), Volume 1, Estado-Maior do Exército, Lisboa 1988.

like General Costa Gomes, who served in Mozambique under General Augusto dos Santos, claimed the 'operation was very negative for us from a counter-insurgency standpoint. It was a mistake to apply conventional methods to a subversive war.'[77] It should be noted, however, that Gomes was involved in the 1961 military coup attempt against Salazar, with Arriaga playing a key role in thwarting it.

Despite the success attributed to Operation Gordian Knot and Arriaga's exuberant media statement that decisive victory was imminent, the war continued to gain momentum, judging from the casualty figures for the subsequent years (see Table I.5.1). Arriaga attributed the reverses to Frelimo's 'third effort', that is, the re-activation of the Tete Front after the setbacks in Niassa and Cabo Delgado in 1970. With the construction of the Cahora Bassa dam in progress since November 1969, Arriaga diverted troops from Cabo Delgado and Niassa to Tete to ensure the project was carried out without hindrance. His request for additional troops and 1 million land mines to be laid on the 800 km-long Tanzanian border, to effectively close it to Frelimo, was turned down due to lack of funds.

The Portuguese defense minister promised Arriaga that he would seek South African material assistance, but the commander-in-chief needed a more rapid solution to deal with an immediate problem. He proposed the construction of *aldeamentos* on a large scale in Tete, but this was delayed by the reluctance of the governor general. Nonetheless, Arriaga's goal of securing the Cahora Bassa project was achieved. In part, this was facilitated by Frelimo itself, which mounted no attacks on the site despite initial pledges against construction. Frelimo opted instead to circumvent the Portuguese troops deployed in the Cahora Bassa region, and avoid the minefields around the dam site, moving southwards into Manica and Sofala, activating these areas in July 1972.

The decision not to attack Cahora Bassa came in the wake of the serious setbacks suffered north of the Zambeze River between September 1968 and mid-1969. The Portuguese Armed Forces were reacting differently to guerrilla infiltration in Tete. Airborne troops were rapidly deployed once a target was identified. Accustomed to previous Portuguese tactics in Cabo Delgado and Niassa, Frelimo military personnel in Tete became virtual sitting ducks before they eventually reviewed their tactics in infiltrating the country from Zambia and in the manner in which they established bases.

As the security situation deteriorated in Tete from mid-1969 onwards, and with incidents beginning to be reported in many areas of Manica and Sofala, the Portuguese government was overthrown in April 1974.

Of the three military fronts Portugal faced in Africa, Mozambique had the largest number of casualties officially reported by Portuguese authorities. Since the start of the war in August 1964 until the signing of a cease-fire in September 1974, 2893 members of the Portuguese Armed Forces had been killed, 1481 in action. The Portuguese attributed the other casualties to accidents with firearms, road accidents and other causes. In June 1969 alone, 101 Portuguese soldiers drowned on the Zambeze River while transporting equipment, almost doubling the previous year's casualty figures. An average of 77.5 per cent of the casualties were troops recruited in Portugal and the remainder were locally recruited personnel. The percentage began to decline after the fifth year of war as the Portuguese increased recruitment of colonial and native Mozambicans.

In Angola, where the war had begun three years earlier, the overall fatal casualty was reported to be 3258. In Guinea-Bissau, where hostilities started in 1963, a total of 2070 troops were killed. As in Mozambique, the percentage of troops killed was higher among personnel recruited in Portugal. The annual average of military personnel deployed in the war fronts between 1961 and 1973 was 117 000 men. In Mozambique, the highest figure for troops deployed was 51 463 men

Table I.5.2 Portuguese Armed Forces Personnel
Recruited for the Mozambique Front, 1961–73

Year	Personnel	Recruited in Mozambique	%
1961	11 209	3000	26.8
1962	11 852	3000	25.3
1963	14 246	5003	35.1
1964	18 049	7917	43.9
1965	22 856	9701	42.4
1966	30 588	11 038	36.1
1967	34 721	11 557	33.3
1968	36 615	13 898	38.0
1969	39 096	15 810	40.4
1970	38 712	16 079	41.5
1971	44 505	22 710	51.0
1972	46 723	24 066	51.5
1973	51 463	27 572	53.6

Source: Resenha Histórico-Militar das Campanhas de África
(1961–1974), Volume 1, Estado-Maior do Exército, Lisboa
1988.

in 1973, compared with 65 592 in Angola, a country about 50 per cent
larger than Mozambique. In Guinea-Bissau during the same period
32 035 troops were deployed (see Table I.5.2).

These and other numbers, however, do not concur with Frelimo
figures. On the second anniversary of the launching of the independence war, Frelimo claimed that over 3000 Portuguese soldiers were
already dead. Most were said to have been killed in 1966 alone, judging
from Mondlane's 1967 New Year address in which he claimed that over
1500 Portuguese soldiers had been liquidated. Taking stock of events in
1971, Frelimo reported 2850 enemy soldiers killed: 1200 in Tete, 1300 in
Cabo Delgado and 250 in Niassa. That is, almost nine times more than
the number of military personnel the Portuguese Armed Forces recorded
as having been killed in the same year, and nearly as much as all those
killed during the ten-year war.[78]

In his book, *Struggle for Mozambique*, Mondlane claimed that by 1967
between 65 000 and 70 000 Portuguese troops had been deployed in the
territory.[79] On 7 March 1968, Mondlane told a meeting at the Royal
Institute of International Affairs in London that one seventh of the
country's population lived in areas virtually under Frelimo control in
Cabo Delgado and Niassa.[80] Based on the 1970 population census, this
represented 1.1 million people, or upwards of 300 000 more inhabitants

than the total population of the two provinces, without taking into consideration the number of peasants the Portuguese had by then forcibly removed from their traditional areas into *aldeamentos*, those living in other areas controlled by the Portuguese, and the considerable number of refugees sheltered in Tanzania, Malawi and Zambia. In the same statement and still referring to the two northern provinces, Mondlane said Frelimo guerrillas were fighting in areas comprising approximately one-fifth of the country. That would imply a guerrilla army with enough personnel – which Frelimo did not have – to be deployed in an area consisting of more than three-quarters of the combined area of Cabo Delgado and Niassa Provinces, and excluding the Portuguese from zones known to be under their effective control.

6
Zambia Backs Frelimo Dissidents

There were efforts to reconcile the Frelimo dissidents. In June 1964, while in Dar es Salaam for an African Liberation Committee meeting, Paulo Gumane held talks with Mondlane. No agreement was reached between Frelimo and Udenamo–Moçambique.

In November, Baltazar Chagonga urged Mondlane to meet the leaders of the other parties in Lusaka with a view to 'uniting all Mozambicans, free of tribal or class segregation'. Chagonga stressed that his party, Unami, 'reiterate[d] its policy as an affiliated Frelimo member, and shall be represented as such within and outside Frelimo'.[81] Responding to Chagonga in typical Portuguese style, Mondlane's missive was harsh and disconcerting:

> There is no Unami party for Your Excellency is aware that such party has never existed. When Frelimo was established on 25 June 1962, Your Excellency lived here in Dar es Salaam with no movement to lead. When it became necessary to ask for your participation in the founding conference, you had to join one of the parties to acquire the right to attend it. Your Excellency submitted your candidacy to the presidency, not as president of Unami, but as a Frelimo member.[82]

Subsequent meetings between Gumane and the Frelimo leadership were held in Dar es Salaam in November, and in January 1965. Gumane proposed that his party could join Frelimo provided that eight of the Central Committee's 15 seats, the vice presidency, and the defense and foreign affairs portfolios were assigned to Udenamo–Moçambique. Mondlane agreed on the vice-presidency and foreign affairs posts. He offered Gumane low-key portfolios like publicity and information, education, and health and social welfare, noting Udenamo would have non-executive powers. Talks between the two organizations were called off with no palpable results achieved.[83]

An attempt to unite all the Mozambican factions in a single front was made in 1965, this time by the Zambian government. The Udenamo factions of Gumane and Gwambe, as well as the MANC and Frelimo, gathered in Lusaka from 24 to 31 March. MANU and Unami were not represented at the meeting, though its leaders agreed in principle with the idea of a united front. Chagonga did not believe a merger would imply the disbanding of his party.[84]

Mondlane rejected the idea of a new organization being formed. Unable to rally the support of the Zambian president, Kenneth Kaunda, in convincing the other organizations to join Frelimo, Mondlane left Lusaka. He would base his decision on the 'unbelievable insolence on the part of other participants and minor Zambian Government officials', the latter a reference to Rankin Sikasula and A Kangwa who chaired the various proceedings.[85]

In a statement issued at the end of unity talks, Kangwa, the Zambian ruling party's under-secretary for Pan-African affairs, pointed out that

> All means by other parties, including myself, to persuade or appeal to FRELIMO to look into the need for UNITY at present; to think twice over their conditions for unity; and to try to bring in suggestions or concessions so as to meet the other parties in one way or the other, failed entirely [...] only three parties were willing to unite [...] FRELIMO members were asked to leave the Conference since they had refused UNITY with other organizations on the conditions agreed by the three organizations.[86]

The other parties agreed to merge under the Comité Revolucionário de Moçambique, Coremo. Like Unami, MANU never joined Coremo. Unami remained active in Malawi, receiving token financial assistance from the Banda government. Its goal remained a negotiated settlement with the Portuguese. The colonial authorities would use Unami as a buffer against Frelimo, and let Chagonga return to Mozambique.[87] He died virtually ignored in Mozambique after independence in September 1988.

Gwambe became Coremo president, Gumane the vice-president, Joseph Chiteje the secretary general, and Fanuel Mahluza the defense chief. The organization drew its membership from a cross-section of Mozambique's ethnic groups.

Immediately, Coremo faced an acute lack of resources to campaign militarily for independence. Although recognized by the OAU, Coremo was never granted assistance by its African Liberation Committee, which was based in and led from Tanzania. Military training was given in China to where Mahluza went in 1965. Former Frelimo members with military experience formed the nucleus of Coremo's Exército Revolucionário Popular de Moçambique, Erepomo. The Zambian government diverted to Coremo military hardware earmarked by the African Liberation Committee for other southern African guerrilla movements based in Zambia. Another source of Coremo's war materiel was South Africa's Pan-Africanist Congress (PAC). In return, Coremo undertook to escort PAC guerrillas wanting to infiltrate South Africa through Mozambique.

Other African countries, particularly Ghana, provided political and diplomatic support for Coremo. Mondlane's apprehensions about this development became evident during an OAU conference held in Accra in October 1965 for which Coremo was invited. Frelimo, Mondlane said, 'has been very badly treated at the conference', adding:

> To start with, the government of Ghana invited Gwambe's delegation. Although they put us in a decent hotel, Gwambe and his delegation stayed at the African Association Centre. Similarly, Diallo Telli's speech was generally against Frelimo and pro-Coremo, alleging that Frelimo refused to join other nationalist movements and to recommend the armed struggle.[88]

Nonetheless, as a CIA report noted, Coremo and other rival organizations, lacked 'the capacity to threaten [the Frelimo] leadership either in terms of external support or political following', and for this reason 'Mondlane seems likely to hang on to his job for some time, largely because he has established credentials as a nationalist in African and other circles abroad'.[89]

Coremo began its war in Tete province's northwestern region at the end of 1965. Subsequently, Coremo guerrillas used the province's northeastern region as an infiltration route. The guerrillas unsuccessfully tried in 1966 to operate in Zambézia's Milange and Morrumbala areas, using southern Malawi as a corridor.[90] What distinguished the organization from Frelimo was that its senior officials took part in military operations, rather than leaving it as a task for the military cadres only. And unlike Frelimo, as an author observed, Coremo's claims of battle victory were refreshingly modest.[91]

In November 1966, Coremo's Central Committee met to review Gwambe's handling of the movement's assets. As in his days as Udenamo leader, Gwambe had failed to give an account of Coremo's finances. Gwambe left the organization, establishing the Partido Popular de Moçambique (Papomo), a party that vanished in the following years. Gumane became the new president, and Amós Sumane the vice-president. Mazunzo Bob was assigned the foreign affairs secretariat.

There was further evidence of internal disputes when a plot to oust Gumane was uncovered. Artur Vilankulu, who represented the organization in the United States, was involved in the plot and is said to have had the backing of Coremo Information Secretary Arcanjo Faustino Kambeu. This led to a reshuffle of the Central Committee in early 1968. Sumane was dropped from the Central Committee. In January that year, he formed the União Nacional Africana da Rumbézia (Unar), a separatist organization based in Malawi and seeking the independence of the territory bound by the Rovuma and Zambeze Rivers. Mahluza replaced Mazunzo Bob as foreign secretary. Three other members were expelled from the organization, allegedly for their close relationship with the Chinese.

Militarily, Coremo began to lose ground from mid-1967 onwards. In early 1968, Mazunzo Bob was reportedly killed in a clash with the Portuguese near the border with Zambia. Bob's death, in the wake of his demotion, caused dissatisfaction among Coremo members who believed he was the victim of a conspiracy. Coremo Deputy Information Secretary Matias Tenda was accused of having killed Bob during the clash, joining Sumane in Malawi afterwards.

In addition to the Portuguese, Coremo guerrillas also had to face Frelimo on the battleground. The first in a long list of clashes between the two organizations occurred in 1968. Two years later, Frelimo arrested a number of Coremo members. In the continuing feuding, Coremo's treasurer Gabriel Machava and two military commanders were killed in a Frelimo ambush near Furancungo in February 1972.[92]

In March, the Zambian government tried to defuse the situation. Mukuka Nkoloso, who liaised with liberation movements based in Zambia, warned Frelimo publicly that its 'future in Zambia would be doubtful if the organization continued with its bad show'. Nkoloso advised Frelimo to 'concentrate on killing the Portuguese oppressors and not their fellow freedom fighters'.[93]

Coremo suffered yet another blow in mid-1968 when Júlio Dzonzi, its deputy defense secretary, was killed by the Portuguese in Manica. At the time, Dzonzi was leading a joint Coremo–PAC column. The South

African guerrillas intended to infiltrate their country through Swaziland once they reached Gaza. The Portuguese claimed to have either killed or captured all of the 12 PAC members of the column. A surviving PAC member was taken into PIDE custody, but was subsequently allowed to 'escape' from a Chimoio jail only to be killed afterwards on the streets of the central Mozambican town by waiting PIDE agents.[94] According to Malhuza, the setback severely disrupted Coremo and the organization never recovered.

Coremo eventually became more of a nuisance than a threat to the Portuguese. Coremo succeeded in gaining some public attention in January 1971 when its forces abducted six Portuguese agriculturists and five Mozambicans working on the Zambeze basin. The six were believed to have been executed by Coremo.

In retaliation, the Portuguese authorities employed token pressure on the Zambian government. Stevedores at the port of Beira boycotted cargo bound for Zambia. But under pressure from economic interests with a stake in Mozambican as well as in Angolan port and railway networks, the Lisbon government never used these fully as leverage against the hinterland countries, particularly Zambia, for supporting nationalist guerrilla movements.

7
Mondlane and Che Guevara

In 1965, Mondlane still hoped that Portugal would agree to a negotiated settlement. He continued to regard the United States as a conduit for pressure on the Portuguese, despite improved US–Portugal relations under the Johnson administration.

In March, Mondlane was reassured of American interest in his organization in the wake of a misunderstanding between Frelimo and State Department officials in New York. Mondlane had instructed the Frelimo delegation to meet the officials in Washington, but when the State Department suggested New York as a venue, its members cancelled the meeting. Informed of the developments, Mondlane asked the American Embassy in Dar es Salaam to confirm urgently the situation as he was under great pressure within Frelimo to issue a public statement condemning the US Government. The State Department responded promptly, asking the Dar es Salaam post to assure Mondlane that there was no change in US policy on seeing Frelimo representatives, and that it had no previous information about the members of the delegation in question, and especially whether they had the Frelimo leader's blessing. The State Department missive added: 'We normally prefer to look to Mondlane himself for discussions on Frelimo matters.'[95]

At the State Department's African Bureau, Mondlane continued to count on Mennen Williams' support. Williams strongly objected in June 1965 to attempts by members of the Johnson administration to review US policy on Portugal and her colonies. He saw proposals contained in the Second Draft of the National Policy Paper on Portugal, as unacceptable to the African Bureau. 'I take strong exception', he said, 'to the proposal permitting Portugal to purchase US military equipment without restrictions on its use so long as there is evidence that

Communist arms, training and/or personnel are being supplied to the nationalists.' Williams added:

> This and other similar statements, including mention of the possibil-
> ity of direct US military support of the Portuguese and even participa-
> tion with the Portuguese against frontier infiltrations, run in the face
> of long established policy and the public stance we have taken in the
> United Nations and in the United States over the last four years.[96]

Williams also objected to giving official encouragement and incen-
tives to US investments in the Portuguese colonies, advising that this
should only happen when the Portuguese publicly accepted a program
of self-determination.

During Robert Kennedy's 1965 tour of southern and eastern Africa,
Mondlane discussed the Mozambique situation with the former American attorney general and other US Government officials in Dar es
Salaam in July. Mondlane confided to Wayne Fredericks that if Portugal
agreed to a plebiscite over the future of its colonies, its terms were less
important than the political process that it would set in motion. Accordingly, Mondlane conceded that eventual independence of Mozambique
did not need to form part of the plebiscite. For him, a single choice
between maintaining the status quo of Mozambique as a Portuguese
overseas province or becoming a member of a Lusophone common-
wealth would in fact be a significant step forward.[97]

In August, the State Department made new proposals to Portugal to
resolve the colonial dispute. Primarily, the United States wanted Portugal to publicly accept the principle of self-determination at some specific time in the future. Secretary of State Dean Rusk told the Portuguese
foreign minister that for the United States self-determination implied
the availability of all options. And the US ambassador to Portugal,
George Anderson, told Salazar in October that if the people of Portuguese Africa were 'to be given a chance freely to express themselves and
to state their preference with regard to their future status, the United
States Government would accept the outcome and would be prepared to
support it'. Anderson noted that the new proposals differed from others
in the past in that they 'offered to Portugal an opportunity to draw upon
the resources of the United States and other NATO allies for the influen-
cing of moderate African states and particularly those contiguous to
Portuguese Africa'. The envoy went on to cite to Salazar Secretary of
State Rusk's suggestion that Portugal provide its friends 'a flag around
which to rally'.

Salazar's response was that a declaration accepting eventual self-determination would play into the hands of African politicians in the Portuguese colonies, anxious for the fruits and benefits of independence. The immediate goal of these politicians, said Salazar, was to become cabinet ministers and ambassadors. The Portuguese premier stressed that Mozambique existed as Mozambique only by virtue of the Portuguese presence and unifying influence. Without these, he added, Mozambique would be nothing more than a number of separate tribes and groupings. Salazar observed that 'Americans in general seem to feel that the civilising of African peoples to the point of adequately governing themselves can be accomplished in a matter of years. Portuguese experience does not confirm this but rather suggests that centuries are required.'[98]

In a nutshell, the Lisbon government saw no need to give in to pressure to abandon its African colonies. Salazar firmly believed Portugal's supposedly civilising mission should continue for a few more centuries until such time as the 'primitive native peoples' achieve what it had not yet been able to accomplish over the past five centuries or so.

It was against this backdrop of Mondlane's apparent moderation of his political agenda and continued liaison with the United States that Cuba presented the Frelimo leader with a proposal that he had no option but to refuse. The Cubans had conceived a plan to engage the United States in simultaneous armed conflicts in the Third World, the aim being to weaken it militarily, ultimately bringing it to its knees. Already engaged in Vietnam, the United States would then be lured to intervene in Africa and Latin America. It fitted in with what Che Guevara had envisaged as the creation of two, three, or more Vietnams.

Cuba was already supporting guerrilla organizations in various Latin American countries. In Africa, which Guevara saw as 'imperialism's weak link', Cuba planned to mount a military campaign against southern Africa's white regimes, using the Congo as a starting point. 'With the backing of the Africans through the [African Liberation] Committee in Tanzania, and with two Cuban battalions', said Guevara, 'I believe we can give a blow to the imperialists at the heart of their interests in Katanga.'[99]

Cuba threw its weight in with the Congolese guerrilla factions fighting the Tshombé government. Southern African guerrilla organizations were asked to supply men to the Cuban-led contingent active in Congo. Angola's MPLA, Zimbabwe's ZAPU, and the ANC of South Africa endorsed the plan, as did the Rwandan guerrillas. Ghana warned Guevara that he would run against difficulties if he relied on Mondlane's assistance, a view shared by Pablo Rivalta, the Cuban ambassador to Tanzania.

Rivalta noted that Frelimo was under strong American influence, its training camps 'contaminated' by Peace Corps. Rivalta advised Guevara to work instead through Marcelino dos Santos in whom he had 'utmost trust'.[100] The two had met for the first time in Prague during a student conference when Dos Santos was exiled in Europe.

Nonetheless, Guevara went ahead and met Mondlane in Tanzania in February 1965. The atmosphere at the meeting, as Guevara wrote in his Congo diary, 'was extremely chilly'. Mondlane, as other guerrilla leaders, opposed the idea of fighting other people's wars. 'Africa', Guevara concluded, 'had a long way to go before it achieved real revolutionary maturity...'.[101]

In October, with the Cubans in dire straits in the Congo, Castro himself urged Frelimo to commit its forces in exchange for much needed military assistance. Despite his meagre military hardware resources, Mondlane remained adamant. He had, some three months before, already refused to accept a group of about nine Cubans wanting to join the Frelimo guerrillas in Mozambique.[102]

Mondlane later remarked that Guevara had behaved 'like a doctor, extremely conceited, without wanting to pay attention to his interlocutors'.[103] For their part, the Cubans lambasted Mondlane for his unsavoury remarks, referring to him as 'the Frelimo president who travels to the United States more frequently than a State Department ambassador'. They accused him of 'never having entered Mozambique to fight with the guerrillas (...) and of having chosen Washington and other major capitals as the "battleground" while Commandant Guevara selected Sierra Maestra, first, and the Bolivian mountains, where he fought until his death, afterwards'.[104]

8
The Rise of Samora Machel

A year after the start of the independence war, Frelimo contained two distinct factions. One, consisting of civilians, represented the front's political leadership and was confined to the Tanzanian capital. The other included the rank and file of Frelimo's incipient army, who enjoyed direct grass roots contact that the former did not.

The military's perception of the political leaders – albeit not totally correct, in view of the restraints imposed by the Tanzanian government – was that they were not fully committed to fighting the Portuguese. Regardless of the efforts the Frelimo political leadership made to ensure its supremacy over the entire organization, the military was gradually developing into a parallel force that could well reduce the politicians to an irrelevant entity, ultimately posing a threat to their very existence. The divergence of these two wings was further widened when Frelimo political leaders rejected the suggestion made by the military commanders to shift Frelimo's headquarters from Tanzania to areas they controlled inside Mozambique.

Ethnicity was another contributing factor. The cluster of southerners in the political wing noted with concern the growing influence of northerners in Frelimo's military apparatus. The Frelimo army, in view of Tanzania's proximity to Cabo Delgado, had drawn its members mainly from the northern provinces, notably the Makonde and the Makua. To correct the imbalance and in the process strengthen their grip on the organization, the political leadership saw to it that people of their own kind would secure command posts in the military structure. As commander-in-chief of the guerrilla army, Mondlane had the prerogative of filling such posts.

That the Frelimo leadership felt uneasy about the mood in the armed forces came into the open during a Central Committee session in October 1966. The session referred to 'the emergence of a certain spirit among several militants who believe there are two types of Frelimo members – the military and the civilians, the first being the superior ones'. The resolution added that 'such a spirit, due partly to shortcomings in our working structures, also reflects a lack of correct understanding by those comrades of the nature of the struggle we are waging'.[105]

Although the documents of this session made no mention of it, a faction intent on seizing control of the organization had emerged in 1965. Calling itself the Mozambique Revolutionary United People's Party (MRUPP), the faction was led by Frelimo vice-president Uria Simango. Other members included Frelimo's defense and security chief, Filipe Magaia, and his deputy, Raúl Casal Ribeiro, as well as Lázaro Kavandame, the provincial secretary for Cabo Delgado. Manuel da Maia, who was in charge of the MRUPP's youth wing, claimed that Tanzanian officials, notably Oscar Kambona and Mustafa Songambele, the commissar for Tanzania's Coast Region, supported the splinter group.[106]

Ironically, the Portuguese, or rather, circles in the Portuguese administration, showed concern over the possibility of Mondlane being ousted from Frelimo's presidency. As Portugal's Navy Intelligence chief in Mozambique told the US mission in Lourenço Marques, the Portuguese 'regard Mondlane as a moderate and would rather have him as Frelimo leader than one of his rivals who could well perform indiscriminate acts of terrorism throughout Mozambique'. The Portuguese had knowledge that 'opposition to Mondlane within Frelimo had increased to the point where rivals boast that he would be removed by the end of the year'.[107]

For its part, the CIA reported in late 1965 that Mondlane had 'doubts regarding his own future in Frelimo'. Like Angola's Holden Roberto, said the CIA, Mondlane

> continues to be regarded as a symbol of political unity, but he is not well known as a leader in the north where the fighting is centered, and opposition to him has grown among other Frelimo figures who consider themselves closer to Mozambique's tribal peoples. None of these individuals possess much personal prestige or following, however.[108]

The Mondlane camp took decisive action to correct the situation. In October 1966, while on a mission to Niassa, Filipe Magaia was assassinated. The official Frelimo version has it that Magaia died in action. But an inquiry conducted by the Frelimo representative in Tanzania's Songea District, from where Magaia's column had departed for Mozambique, showed that he was killed by one of his own men with the connivance of at least two others. The inquiry pointed out that during interrogations, the assassin confessed that he acted on orders received in Nachingwea, a recently established Frelimo military training camp in southern Tanzania.[109]

Though possessing a southerner surname, Filipe Magaia was a Makua at heart. His father, a nurse, had been transferred from southern Mozambique to Zambézia where he married a local woman. Born in 1937, Filipe Magaia spent his childhood in a Makua environment, leaving Zambézia for Lourenço Marques for his secondary education. Conscripted into the colonial army, Magaia rose to the rank of non-commissioned officer. Upon his discharge, he worked for the railways in Beira. He fled to Tanzania in 1962, and in January the following year was sent to Algeria for guerrilla warfare training.[110] With the expulsion of João Munguambe, Magaia was made Frelimo's defense and security chief.

Magaia favoured a guerrilla army representing a cross-section of Mozambique's ethnic groups. He is on record as having taken issue with the disproportionate representation of Makonde and Makua in the Frelimo army, stressing that a diverse ethnic representation would be more appropriate. A career soldier, Magaia is said to have commanded the support of the Frelimo armed forces, his Makua background undoubtedly having contributed to that.[111]

At Magaia's funeral in Songea, Mondlane announced what had been planned well in advance at the highest level. Samora Machel, the commander of the Nachingwea camp who had accompanied Mondlane from Dar es Salaam, was to replace Magaia. Regardless of his rank and length of service, Casal Ribeiro would serve under Machel.

Like Mondlane, Machel was also from the southern province of Gaza. Born in 1933, he joined Frelimo when he was 30. A nurse by profession, Machel was sent for military training in Algeria in June 1963. Back in Tanzania in April the following year, he was assigned to the Frelimo camp at Kongwa, replacing Simão Tobias, a Makonde, as its commander. Machel's appointment to the defense and security department of Frelimo was without the knowledge of the Frelimo vice president, Uria Simango, who is known to have objected to not being consulted.

For those aligned to Magaia, his death was a conspiracy by the southerners. 'The whole extent of the conspiracy', said Manuel Tristão, the Songea representative, 'unfolded before my eyes rapidly, but clearly. When at the funeral Machel, in a sarcastic tone, came to me and said, "So, old chap, what are you going to do now that your boss is dead?", I realized the dimension of the whole cabal.'[112]

Following Magaia's death, Frelimo made a concerted effort to effectively establish control over the armed forces. The Department of Defence and Security was disbanded, and in its place two separate departments established. Samora Machel retained the defense portfolio, while security was assigned to Joaquim Chissano. A National Command Council was formed to oversee all military operations. Based at Nachingwea, the Council met every two weeks under the chairmanship of the Frelimo president.

With the new military structure in place, the Frelimo leadership moved on to consolidate its position in all branches of the armed forces. For his role during this period, Machel was singled out in the Frelimo Central Committee report to the II Congress of 1968, for his 'political line and military discipline, without which our struggle might not have progressed'.[113]

Those whom Magaia had appointed or seen to be loyal to him were removed and in some instances, so claim former Frelimo members, summarily executed. Men trusted by Machel, mostly from southern Mozambique, filled the vacant posts.

Dinis Moiane, a southerner, became the new Nachingwea commanding officer. Augusto Mtuku, a Makonde, was dismissed as Frelimo's logistics chief in Mtwara.[114]

Rui Vilanamuali and Agostinho Mbaua, commanders of the Mkalapa and Mponda bases in Niassa, were allegedly executed in 1967. The two were natives of Zambézia. Early in 1968, Lino Abraão, a military commander from Zambézia stationed in Niassa, who had been outspoken in condemning Magaia's assassination, was arrested and taken to Cabo Delgado where he is said to have been executed. For the same reason, Magaia's secretary, Luís Njanje, otherwise known by his *nom de guerre* as António Canhemba, was reportedly executed at Base Beira's 1st Sector in Cabo Delgado.

Complaints of ill treatment meted out to combatants and civilians alike began to reach the Frelimo headquarters in Dar es Salaam. Those fleeing Nachingwea spoke of a witch-hunt whereby anyone suspected of being opposed to the Frelimo leadership was detained and subjected to a public trial. Those found guilty were executed in Nachingwea, a common site having been the pit latrines built in the precinct of the centre.

Subsequently, executions were carried out in Frelimo bases inside Mozambique, to where those found guilty by the kangaroo court hearings in Nachingwea began to be sent. According to Uria Simango, the complaints, notably from Cabo Delgado, reached alarming proportions at the beginning of 1967.[115]

Towards the end of 1967 and early 1968 the situation grew worse, leading Cabo Delgado provincial secretary Lázaro Kavandame and his chairmen to accuse the Frelimo leadership of giving *carte blanche* to the army to kill as it pleased. Cabo Delgado even had a People's Court on the Nangade highlands. Sentences passed by the court included corporal punishment. The accused were given anything between 15 and 80 lashes. Another form of punishment consisted of tying a prisoner's hands behind his back with a rope, which ran across his mouth. Often the prisoners were tied in a squatting position with their legs around a tree. Executions were carried out by strangulation, blows with the butt of a rifle, stabbing, or even burning with firebrands.

Fearing for their lives, many of Frelimo's rank and file opted to leave and others went into exile. Some fled Tanzania altogether. Manuel Lisboa Tristão left for Kenya, and Joaquim Machado, a Makua who had served as deputy commander of the Nachingwea military centre under Machel, for Malawi in 1967. In September, Luís Arranca Tudo left his military base in Niassa Province and sought political asylum at the Portuguese Embassy in Malawi.

Life inside the Frelimo bases became so unbearable that those sent there as punishment, where they would most certainly face execution, were left with two options. One was to attempt an escape to Tanzania, where they would invariably be detected by the Nyumba Kumi-Kumi, the country's ten-house cell system, whereby all members of every ten houses were supposed to know one another, and expected to report to the cell's head any visitor or stranger. The other option was to surrender to the Portuguese, which many did as a way out of their predicament, only to be hunted down as traitors after independence.

9
Student Unrest

The October 1966 session of the Frelimo Central Committee had also addressed the organization's educational program.[116] Frelimo was apprehensive that IM students enjoyed more privileges than others, were out of touch with the liberation movement and that there was a danger of them evolving into an elite. Of particular concern were those students who tended to look down on the guerrilla fighters, who, for lack of a formal education, were regarded as an inferior class.

Upon completing two years of secondary education at the IM, students were normally sent to the African-American Institute-operated college in Dar es Salaam. Afterwards, they were placed in foreign universities, notably in the United States, on scholarships obtained by the Mozambique student organization, Unemo, and Frelimo.

In January 1967, Frelimo Education Secretary Armando Guebuza told students that the Central Committee had decided that it was no longer necessary to rely on the Dar es Salaam college because the same curriculum would be introduced at the IM. The IM would now be a Portuguese medium school with English taught as a second language. During school holidays, students, including those from primary schools, would undergo military training at Nachingwea. Students who failed twice in the same year would join the ranks of the Frelimo army. Those studying abroad were told not to register for the next higher course of study 'without first interrupting their studies for at least one year in order to participate directly and closely in another task of national liberation . .'.[117]

The students, primarily from central and northern Mozambique, rejected the Central Committee decisions. They argued that Frelimo had no jurisdiction over either the students or the IM, and that the latter had been created as an independent educational establishment. Those studying abroad assumed that participating 'directly and closely in another task of national liberation' was like going to 'São Tomé', as they derogatorily called Nachingwea in a reference to the West African island which the Portuguese used as a penal colony. And they feared that the possibility of ever being able to proceed with their studies abroad would be remote.

In an unusually strongly worded statement, Frelimo lashed out at 'students in the United States [. . .], who, instigated by imperialists and for purely egotistical reasons and their corruption, refused to interrupt their studies'.[118] It is questionable whether Mondlane, who signed the statement, had actually written it. The way he referred to himself in the third person throughout the document was uncharacteristic of his style, matching Marcelino dos Santos' rhetoric instead.

The students stated that they had no quarrel with Frelimo as such, but only its president, 'who is an imperialist representative disguised as a Mozambican nationalist [who failed] as leader of a truly revolutionary Mozambican party'. The students questioned Mondlane about the 'mysterious deaths' of people such as Filipe Magaia, and the fact that there were Mozambicans fleeing not only from the Portuguese, but also from Frelimo.[119] Nonetheless, Frelimo did not give way. This encouraged the growing unrest that had been gaining momentum at the IM and served to alienate most of those studying abroad.

The IM had become an ideologically charged melting pot. In direct contact with Maoist theories and influenced by the Cuban revolution, most students felt a natural antipathy towards Western influence within Frelimo, which Mondlane's lifestyle and political standing epitomized.

The IM students found sympathy for their grievances in Mateus Pinho Gwenjere, a Catholic priest recently arrived from Mozambique. Gwenjere, a staunch opponent of Portugal, had in fact been instrumental in dispatching students from Catholic missions in central Mozambique to Tanzania, using Malawi as a corridor. The priest was no longer safe and could not count on the protection of Bishop Soares de Resende in Beira, who was influential among the Portuguese authorities, even though he was harshly critical of their administration. As the colonial police periodically detained him for questioning, Gwenjere decided to skip the country in June 1967.

In Tanzania, the 40-year-old priest from Sofala went through the same formalities as any ordinary recruit, even receiving military training at Nachingwea. He wanted to join the guerrilla forces inside Mozambique, but Mondlane discouraged him from doing so. Impressed by the priest's intellect, which stood out from the majority of refugees of rural origin, Mondlane preferred to have him in Dar es Salaam instead. He introduced the priest to the higher echelons of the organization, and even offered him the post of dean of the IM. Gwenjere turned it down, saying that as a priest he could not become involved in managerial tasks. At most, he would agree to counsel the students. He accepted Mondlane's suggestion to testify before the United Nations in New York, to let the world know of his recent experiences in Mozambique. Not only that, Mondlane arranged for the priest to meet the Kennedy brothers in Washington. Mondlane was to regret having brought Father Mateus into Frelimo's inner circle. 'I made a terrible mistake', acknowledged Mondlane a few months later.[120]

Accompanied by Uria Simango, the priest left for New York in October. It was during their tour that Simango gave Gwenjere an account of the situation prevailing in Frelimo. Simango spoke of the summary executions of Frelimo members in Tanzania and Mozambique, attributing this to a plan conceived by southern Mozambicans to secure their supremacy in the movement. Reflecting the mood among a great many Frelimo members, Simango saw the presence of whites in the organization as having a detrimental effect on the independence struggle for they were certainly Portuguese agents. Simango spoke of the rampant dissatisfaction among the military in view of the heavy-handed methods employed after Filipe Magaia's death. There were also complaints of acute shortages of war equipment on the battlefront. Frelimo commanders claimed that the situation had worsened ever since Tanzania decided to divert weapons, which the OAU Liberation Committee had earmarked for Frelimo, to the Biafran secessionists in Nigeria.

Back in Dar es Salaam, Gwenjere was assigned to a Frelimo nurse training facility operating next to the IM. Being in close contact with the students, he became aware of their grievances, notably complaints of rampant tribalism. They believed the Central Committee decisions were yet another indication that the Frelimo leadership wanted to prevent non-southern Mozambicans from making it to the top.

It did not take long before the priest campaigned to rally the support of the Makonde-dominated armed forces and the Council of Elders. The Council consisted of old Makonde traditional chiefs on whom Frelimo had from the outset relied to communicate with the rather individualistic Makonde people. But the Council had since been kept at arms' length by Frelimo, particularly its Marxist orientated members who regarded it as feudal. Gwenjere's support base in Dar es Salaam spread right to the office of the second Tanzanian vice president where powerful people dealing with refugee affairs favoured Father Mateus. His idea was to replace Mondlane with Simango.

Encouraged by Gwenjere's attitude, the students adopted an even more militant posture towards the Frelimo leadership. They outspokenly criticized the presence of white Mozambican teachers at the IM, whom they regarded as a colonialist influence. Mondlane himself was not spared. Educated in the United States, married to a white American woman, and leading a typical western lifestyle in Dar es Salaam, Mondlane could only be an 'imperialist agent'.

Frelimo attempted to defuse the situation by having the priest removed from the scene. Gwenjere claimed that a guerrilla soldier had been hired to kill him, but confessed to the priest what his plans were. Frelimo then turned its attention to the students. On the night of 6 March 1968, the Frelimo defense and security chiefs, accompanied by two military commanders, entered the IM installations to arrest the student ringleaders. They were after Daniel Chatama, whom they saw as being behind the student unrest. Shots were fired within the IM where the two commanders were manhandling the students in their dormitories, throwing some of them off their beds. The Tanzanian police were alerted and intervened, arresting the raiding party. Frelimo defense chief Samora Machel and Aurélio Manave, one of the commanders, spent the night at the Kurasini police station, but were released on bail the next morning.

Fearing that in retaliation Frelimo would round them up and send them to Nachingwea, the students left the IM. Some of them sought refuge at Gwenjere's house. They refused to heed Frelimo's calls to return to the Institute. In May, Frelimo ordered the closure of IM, and decided that the students would be sent to Nachingwea. The students resisted this and asked for the protection of the Tanzanian authorities whose immediate response was to keep them in Dar es Salaam's remand prison for about a week. Afterwards, they were sent to the Rutamba refugee camp in southern Tanzania.

About a year later, most of the students fled to Kenya, joining former Frelimo guerrillas who had been fleeing in droves after the 1966 purges. They were all granted refugee status. With scholarships provided by the International University Exchange Fund and the UN Development Program, the students were allowed to enroll in Kenyan schools. The Joint Refugee Services of Kenya gave them food and shelter.

As for the whites in Frelimo, the Tanzanian government told them to leave the country because it believed racial tension had played a role in the dispute. Frelimo assigned the teachers to its office in Algiers. They returned permanently to Tanzania some two years later.[121]

10
Crisis within Frelimo Mounts

The disputes within Frelimo were far from over. The Makonde element decided to settle the dispute once and for all. Makonde guerrillas in particular continued to believe that Frelimo had been infiltrated by the Portuguese and the movement's senior members, including Mondlane, were part of the plot. They were convinced that all military plans were passed on to the Portuguese in advance, and this could be the only explanation for the ambushes they encountered as soon they crossed the Ruvuma River into Mozambique.

On 9 May 1968, armed with clubs and knives, a group of Makonde guerrillas marched to the Frelimo headquarters in Dar es Salaam with the intention of killing the entire leadership. They could not find Mondlane because he was out of the country. The assailants turned to the Frelimo security chief, but Chissano managed to escape with several others. Less fortunate was Mateus Muthemba, a former primary school teacher of Mondlane. He was knocked unconscious, dying of head injuries afterwards.

Meanwhile, with the support of guerrilla fighters loyal to Lázaro Kavandame, Gwenjere was committed to continuing his plan to oust Mondlane and have Uria Simango as the new Frelimo leader. The plot was known to, and might have even had the blessing of, several Tanzanian officials of Makonde extract who supported the idea of a Mozambique liberation movement dominated by their brothers from across the border. To Gwenjere's disappointment, Simango had a failure of nerve and refused to head a revolt against Mondlane. Simango preferred to deal with the situation at the next Frelimo Congress in 1969.

However, Kavandame and the Frelimo chairmen for Cabo Delgado called for a special Congress session in 1968 during which they intended to back Simango's bid for the presidency. Other provincial secretaries endorsed the call for an early Congress.[122] Mondlane agreed that it would be held in July 1968, but instead of in Tanzania as requested, he decided that it would take place in Niassa. He and his supporters felt safer if the event took place in an area where the Makonde would not feel at home. The Cabo Delgado chairmen boycotted the Congress, alleging that there was a plot to kill them if during the proceedings they disagreed with the leadership's views. The absence of 12 Cabo Delgado delegates to the Congress, Simango claimed, robbed him of the Frelimo presidency.[123] The Cabo Delgado chairmen refused to endorse the decisions of Congress.

At a meeting in Mtwara, southern Tanzania in August, to which TANU was invited, the chairmen vented a long list of grievances that had put them at odds with the Frelimo leadership. The Frelimo leadership was blamed for the spate of executions of combatants and civilians both in Tanzania and Mozambique. The chairmen rejected Mondlane's leadership and demanded his resignation or else they would part company. They decided that the Makonde woman to whom the Council of Elders had given the magic potion to protect Mondlane's life should surrender it because the Frelimo leader no longer deserved to be guarded by ancestral Makonde spirits.

At the Mtwara meeting, Mondlane failed to win back the support of the Cabo Delgado secretary, who instead launched a vitriolic attack on Frelimo and its leaders. Kavandame is reported to have told Mondlane, in the presence of Tanzanian Minister of State Lawi Sijaona, that Frelimo was a tribal-oriented organization. He took issue with the few Makonde students who had been expelled from the IM, claiming that they had been discriminated against. Kavandame then listed the names of those who had been executed on Frelimo's orders, but the Portuguese were blamed for it.

Sijaona allayed Mondlane's fears, assuring him that Tanzania would not side with the dissidents against him.[124]

Despite Mondlane's efforts, Kavandame and his men went ahead with their plan. They established 'road committees' so that no other Frelimo member operated in Cabo Delgado. In September, the Tanzanian government ordered a two-month closure of the border with Cabo Delgado to prevent Frelimo members from killing each other once inside Mozambique. Shortly after the border reopened, Frelimo sent its deputy chief of operations, Paulo Kankhomba, to Cabo Delgado to reorganize Frelimo's structures in the province, relieving those loyal to Kavandame from their posts. On 22 December 1968, as he was about to enter Cabo Delgado, a group of Frelimo youth leaguers waylaid Kankhomba, stabbing him to death. The Tanzanian police arrested several suspects, but none of them would reveal who had instructed them to commit the murder.[125]

In Washington, the State Department viewed the crisis Mondlane faced with apprehension. An August 1968 memorandum for the Secretary of State noted that 'Mondlane is probably in trouble. His often lofty and almost patrician manner has lost him support of some younger and more radical members of the party.' The memorandum continued:

> Unless he condescends to palaver in the traditional African manner with his followers and thrashes out their problems – and his – he may be in danger of losing Frelimo's leadership or, at least, of seriously weakening his position.[126]

In the wake of the August 1968 Mtwara meeting, Gwenjere put the final touches to his plan to hold fresh elections for a new Frelimo president. Delegates from Cabo Delgado, Mtwara, Zanzibar and Zambia had arrived in Dar es Salaam for the election scheduled for 3 January 1969. The priest was confident of the success of his move, not only because of the support he had from Frelimo's rank and file, but also from influential Tanzanians. Through J Matola, a Makonde police superintendent in the Dar es Salaam area, Gwenjere had gained access to Lawi Sijaona and Tanzania's second vice president, Rashidi Kawawa.

Mondlane, however, took swift action to reverse the virtual state of anarchy afflicting Frelimo. On 28 December, Gwenjere was arrested and confined to the Archbishops House in Tabora, western Tanzania. On 3 January 1969 the Frelimo Executive Committee suspended Kavandame from his provincial secretariat post.

Mondlane's endeavour to consolidate his position was cut short. On the morning of 3 February 1969, he was killed in a bomb blast at Betty King's house in Oyster Bay. King, who had since ended her association with the IM, worked at the time for a Tanzanian gemstone firm. She was put into police custody as a suspect.

11
Mondlane Assassinated

The full circumstances surrounding Mondlane's assassination shall only be known when Tanzania discloses the findings of its investigations conducted with the help of Scotland Yard and Interpol. Tanzania's decision not to publish them at length could be explained by its reluctance to reveal the level of disunity and squabbling that plagued Frelimo throughout its stay in that country and the involvement of Tanzanian officials with those opposed to Mondlane. These and other motives are certainly behind Frelimo's adoption of a similar attitude to the case. Instead of telling Mozambicans the entire extent of what really happened in the turbulent years of exile, which culminated in the death of its first president, Frelimo has made use of the assassination to discredit its opponents and justify the action taken against some of them.

Two days before his death, Mondlane met officials of the Tanzanian second vice president's office, informing them of his concern about Kavandame's activities. Mondlane noted that Kavandame and his followers were acting with the tacit support of Tanzanian officials. These, the Tanzanian police later revealed, included Lawi Sijaona and M Kalimaga, TANU's chairman for the Mtwara region. Earlier, Rashidi Kawawa had told Mondlane that the Tanzanian government could no longer guarantee his safety.[127]

Despite Mondlane's worries and the recent developments within Frelimo, particularly the attempt to assassinate him in May 1968, no precautions appeared to have been taken by the movement's Security Department. In fact, security was by all accounts slack. A senior Tanzanian Criminal Investigation Department (CID) officer revealed that the parcel-bomb that killed Mondlane had reached the Frelimo headquarters in Dar es Salaam on or before 1 February, but the Frelimo messenger could not recall having collected it from the post office. At least three people remembered seeing the parcel before the blast.[128] And what baffled the police most was that no security checks had been performed on the parcel itself, especially since it was addressed to the Frelimo president. The CID officer said Simango, whom Frelimo would later accuse of involvement in the assassination, had even slid the parcel's paper wrapper down to read the title of the book. Realizing that it was in French, which he could not read, Simango slid the wrapper back up again.[129]

Ten days after Mondlane's death, a further parcel-bomb similar to the one sent to him was received at the Frelimo headquarters, but addressed to Marcelino dos Santos. In March, a third parcel was discovered. Like the previous two, it had been posted in Dar es Salaam, but this time to Uria Simango in Nachingwea.

As Dar es Salaam was agog with rumours of an American conspiracy, the United States sought to put the record straight, at least in the eyes of Mondlane's widow. In a message of condolence to the widow, the Americans regretted 'the tragic death of [her] husband whose idealism, courage and intellect were so widely admired'.[130]

Portugal was quick to deny any involvement in Mondlane's death. In a statement issued the day after the assassination, Portugal attributed it to faction fighting within Frelimo. 'Although Eduardo Mondlane was educated in the United States', read a Foreign Ministry statement, 'some of his associates were trained in Prague, the People's Republic of China and in the Soviet Union, which explains the major dissent within the organisation.'[131] Despite the fact that the assassination occurred at the height of much infighting within Frelimo, evidence suggests that the PIDE had an hand in the case and might even have connived with some of the movement's dissidents. PIDE officials in Lourenço Marques are known to have celebrated when they learned of Mondlane's death. In 1964, the PIDE had considered assassinating Mondlane. In 1967, the PIDE in Lourenço Marques began planning an operation to that end. Codenamed Barbarossa, the operation consisted of sending a hit squad to Dar es Salaam during the peak tourist season.[132] Former PIDE inspector Rosa Casaco has hinted that the parcel-bomb that killed Mondlane was assembled in Lourenço Marques by Casimiro Monteiro, one of his colleagues.[133] Monteiro, who had been transferred from Lisbon in 1965, specialized in explosives.[134]

Indeed, a bomb disposal expert assigned to the Canadian Training Mission in Tanzania who defused the parcel bombs sent to Marcelino dos Santos and Simango, revealed that they had been assembled professionally. The batteries used to switch the detonators were of Japanese origin. Interpol learned from the Japanese police that the batteries were part of batch manufactured in August 1968 and exported to a Lourenço Marques firm in that month.[135]

Further evidence of Portuguese involvement came from Rebello de Souza, the colonial governor general of Mozambique. De Souza admitted that he 'was intrigued by the fact that the first REUTERS' reports from Dar es Salaam said Mondlane had been killed by a rifle shot'. The governor general told a US diplomat the day after the assassination that the Portuguese government 'thought that the use of a time-bomb was much more typical of the Makonde'. De Souza added that 'if it should turn out that Mondlane had been killed with a rifle, this would make the causes of the assassination even more obscure'. In any event, he reiterated the Portuguese Foreign Ministry's standpoint, adding that 'to blame the Portuguese would be to give Portuguese capabilities in Tanzania too much credit, even if they had been so minded which of course they were not'.[136]

In continuing their investigations, the Tanzanian police were surprised at the reaction of the IM students to Mondlane's death. They were overjoyed, and some even toasted his death, hoping that either Simango or Gwenjere would take over the reins of Frelimo.

As the police gained a broader picture of the conflictual situation within Frelimo, they centered their attention on the Makonde element. The police were particularly interested in questioning a Makonde believed to have been responsible for the death of Paulo Kankhomba in December. They had learnt that the man had meanwhile sent another group of Frelimo youth leaguers to Dar es Salaam with the aim of killing Mondlane. Learning that the police were after him, the Makonde vanished.[137]

A week after Mondlane's death, the CID questioned Kavandame in Mtwara, but his answers were incomplete and often contradictory. Kavandame was evasive, and tried to monopolize the conversation. In trying to establish the facts at Mtwara, the Tanzanian police felt increasingly frustrated because the local police commander was reluctant to take action against Kavandame. The commander feared the regional TANU chairman, M Kalimaga, a Makonde and a personal friend of Kavandame. The police commander actually left Mtwara for Lindi when he learned of the pending CID investigation and did not return while the investigators were in town. The CID could not get any help from the commander's subordinate inspectors either. When the CID decided to arrest Kavandame he had already slipped into Mozambique, defecting to the Portuguese in March.[138]

In its investigations at Mtwara, the CID found out that Kavandame had amassed a great deal of money from his handling of trade with Frelimo-controlled areas in Mozambique. In terms of an arrangement between Frelimo and the Tanzanians, Cabo Delgado peasant farmers took produce across the border. The Tanzanian government would then buy it covertly and place the money in Kavandame's personal bank account. Kavandame was then supposed to buy manufactured goods to send to Mozambique, but apparently very little reached Cabo Delgado. At the time of his questioning by the CID, Kavandame had 20 000 shillings in the bank, and owned several farms in the Mtwara region.

Kavandame has been represented by the Frelimo camp as standing for corruption and greed, only keen on replacing the colonialists, and his differences with the movement's leadership were merely because it opposed his methods. Yet, the resources Kavandame amassed suggest that there was more to it than straightforward corruption. That Kavandame had specific political goals in mind was evident from the military training of Makonde youths loyal to him given at one of the farms registered in his name. As the CID learned, Kavandame's youth leaguers were better fed, dressed and equipped than the Frelimo guerrillas themselves. He had almost complete control over Council of Elders members in Mtwara.[139]

For the Frelimo dissidents in Tanzania, the writing was clearly on the wall. With the prospects of bringing down the Frelimo leadership thwarted, they became disillusioned. In Dar es Salaam, members of the Council of Elders, according to the Tanzanian police, were most upset that the Frelimo leadership had not fallen into their hands as a result of Mondlane's assassination.[140] The defection of Kavandame created a sense of confusion in the ranks of the dissident faction. Several Frelimo commanders deserted the organization. Some mingled with the Tanzanian population, but others, with Frelimo hot on their heels, fled to neighbouring countries, including Mozambique. Others were not so lucky. The Tanzanian police arrested whoever Frelimo indicated to them as troublemakers, and interned them in detention camps in Dabalo and Tabora, in central Tanzania. Gradually, most of the Mozambicans fled the camps and settled in Kenya, like Gwenjere who escaped in December 1972.

The taking of Betty King into police custody reflected Tanzania's suspicions of Western involvement in the assassination. The police dossier on King made what the US ambassador described as 'unsupported allegations that the firm for which she worked was the arm of an American intelligence organisation'.[141] The Tanzania Intelligence Service (TIS) believed that certain Western governments, not necessarily supportive of the Lisbon regime, had unwittingly caused the death of Mondlane. By deliberately promoting dissent within Frelimo so as to weaken the pro-Communist elements around Mondlane, reasoned the TIS, those governments created a force that eventually grew out of their control.[142]

12
Frelimo after Mondlane

After Mondlane's death Simango was appointed Frelimo's interim president. Under the movement's constitution, he would stay in office until the next Congress. However, he faced immediate opposition from other Frelimo members.[143]

To forestall the possibility of the Simango camp seizing power after the assassination, those allied to Mondlane quickly informed the Frelimo commanders inside Mozambique that there had been a bomb blast at the movement's headquarters, in which Mondlane, Simango and other leading officials had all been killed.[144]

On 11 April, the Frelimo Central Committee began an eleven-day session during which Simango came under strong criticism. Despite his efforts to defend himself, Simango lost the interim presidency of Frelimo. The Central Committee opted for the creation of a three-man Presidential Council, including Simango, Machel and Marcelino dos Santos. Simango did not oppose this, realizing that, as in the second Congress, he would not count on the backing of his Makonde allies as the latter had been thrown into disarray in view of Kavandame's defection.

The southerners and the Marxist tendency within Frelimo, which faced the same ethnic and racial hostility from the northerners, used the Council to consolidate their position. They saw no reason for retaining Simango as they knew of his close association with the so-called reactionaries in Frelimo.

The purges that started in 1966 continued after Mondlane's death. In the wake of the April Central Committee session, Silvério Nungu was demoted as head of the Department of Administration and sent to Cabo Delgado. In June he was tried by a people's court for alleged corruption. Simango claimed that Nungu, a former Udenamo member from Sofala, was forced to write a declaration admitting his guilt, and afterwards was beaten until he lost consciousness. The following day, the Frelimo guards hung him by the neck and pierced his stomach with a bayonet. He died on 18 June.[145] As in the case of Magaia, the real cause of Nungu's death was not reported. Frelimo attributed it to a hunger strike. Also allegedly executed in 1969 was Barnabé Thawe who once served at the Frelimo office in Songea.

Simango interpreted all this as an effort by his two partners in the Presidential Council not just to undermine his position, but to eliminate him. On 3 November 1969, Simango released a paper entitled 'Gloomy Situation in Frelimo' in which he exposed the internal friction that had plagued the organization since its founding. He claimed that the situation became more serious towards the end of 1965, culminating with Magaia's assassination and the execution of Frelimo fighters and civilians in Mozambique. He spoke of 'a general demoralization among many members of the Central Committee and their quitting of the organization', adding that 'this situation is unavoidable as long as exist a group within that is determined to liquidate others physically for political or material gains'. Simango pointed out that 'instead of fearing the Portuguese colonialist, we go insecure and distrustful of one's own brother, for he does not care to kill others'.

Simango distanced himself from those, who, in the wake of Mondlane's death, had found it appropriate to steer Frelimo ideologically towards the Eastern bloc. As he saw it, Frelimo should not allow itself to be divided between scientific socialism and capitalism. He rejected the notion that the movement was establishing a socialist system in the country. To claim this, he said, merely showed ignorance on the part of its proponents. He warned against antagonizing the domestic bourgeoisie, which should instead be accepted into Frelimo so as to contribute to the independence struggle.

As a solution to the crisis, Simango outlined a six-point plan that called for the restoration of democratic methods of operation; the abolition of nepotism and tribalism and equal treatment for all ethnic groups; adherence to the basic principles of Frelimo's constitution; the creation of an atmosphere that would draw students back to Frelimo; reconciliation with all Frelimo deserters, and an end to the execution of guerrilla fighters. He demanded the resignation of Machel, Chissano and Marcelino dos Santos, stating the need for them to be put on trial in view of their execution of many Frelimo members. In a calculated move, Simango said that 'failure to comply with these demands will mean my immediate resignation'.

Simango was confident that the military, due to the recent dispute between the Makonde and the Frelimo leadership, would rally in his support. He believed that prospects of continued leadership of Frelimo for the other Presidential Council members were slim without the military's support.

On 8 November, the Frelimo Executive Committee met to discuss Simango's paper. The Committee denied all the charges, noting that the accusations were aimed at denigrating senior Frelimo officials in view of their true nationalism, patriotism and revolutionary standing. The Committee added that the paper had been inspired by Simango's personal ambition. The Executive Committee did not actually expel Simango, deciding instead to suspend his membership of the Presidential Council until the next Central Committee session.[146]

Several critics of Simango, not necessarily aligned to his opponents in Frelimo, felt that his November 1969 stand had been long overdue. They pointed out that his condemnation of the politically motivated killings was unconvincing, considering his own knowledge of them at the time, and even, as some have suggested, his own tacit approval. So much so that when the Tanzanian authorities raised some of the allegations contained in Simango's paper with the Frelimo officials concerned, they retorted that Simango himself had been a party to the decisions about which he was now complaining. This is said to have prompted the Tanzanian police to remove Simango from Dar es Salaam and keep him with other Frelimo dissidents at a camp in Dabalo.

But Josefate Muhlanga, Simango's brother-in-law, suggests that the decision to deport Simango to Dabalo had more to do with his public condemnation of the Tanzanian government's appropriation of military equipment earmarked for Frelimo, which was either sent to the Biafran secessionists or used by the Tanzanian armed forces.[147]

Before the Frelimo Central Committee met to take a final decision on Simango, he left for Cairo. Eventually, during a session held in May, the Central Committee decided to expel Simango from Frelimo, and that he 'ought to be subjected to people's justice in Mozambique'. As for the Presidential Council, the Central Committee abolished it after 'realizing that the reasons that had led to its establishment were no longer valid, and that it was now possible and appropriate to further centralize the leadership'.[148] Samora Machel was designated Frelimo president and Marcelino dos Santos the vice president. As with the April 1969 Central Committee decision to establish the Presidential Council, the May 1970 session disregarded Frelimo statutes, which stated that Frelimo's president and vice president should be elected by Congress.

Internally, Frelimo continued to be plagued by the same problems that had characterized it since its inception. Reports of executions of Frelimo military personnel continued to reach Tanzania. In October 1969, ten guerrillas suspected of being Gwenjere sympathizers were publicly executed in the Catur region of Niassa Province. This was said to have sparked off a new wave of defections of guerrillas to the Portuguese, while others sought refuge in Malawi and Tanzania.[149]

Defections of both junior and senior Frelimo members continued to be reported. In 1969, Casal Ribeiro abandoned Frelimo and settled with his family in northern Tanzania. In July of the same year, António Almeida, Frelimo's provincial military commander for Tete, abandoned the organization amid claims that he was collaborating with the Portuguese. Four months later, Alexandre Magno, Frelimo's first secretary for Zambézia, defected to the Portuguese. Several other Frelimo members, including Samuel Dhlakama, Gabriel Simbine, Eduardo Mbateya and Eli Ndimeni sought political asylum with the Tanzanian government,[150] but most of them returned to Frelimo. Aligned to this group was Miguel Murupa, an American-trained economist who had been serving as Frelimo's deputy secretary for foreign affairs. The Tanzanians handed Murupa and others over to Frelimo. As a disciplinary measure, Frelimo sent them to Cabo Delgado. Fearing that he would meet the same fate of others in his circumstances, Murupa escaped once inside Mozambique, turning himself over to the Portuguese in November 1970.[151]

The following year saw the defections of João Abílio Andrade, Fernando Timóteo Bila, Joaquim Nhaunga, and Januário Napulua. In March 1972, Wills Kadewell, a former Frelimo first secretary for Niassa, defected to the Portuguese, alleging tribal disputes with the Frelimo leadership.[152]

Four months later it was the turn of João Craveirinha, a nephew of the Mozambican poet. Craveirinha, who worked under Jorge Rebelo in Frelimo's Information Department, spoke of religious persecution within the organization and of a systematic campaign against intellectuals.[153]

Frelimo commanders Lumbela and Muhate, the latter trained with Joaquim Chissano in the USSR, also defected to the Portuguese. Lumbela had learned that he was to be executed for having disagreed with his seniors.

Ideologically, Frelimo made its realignment with the Eastern bloc countries even more obvious. Frelimo regarded them as its 'natural allies'. From 1970 onwards, Frelimo strengthened its ties with the Moscow-aligned Portuguese Communist Party, PCP, and its armed wing, the

Acção Revolucionária Armada, ARA. In Portugal itself, ARA undermined the regime's colonial war effort in daring commando operations. In October 1970, ARA placed explosive charges on board the *Cunene*, a ship docked at the port of Lisbon and loaded with war materiel for the Portuguese Armed Forces fighting in Africa. In March 1971, ARA destroyed 30 aircraft at Tancos, the largest Portuguese military complex.[154] In April, the Portuguese ship *Angoche* was hijacked while sailing with military equipment along the Mozambican coast. Its crew of 44, believed to have been taken to Nachingwea, has never been seen alive again.

After the 1965 Che Guevara fiasco, the Cubans finally succeeded in cementing their relations with Frelimo. Until then, Mondlane had ensured a balanced East-West position as well as an independent position within the Sino-Soviet dispute.[155] The Machel-Santos leadership eventually sided with the Soviet Union and those under its sphere of influence, turning its back on the Chinese. It was as if Mondlane's death had come as a blessing in disguise.

The centralization of power, to which the May 1970 session of the Central Committee alludes, saw the consolidation of Frelimo's 'correct line'. The latter represented the self-styled revolutionary faction within Frelimo with Samora Machel and Marcelino dos Santos at its head. Its claim to legitimacy dates back to the Second Frelimo Congress of July 1968 which marked the defeat of the Simango-Gwenjere-Kavandame alliance. The revolutionaries' Marxist outlook developed only after Mondlane's demise, though attempts have since been made to present it as a legacy of the original Frelimo leadership.

The defeated alliance and its followers within Frelimo were to become known as the 'reactionary line'. In Frelimo's view, the reactionary line espoused the principle of a quick military victory, as opposed to the concept of protracted struggle followed by the revolutionaries. It was racist and tribalist in its outlook, and bent on replacing the Portuguese colonial system with other forms of economic exploitation and political oppression.

But that ought to be put in the right perspective. The so-called revolutionaries were once party to the idea of a rapid military victory against the Portuguese, as seen in their 1964 effort to simultaneously start operations in areas as distant from the Frelimo headquarters as Tete and Zambézia as well as in provinces south of the Save River, including the Mozambican capital. It was Mondlane, who, after all, had predicted the fall of the Portuguese colonial regime in a matter of five years.

The revolutionaries' stated intention of doing away with tribalism not only within Frelimo, but also in the country as a whole smacked of pure rhetoric for it reflected the views of an ethnic group that had succeeded in consolidating its power at the expense of other groups.

Purportedly non-racial, the new Frelimo leadership was willing to accept Mozambicans of different racial backgrounds in its midst. But that had strings attached – white, brown and yellow had to subscribe to the revolutionaries' views, otherwise they would all be dismissed as settlers or agents of colonialism, a theme that Frelimo would continue to harp on well after independence.

In essence, the role of the revolutionaries clearly showed that in fact they were the ones committed to a political, social and economic program of action that, in practice, did not differ much from the tenets of the colonial era. The heavy-handed manner in which they went about implementing their program merely ensured the continuation of the conflict that had not only pitted Mozambicans against one another within Frelimo, but also kept its leadership at odds with those it sought to rule. Whereas at independence the Frelimo program was implemented nation-wide, the proportions the conflict acquired were of necessity much larger. It was as if the tradition of conflict that had been the hallmark of Frelimo ever since its founding days refused to let go.

Part II

Independence

1
Portugal Transfers Power to Frelimo

A priority in General António de Spínola's agenda once appointed new
Portuguese head of state following the Armed Forces Movement (MFA)
coup of April 1974 was to unravel the colonial crisis. But he intended to
accomplish this by implementing the plan he had elaborately dealt with
in his book *Portugal e o Futuro* published just prior to the coup. In a
nutshell, Spínola's plan was in no way designed to alter the colonial
status quo. As he argued, 'without the African territories, [Portugal]
would be confined to a corner of Europe (...) and its independence
totally compromised'. Spínola wanted to establish a Lusophone community of nations by granting greater autonomy to the colonies,
though maintaining intact the umbilical cord with Portugal. The
peoples of the colonies would be given a say in the running of their
own affairs, and put on an equal footing with the respective white communities. As for the nationalist movements fighting for independence,
Spínola dismissed them as 'non-representative of the spirit of African
emancipation'.[1]

A month after the coup, Portugal began exploratory talks with
Frelimo in Zambia. Unhappy with the outcome of the talks, Frelimo
stepped up its military operations. The Portuguese Military Command
in Mozambique reported incidents in Manica and Cabo Delgado. For
the first time since the start of the war, Frelimo resumed operations
in Zambézia in July.[2] The Portuguese reported that a 300-strong
Frelimo group approached their garrison at Omar on the south bank of
Rovuma River in Cabo Delgado on the night of 31 July. Using
megaphones, Frelimo reportedly enticed the military personnel to a
meeting near the airstrip, saying that the war was over. Unarmed, the
137 Portuguese soldiers proceeded to the airstrip, only to be surrounded
and taken prisoner to Tanzania. Frelimo's version of the incident was

that the garrison had surrendered after being warned of an imminent attack.

Amid these reports, the MFA ordered the troops on the ground to limit their operations to a mere defensive role. On 23 July, the MFA committees in Cabo Delgado and Tete stated that they would declare 'a unilateral cease-fire if a full-fledged cease-fire accord had not been reached with Frelimo by the end of the month'. From that month onwards, the MFA committees 'would refuse to supply the troops on the ground'.[3] Without consulting Spínola, the MFA resumed talks with Frelimo in Europe as well as in Dar es Salaam. To facilitate the negotiations between the two, Zambia turned its back on Coremo, barring it from talks with the Portuguese delegation that had arrived in Lusaka in early June. Coremo offices in Lusaka were ordered to close down, while the Zambia National Defence Force rounded up Coremo guerrillas assembled in bases on the Mozambique border. Those arrested were subsequently handed over to Frelimo in Tanzania.[4]

In Mozambique itself, the liberalization brought about by the Portuguese military coup resulted in the formation of an unprecedented number of political organizations. Among the first to surface with a political agenda was Máximo Dias, a 37-year-old lawyer of Goanese extraction born in Zambézia Province. With the agreement of the Portuguese, Dias launched in February 1974 the Grupo Unido de Moçambique (Gumo), which sought to protect the rights of ethnic minorities with the advent of a majority-rule government. According to Dias, the domestic intelligentsia, including Mário da Graça Machungo, an economist trained in Portugal who had opted to work within the colonial establishment, as well as Salomão Munguambe and Domingos Arouca, endorsed the Gumo idea.[5] Arouca had just completed a jail sentence after his arrest by the PIDE in 1964 for sedition.

Also active was Joana Semião, a 37-year-old Makua from Nampula who had split with Frelimo in 1968. After a spell with Coremo, she returned to Mozambique in 1971 and began a teaching career, first in Beira and afterwards in Lourenço Marques. Semião had made her political agenda known in January 1974. Although in the past she had espoused violence as the only means of resolving disputes, Semião was now willing to work with the Portuguese government to fulfil the aspirations of Mozambicans. Like Dias, Semião appealed to the ethnic minorities in the country, urging them to form 'an internal front', which, 'in co-operation with the Portuguese government, would strengthen the participation of leading elements of the [black, mulatto, white, Indian and Chinese communities] in the running of public affairs'. Semião spoke of a 'Mozambicanization' of the country's political life, but she stressed that she did not want it to 'evolve in a catastrophic manner'.[6]

Dias and Semião worked together, but for a short period. Although in the wake of the April 1974 coup Dias had favoured a 'progressive political autonomy' for Mozambique 'within the existing Portuguese political institutions', in less than a month he made a political U-turn. In the event of a Frelimo political democratic party being established in Mozambique, Gumo, he said, would immediately join that party, forming the one and only united, peaceful and active front until the final victory of the people of Mozambique.[7]

Unlike Dias, Semião not only remained committed to Gumo's initial goals, but also came to adopt an openly hostile position towards Frelimo. The two split, and Semião campaigned from then onwards to bring all exiled political leaders under the umbrella of a single organization. Semião secured the support of the Mozambique African National Congress (MANC), now under the leadership of António Makulube, and other Gumo officials opposed to Dias. In June, she went to Malawi to meet Coremo officials who had since fled Zambia to escape arrest. Other of Semião's lieutenants met Frelimo dissidents in Nairobi.[8] The exiled Mozambicans agreed to work together and return home to campaign for the independence elections.[9]

The first to arrive in Mozambique in early July was Uria Simango. He had joined Coremo after parting company with Frelimo. Simango stressed the need for all Mozambicans, regardless of their colour or race, to play a role in the new Mozambique. In August, Simango and others announced the formation of the Partido de Coligação Nacional, PCN. Simango was elected president and Paulo Gumane the vice-president.[10] Basílio Banda, who had been Gwenjere's private secretary when the Catholic priest campaigned for the ousting of Mondlane, became PCN's secretary-general. Coremo's information secretary Arcanjo Kambeu was put in charge of PCN's foreign affairs, and Frelimo dissident Manuel Tristão became its organizing secretary. The information portfolio was assigned to Nasser Mbule, another Frelimo dissident exiled in Nairobi in 1971. Semião was put in charge of education and culture, while Gwenjere became PCN's national adviser. Not listed in the PCN's membership was Miguel Murupa although he was the one who suggested the name for the coalition party. In its first public statement, the PCN said Mozambicans should be granted immediate independence through a democratic process. In a clear reference to Frelimo, the PCN said:

the future of Mozambique should not be compromised by any accord negotiated and reached between the Lisbon government and any organization or political group to the exclusion of others. No organization should claim the right to be the sole and legitimate representative of the Mozambican people without being put to the test of democratic process.

For the PCN, the 'the solution to Mozambique's colonial problem can only be found by means of a multiracial society which respects the views, traditions and culture of the various races, and social and ethnic layers forming part of the people of Mozambique'.[11] But the PCN's appeal had been overtaken by events. Some two weeks after the launching of the PCN the Portuguese government and Frelimo signed the Lusaka Accord whereby sovereignty rights were transferred to Frelimo and independence would be declared in the following year on the occasion of the organization's 13th founding anniversary.

President Spínola had been effectively outmanoeuvred by the MFA faction committed to an unconditional transfer of power to Frelimo. Without Spínola's knowledge, MFA member Major Melo Antunes had been conducting secret talks with Frelimo since July. Spínola's attempts to include in the text of the Lusaka Accord a clause stating that the Mozambican people would 'freely and democratically choose the country's political and social regime' was turned down during the 5–7 September talks in the Zambian capital, with the Portuguese delegation making no effort to see to it that Spínola's wishes were complied with. Spínola eventually resigned as head of state on 30 September, for he believed the internationally recognized principles of decolonization had been 'misrepresented with the deliberate intention of replacing them with undemocratic measures, detrimental to the real interests of the African peoples'.[12]

2
Jorge Jardim – Myth and Reality

Also overtaken by events was Jorge Jardim, an influential Portuguese who had been living in Mozambique since 1952. An agronomist born in Lisbon in 1920, Jardim began his political career in Salazar's cabinet as under secretary of state for commerce and industry. A dedicated Fascist influenced by the likes of Spanish Falangist leader Primo de Rivera, Jardim resigned from the cabinet in 1952 over differences with his minister's liberalization of the commercial sector.[13]

But as a Salazar protégé, Jardim's political career was far from over. Over the next 16 years, the Portuguese dictator assigned him a variety of special tasks in India, Brazil, Angola and Mozambique. Jardim established a permanent base in Mozambique in 1952 as managing director of the Lusalite asbestos company near Beira owned by the Abecassis, a Portuguese Jewish family. His political brief in Mozambique included fostering friendly relations with neighbouring independent countries, notably Malawi and Zambia, so as to discourage them from following Tanzania's path and allowing their territories to be used as sanctuaries for independence movements.

He did this with relative success in Malawi, using Mozambique's ports and railways facilities as well as his business contacts in Portugal as bargaining chips. Malawi even appointed Jardim as its consul general in Beira. Cooperation between the two governments extended to the security field, with Portugal providing military hardware and training to the Malawi Young Pioneers. Information on the threat posed by Malawi's domestic and exiled opponents was regularly passed on to the Malawian authorities.

Zambia's Kenneth Kaunda proved to be a more difficult case to handle. Although Kaunda did not establish formal relations with Portugal, he made extensive use of Mozambican as well as Angolan railways and ports in tandem with his support for the independence movements.

Portuguese society under dictatorial rule evolved around spheres of influence at the crest of which flourished the protégés and friends of the regime. The regime promoted nepotism as a means of consolidating its power. The cult of subservience and dependency was nurtured across the nation, with those in influential positions revered by people wanting to curry favour with a view to promoting their personal interests. In the specific case of Jardim, he soon gained in Mozambique the reputation of Salazar's right-hand man. Jardim built around himself an aura of prestige and influence, all too happy to let the gullible fantasize about the real extent of his political clout, the 'private armies' that he never owned, and his financial resources. Jardim once represented the Mozambican constituency in Lisbon's one-party National Assembly. Soon, companies willing to establish a foothold in the colony, or to expand their business activities, protect their interests and be in the good books of the powers that be, saw it appropriate to bring Jardim into their fold. In addition to Lusalite, Jardim's second main source of income was as managing director of the Sonarep oil refinery owned by the industrialist Manuel Boullosa. A string of other companies offered Jardim nominal posts in their administration boards at a generous remuneration. At the peak of his career, Jardim served in about a dozen firms, ranging from insurance, mills, the news media, sugar estates, and suppliers of rolling stock for the armed forces.

Outsiders saw Jardim, mistakenly, as the wealthiest man in Mozambique, on par with the Rockefellers or the Oppenheimers, though his overall income obviously placed him well above the average Portuguese in the colony. Jardim's access to the government's secret fund contributed to that erroneous perception.

Jardim developed his own political agenda for Mozambique. He accepted Frelimo and Coremo as a reality, but saw no reason why he should not also be politically active, playing a controlling role in an independent Mozambique. He began to contemplate more seriously this possibility after Caetano replaced a senile Salazar in 1968. If until then Jardim felt obliged to remain loyal to Salazar, who was even the godfather of one of his 12 children, to Caetano he had little or no obligations. 'Now that Salazar is gone', said Jardim to one of his confidants, 'I have my hands free to do something for Mozambique.'[14]

Realizing that the solution to Mozambique's colonial dispute had to be found at the negotiating table, Jardim sought Kaunda's mediation in a negotiated independence settlement with Frelimo. Without Lisbon's knowledge, Jardim met the Zambian leader in Lusaka in July 1973. Subsequent discussions were held with Kaunda's personal assistant, Mark Chona.[15]

The Zambians succeeded in leading Jardim through a path which he had certainly not wanted to follow. Instead of only tackling the Mozambican question, the Zambians included the other Portuguese colonies in the agenda. Chona saw to it that Frelimo was kept informed of the developments, but at Frelimo's request the Zambians never brought the two together. Frelimo preferred to wait and engage Portugal in talks only once the situation was clearer. Jardim's initiative was seen in Frelimo circles as an indication that the colonial edifice was finally beginning to crack, and assumed that he was acting on behalf of the Lisbon authorities. Frelimo encouraged the Zambians 'to continue talking to Jardim and to tell him that Frelimo was very interested'.[16]

Chona presented Jardim with two memoranda on a framework for independence. Portugal would agree to grant independence to its territories, pending negotiations with the independence movements. Zambia would facilitate such negotiations. To entice Jardim and, through him, the Portuguese government who the Zambians too assumed was behind Jardim's initiative, the memoranda emphasized the upholding of Portugal's political, cultural and economic interests in the future independent countries. Although this purported to be the views of the independence movements, none of it reflected Frelimo's own program for Mozambique.

With the memoranda in his hands, which he personally decided to call the 'Lusaka Program', Jardim did not know quite what to do next. He had gone to Lusaka without a mandate from Caetano or any of his ministers. An initiative of that magnitude required a power base from which to proceed, which Jardim lacked. In his memoirs, Jardim admitted that to build such a power base he tried to enlist the support of Colonel Diogo Neto, the Portuguese Air Force commander in Mozambique. Col. Neto, however, was also the MFA representative in the colony. And Major Águas Varela, the officer commanding the Special Intelligence and Intervention Services (SEII), with which Jardim had long been involved, was another MFA member. General Arriaga, the man on whom Jardim thought he could count, had just ended his assignment in Mozambique in July 1973. Jardim's so-called 'private armies' could not be counted upon either for the locally recruited commando units had always been under the effective control of the Portuguese Armed Forces. In fact, Colonel Pinto Ferreira, the commander of the units, had embraced the MFA's leftist wing. Jardim would describe him in his memoir as 'a commander that had lost prestige'.

As rumours of Jardim's visits to Lusaka reached Lisbon, action was taken to curtail his movements. The Abecassis family was advised to dispense with Jardim as Lusalite's managing director. To compensate, Lisbon offered Jardim the post of ambassador to Malawi. Before being dismissed from Lusalite, Jardim resigned from the company in early 1974.[17] If any questions still hung in the air about Jardim's personal financial clout, his departure from Dondo and the need to find alternative accommodation served to clarify the situation. He had just about the right amount in his bank account to buy a house in Beira's beach front on sale for the equivalent of US$75,000 at the then rate of exchange.

When Jardim sensed that he had placed himself in a cul-de-sac, he knocked at the doors of acquaintances in Portugal to where he returned in February. In Lisbon, he showed his 'Lusaka Program' to Arriaga, but to his surprise, the general told him that to endorse the plan would be to betray Portugal.[18] Besides, not many months earlier, Jardim had antagonized Arriaga and several members of the Portuguese Armed Forces hierarchy over his handling of the Wiryamu massacre in Tete. Despite repeated denials by the military, Jardim presented evidence to Caetano showing that an armed forces unit had in fact committed atrocities in Tete. As a result, the Tete governor and military commander, Colonel Armindo Videira, lost his job, and Arriaga was brought into disrepute. Not only that, Jardim provoked the wrath of the Portuguese Special Forces whose 6th Company had been responsible for Wiryamu. Although Jardim's main goal in investigating Wiryamu had been to settle a personal score with Videira, his biographer suggests that Jardim merely wanted to appear in the eyes of Kaunda, and through him, the Tanzanian and Frelimo leaders, not as a symbol of colonialism, but as a humanist who even uncovered war atrocities.[19]

A week before the coup in Lisbon, Jardim showed the memoranda to Caetano, but the Portuguese premier felt he had gone too far, and was never to raise the issue until he was deposed. For Caetano, Jardim had 'treacherously concocted a "Lusaka program"'.[20]

In the wake of the coup, Jardim decided to publicize his Zambian initiative. If until then Jardim had upheld Lisbon's colonial policies, all of a sudden he appeared as an apostle of independence. Jardim's dual agenda had of necessity to be interpreted as opportunistic by his political adversaries who descended on him with all their might in view of his overnight reversal of character. Particularly vociferous were long standing opponents of the old regime, who, after the coup, operated under the banner of the Democratas de Moçambique, a pressure group consisting primarily of lawyers from the colony's middle class. Among them were four barristers who had recently defended two Catholic priests charged with sedition. Ironically, Jardim, the private investigator of the Wiryamu massacre, had masterminded the arrest of the priests and wanted to silence one of them for exposing in a homily the atrocities committed by the Portuguese Armed Forces in the very province of Tete.

Jardim desisted from engaging in public debate with the Democratas de Moçambique. He remained convinced that the Lusaka memoranda could form the basis of a negotiated settlement with Frelimo, and was particularly hopeful that Zambia would ensure his role in independence talks. The rapidly changing political situation proved him wrong. Given that after the June meeting in Lusaka, officials of the new Portuguese government and Frelimo continued to hold talks elsewhere, the Zambians realized that Jardim had to be scrapped. Embarrassed by having agreed to meet Jardim in the first place, particularly in view of his inflated claims about the 'Lusaka Program', the Zambians were at pains to downplay the Jardim initiative which Kaunda had previously praised. Unconvincingly, Chona would claim that he and Kaunda had taken Jardim for a ride.[21]

The Democratas de Moçambique continued with their campaign to promote Frelimo, echoing its claim to sole and legitimate representativity. Acting as a de facto Frelimo front organization, the Democratas vilified other political forces, portraying them as neo-colonial outfits. For this they counted on the support of leading intellectuals and university students grouped in the Associação Académica de Moçambique (AAM). Liberal journalists who had gained the upper hand in newsrooms until recently serving the colonial establishment added their support. As a whole, the Democratas and their followers constituted themselves into a powerful Frelimo spearhead operating in Mozambique's urban areas where the movement was eager to establish a foothold.

3
The Long Arm of Frelimo

On 7 September, as Portugal and Frelimo signed Mozambique's independence accord in Lusaka, a group of Portuguese settlers and white Mozambicans stormed the radio station in Lourenço Marques to voice their opposition to the deal. The Movimento Moçambique Livre (MML) was thus born. To all intents and purposes it was a movement opposed to independence and perceived by the majority of the population as wishing to maintain intact the colonial links.

Taking advantage of this rare opportunity to air their views nationwide, the PCN used the MML platform to state its opposition to the independence accord, and insist on the holding of free elections before Portugal relinquished its powers. The PCN's association with the settler uprising was to haunt its leaders for the rest of their lives. Frelimo used this as evidence that they too stood for a neo-colonial alternative.

Under pressure from the Portuguese authorities, the MML crumbled four days after it had come into being. Its leaders could not even count on the support of the South African government which did not want a repetition of Rhodesia's whites-only independence. In fact, Pretoria had realigned its foreign policy with a view to safeguarding the apartheid regime.

In October, South African Prime Minister John Vorster announced that in terms of what he had recently discussed with African and European leaders, South Africa would ensure peace and stability in southern Africa. The long-standing Rhodesian dispute was to be settled once and for all, and black governments allowed to take over in Mozambique and Angola. In return, South Africa would not be harassed for its apartheid policy.

The Vorster government saw to it that any signs of support from whatever quarters within South Africa towards the MML or any other force opposed to a Frelimo take over would be squashed. The Bureau of State Security, BOSS, aborted an invasion of southern Mozambique by the South African Army before independence was declared.[22] Arrangements for the invasion had been made with António Champalimaud, a Portuguese industrialist with vast economic interests in Mozambique, and South Africa's Directorate of Military Intelligence.[23]

Before the signing of the independence accord, the South Africans had advised Uria Simango not to take any drastic action against Frelimo. They warned him that Lourenço Marques was surrounded by Frelimo guerrillas, and that without arms, the PCN did not stand a chance.[24] Similarly, the Rhodesians snubbed Simango when he attempted to meet cabinet members in Salisbury to enlist support for his party. He was told by a Rhodesian intelligence (CIO) officer in October that 'there would be no question of him being accorded the type of interview he had requested until it had been ascertained whether his plans and intentions justified a recommendation for such action'.[25] The Rhodesians wanted Simango to do the impossible, considering that in terms of the independence accord, no political opposition would be allowed. 'Before Rhodesia would give consideration to his request', the CIO recommended that:

Firstly, he had to provide proof that the numerous opposition groups had united to form a cohesive body with an elected leadership; secondly, to provide convincing evidence of the viability of their plans as an opposition party which could lead to success in the attainment of their aims; thirdly that they possessed an organizational structure within Mozambique with which to gain the support of the populace.[26]

With the Frelimo-led transitional government in place in Lourenço Marques, Frelimo gave priority to the suppression of all forms of opposition either at home or abroad. Frelimo's security chief, who was designated prime minister in the transitional government, would meticulously execute a plan conceived by his peers in Tanzania, whereby Mozambicans known for their recent and past stand against Frelimo were all marked for arrest if in Mozambique, and abduction if living abroad. Others, such as the exiled students from the defunct IM, were encouraged to return home, but were promptly arrested upon arrival at the country's airports. Portugal became an accomplice to the plan, actively assisting Frelimo.

Frelimo soldiers entered Simango's residence in Beira in early October to arrest him. Since he had left the country before the wave of arrests started, they took his wife. Her three minor children were left unattended and would never see her alive again.[27]

Portuguese security policemen arrested Joana Semião shortly after her arrival from Malawi at Beira's airport, handing her over to Frelimo. Other detained PCN members were sent to a newly established Frelimo military barracks west of Beira where Frelimo army deserters were being kept.

Having learned that Simango was in Kenya, Frelimo sought help from Malawi for his arrest. In November, Albert Nqumayo, a Malawian minister and secretary-general of the ruling Malawi Congress Party, invited Simango to travel to Blantyre as a matter of urgency in view of a pending cabinet meeting during which the situation in Mozambique would be discussed.[28] Shortly after arrival in Blantyre, Simango was taken to the Milange border post and handed over to Frelimo military officers. Without realizing it, Simango had been lured into a trap. Subsequently, Frelimo had the Mozambican media reporting Simango's arrest 'inside Mozambique'.[29]

Also in November, the Malawians arrested the PCN vice-president, Paulo Gumane, and ten other PCN officials. Like Simango, they were all handed over to Frelimo at Milange.[30] Awaiting them was João Honwana, Frelimo's security chief for Zambézia. He had the prisoners tied against an army truck's bodywork, their heads upside down, and driven to the Frelimo military camp at Mônguè. Simango and Gumane were set aside and flown to Tanzania.[31]

Judas Honwana, who had split with Frelimo in the early 1960s to become Coremo's information vice-secretary, fell into a similar trap to Simango. Living in Cairo at the time, he was lured to Tanzania by Marcelino dos Santos. Posing as Simango, Dos Santos sent a telegram to Honwana, asking him to attend a reconciliatory meeting with Frelimo in Dar es Salaam. Travelling expenses were to be covered by Frelimo, said Santos in the telegram. Upon his arrival in Dar es Salaam, Honwana and his family were arrested and taken to Nachingwea.

Raúl Casal Ribeiro, who, after parting from Frelimo, had been living with his family in northern Tanzania, was also taken to Nachingwea. This time, Frelimo had requested the assistance of the Tanzanian police.

Ribeiro and more than 300 other political detainees, whom Frelimo had rounded up since the inauguration of the transitional government, were paraded in Nachingwea during a show trial in April 1975. Sérgio Vieira, serving at the time as Samora Machel's private secretary, organized the proceedings. With the promise of pardoning, in keeping with 'Frelimo's prestigious tradition of clemency', Vieira and his staff extracted self-incriminating confessions from the detainees. Others, such as Simango, were reported to have made confessions under duress. Reminiscent of the Stalinist era, the detainees were then instructed to make public confessions of guilt, portraying themselves as enemies of the people, guided, not by any ideology, but by foreign interests. They all pleaded with Frelimo to show them the way.

Individually or in groups, the detainees were paraded before a tribune of honor presided over by Machel who acted as both prosecutor and judge. Frelimo military personnel stood by in a deliberately intimidatory presence. High-ranking Tanzanian officials lent an air of dignity to the travesty of justice by rubbing shoulders with leading Frelimo members at the tribune. Frelimo cronies working as foreign correspondents in Dar es Salaam were on hand to report on the event in a manner that suited first and foremost the purpose of the exercise.

For Frelimo, Uria Simango's presence at Nachingwea was the accomplishment of at least part of the pledge it had made nearly five years earlier to have him stand people's justice in view of the publication of his paper, 'Gloomy Situation in Frelimo'. As Simango entered the precinct to read a lengthy confession partly drafted by Vieira, in which he retracted all his previous statements, the audience, consisting of Frelimo's rank and file, burst in unison, singing 'Simango, You're a Sell-out, Simango, You're a Traitor'.

Throughout his confession Simango clearly indicated that he had been well rehearsed for the parody at Nachingwea. Concurring in verbatim with the Frelimo Executive Committee communiqué issued in the wake of the publication of his paper, Simango said he had written it because he was 'blinded with ambition' and wanted to 'denigrate the Frelimo leaders'.

After recalling the 'humane treatment' Frelimo had accorded to him, Simango then portrayed the PCN as 'an instrument to fight Frelimo' in multiparty elections, an anathema for Frelimo at the time. Simango completed his statement by asking to be re-educated and that his personal case should be used as an example for the coming generations.[32]

As if to comply with Simango's request, Machel told the audience that the PCN leader and the other political detainees would be re-educated. They were sent to re-education camps in Cabo Delgado and Niassa.

Absent from the Nachingwea show trial was Gwenjere. The priest, who had returned to Nairobi, was abducted from Kenya and sent to Mozambique by the Tanzanian security police. J Matola, the Dar es Salaam police superintendent who had befriended Gwenjere during Frelimo's 1967–68 crisis, showed up at the priest's, posing as an opponent of the Tanzanian government. In reality, he was part of the Tanzanian delegation to the East African Community headquarters in Nairobi. Matola suggested that Gwenjere should meet Tanzanian 'dissidents' in Mombasa to discuss ways of ousting Nyerere. With Nyerere out of the way, Matola reasoned, it would be easy to prevent Frelimo from consolidating its political power in Mozambique. As arranged, on 5 March 1975, Gwenjere met Matola and three other Tanzanians. But instead of heading to Mombasa, the car in which they were traveling took the road south to Namanga, on the border with Tanzania.[33]

Encouraged by Frelimo's reconciliatory remarks that 'the past ought to be buried', some of the former IM students returned home from exile. On arrival, however, they were promptly arrested, and languished the next few years in jails. 'Frelimo, comrade', said a party official when detaining a student just arrived at the airport of Beira, 'has a long arm and wherever you are we will always get you'.

Other former students and Frelimo guerrillas who had been living in Kenya and who had opted not to return home at independence were faced with the possibility of being forcibly repatriated to Mozambique. The UNHCR decided that since Mozambique had become independent, refugee status no longer applied to them. Indifferent to the reasons why so many Mozambicans had left for Kenya in the first place, the UNHCR informed the Kenyan authorities that it would be available for assisting them in repatriating the refugees to Mozambique. As a last resort, the refugees staged a demonstration outside the UNHCR office in Nairobi in October 1976, eventually making the Kenyan government review their case. They were allowed to stay in the country well into the 1990s when transition to democracy in Mozambique became irreversible.

Frelimo, however, left no stone unturned in its attempts to have all refugees back home. After independence, the Frelimo government persuaded several countries, and even non-governmental organizations and other institutions that had granted scholarships to Mozambican students in exile, to cancel their assistance. If they were unwilling to return home, the Frelimo government saw to it that at least they would have a difficult life wherever they lived.

4
Totalitarian State

Mondlane, wrote his widow when Mozambique had been independent for over a decade, would not have agreed with decisions taken after independence, 'many of them allied to the violation of the idea of the right to individual freedom'. She believes that Mondlane 'would have debated how to balance this freedom with what would benefit the whole group'. There was, however, one idea that would not have been violated under Mondlane – 'that ideology is not more important than people'.[34]

The very nature of the independence accord Portugal signed with Frelimo precluded the fulfillment of that ideal. Mozambique merely shifted from one form of totalitarianism to another – specifically, from Fascism to Leninism. Frelimo's goal was to regiment Mozambican society in terms of the role that it accorded to itself as the 'leading force of the state and society' as provided for in a Constitution of its own making.

Executive, legislative and judiciary powers were vested in Frelimo. As party leader, Samora Machel was also the head of state and government, the speaker of parliament, and the chief justice, in addition to being the commander in chief of the Armed Forces. The executive branch was answerable only to the Frelimo Political Bureau.

Frelimo saw this as a clear-cut example of a real democracy, embodying the aspirations of the proletarian and the peasant classes of which it claimed to be the vanguard party. The new Mozambican regime, as Machel indicated, was prepared to go to great lengths to impose the will of those classes, even if it meant 'forcing those who refuse to accept such an imposition, and to repress those who oppose such a will'.[35]

The People's Assembly, as parliament was known, consisted of 210 members appointed by Frelimo. Although described as the supreme organ of state, the People's Assembly was a mere rubber stamp forum that met for four-day sessions twice a year to ratify legislation adopted – and in many instances already in force – by the party through cabinet.

In March 1979, the Frelimo government drafted the death penalty law, which was ratified by parliament in June the same year. Before that, ten people were sentenced to death and executed by firing squad the day after sentence was passed. As in all previous and subsequent sessions of the People's Assembly, voting of the death penalty law was unanimous. That the defendants had been tried for offenses allegedly committed before the introduction of the death penalty, and that they had been executed in disregard of the right to appeal as stated in the law, not to mention that executions should only have been carried out five days after the passing of the sentence, did not seem to be a cause for concern to the People's Assembly.

The peculiarity of the Mozambican parliamentary system came to light again when government decided to extend the death penalty to smuggling, and to reintroduce the much-hated colonial practice of corporal punishment. It was only after a number of people had retro-actively been sentenced to death and to flogging under the terms of the new legislation that the People's Assembly ratified the new laws.

The government's 1975 decision to abolish private law chambers created a vacuum in the Mozambican judicial system. To replace them, a National Legal Consultancy and Assistance Service would uphold the citizens' legal rights. At the end of 1984, however, the service had not as yet been operational. Lúcia Maximiano, a jurist tasked with creating the service, admitted in December that year that very little could be said about the organization and functioning of the service, noting that people went to court without any means to defend themselves, without knowing how their interests could be upheld, and whom they should approach for assistance and consultation.[36] The service only became operational in December 1986. In the interim, 'people's justice' was applied arbitrarily by party organs and government security agencies, namely those under the Ministries of Defence, the Interior, and Security.

In its unbridled quest for asserting itself as the leading force of state and society, Frelimo demanded that Mozambicans conformed with its political line unconditionally. 'Unity of thought' became a feature of Mozambique's new political vocabulary. The eradication of all forms of organized political opposition having been successfully accomplished before independence, Frelimo turned on its own supporters. The uni-versity student association, AAM, which had campaigned for an inde-pendent Mozambique and adopted a pro-Frelimo stance during the colonial days, saw its activities curtailed. Says a former AAM member:

In view of the Association's democratic tradition and its posture as a promoter of free debate and dissemination of ideas, Frelimo felt that in the future it could become the rallying point for the country's intelligentsia, a threat to the establishment.[37]

The youth, women, teachers, journalists, writers, students and workers, in fact people from all walks of life, were grouped into so-called mass democratic organizations. These were Frelimo-controlled outfits bank-rolled with state funds and designed to ensure that the government's program of action was implemented at all levels. Eventually, children were also grouped under the Organization of Successors to the Mozambican Revolution.

In the specific case of workers, Frelimo wanted them organized under Socialist Unions operated by the party. As Machel put it, the unions were 'an army of the party', and under Frelimo's leadership, the unions would organize the Mozambican workers.[38]

Party cells were established at workplaces and in residential areas. In the case of residential areas, Frelimo borrowed from Tanzania's ten-house cell system, dividing cities into communal wards. Party members living in a ward became responsible for each of the blocs making up that ward, and blocs were divided into units of ten families each. A party member saw to it that every family was registered at the local party committee. Every family unit was supposed to report to the bloc chief the presence of any visitors within 24 hours of their arrival. To ensure compliance, the bloc chief, accompanied by armed militiamen, could conduct random house searches at any time of the day. A Frelimo Political Bureau member explained that:

> The head of the residential bloc, the head of the 10 families and the person responsible for a building must know each person living in the area under their responsibility, know what they are doing, their source of income and how they live. Every movement by strange persons must be immediately noted and reported to the authorities.[39]

Only registered families were given access to hospitals, clinics, schools and community shops. With the introduction of rationing cards for basic commodities – due primarily to the regime's regimentation policy, but subsequently necessitated by the declining economy – only duly registered residents were entitled to their monthly allocations.

People wishing to travel outside their residential areas either within their province or to other provinces were required to carry the *guia de marcha*, a travel document issued by the respective party committee on recommendation of chiefs of a given residential area.

Sports and recreational clubs and associations were abolished and placed under the jurisdiction of the various government ministries.

Mozambicans' musical and literary tastes, the films they watched and the way they dressed, all came under Frelimo scrutiny. As Machel had directed, Mozambicans had to rid themselves of all 'manifestations and influences of the bourgeoisie's decadent sub-culture'.

At its first national conference five months after independence, Frelimo's Information and Propaganda Department, DIP, announced the creation of a national film distribution network controlled and led by the party, which would be fundamentally geared toward the dissemination of films produced and directed by the DIP.[40] The conference decided that the national radio's Western art music channel should be restructured to 'eliminate its self-evident elitism' and include 'music from countries that are ideologically aligned to Mozambique'. As for publications on sale in the country, the DIP saw them as material that 'appealed to a minority and promoted imperialist principles'. Audio materials were 'extraneous to party principles and pernicious to the creation of a new man'. The party would from then on 'centralize the import and export network of books, records and tapes, and control and oversee their production'.

Authors had to toe the party line if their work was to see the light of the day. Mozambican author Raúl Honwana waited for 17 years before his book was finally published. The party-controlled publishing company had, in Honwana's words, 'the right and the power to interpret things on their own. My work was interpreted as biased.'[41] Dr David Aloni, a sociologist, was sent for re-education for publishing a book without first seeking permission from the party. What made Aloni's case worse was that in his work he had questioned whether African socialism was not rooted in Africa's traditional society, a much-contested theme under the new political order.[42]

Janet Mondlane was prevented from publishing a biography of Frelimo's first president. According to Eduardo Mondlane's widow the party feared that a book about her late husband could obscure Samora Machel whose image as a leader needed to be promoted, particularly in southern Mozambique.[43]

The news media was yet another area placed under government control. It was the Information Ministry's prerogative to appoint editors and reporters to the various media outlets. In line with the DIP conference, Mozambican journalists had 'to subordinate themselves to Frelimo's discipline and guidelines both in context and format'. Clarifying DIP's ruling, Jorge Rebelo, Frelimo's chief ideologue, said the Mozambican media had 'to reflect and disseminate the political line of our party'.[44]

To achieve this, Machel believed that it was 'necessary to politically organize journalists as a whole in a structure of their own; a structure that promotes the journalists' unity of thought and of action . . .'[45] Such a structure was the National Organization of Journalists, the ONJ. Frelimo saw the ONJ as a conduit for reversing 'the journalists' petty bourgeois origin, and their inexperience in organized political struggle and lack of a partisan spirit'.[46]

In due course, the ONJ was able to control the domestic and external dissemination of news. Mozambican-based correspondents for foreign news agencies, radio services and an assortment of publications were by and large drawn from the Information Ministry's pool of journalists. The ONJ was also able to secure a foothold in the newsrooms of foreign media organizations, notably broadcast services. As a matter of policy, various foreign broadcast organizations recruit journalists from the countries to which they transmit. The Frelimo government went out of its way to expedite the hiring of its own media personnel by organizations like the BBC, the Voice of America or Radio Deutsche Welle which employed them in their Portuguese language services.

As for the foreign print media, the Frelimo government, in conjunction with the one-party regimes in other Lusophone African countries, bankrolled *África*, a fortnightly once published in Lisbon. Funds for this publication, according to former Cape Verde Prime Minister Pedro Pires, were channeled through the security services of the respective countries. *África*'s editorial policy was outlined by the governments of those countries.[47]

5
Political Police

Four months after independence, the Frelimo government instituted the Serviço Nacional de Segurança Popular, otherwise known as Snasp. 'A juridical monstrosity' was how a Mozambican jurist described the presidential decree establishing this political police.[48]

Snasp's powers included the right to conduct searches and to arrest people without a warrant. It had the authority to decide on the fate of its detainees who could either be referred to the judicial police for further action, or be taken directly to a court of law. A third option, which Snasp used liberally, was to dispatch its detainees to re-education camps, by-passing the judiciary. Some of the re-education camps set up in the country during the transition to independence were placed under Snasp's jurisdiction. The powers conferred on Snasp specifically stated that people under its investigation were not covered by a clause of the Penal Procedural Code in force in the country, which accorded a defendant, within seven days from the date he/she was charged, the right to challenge the charges faced, and to name witnesses and legal counsel. Snasp was also entitled to confiscate property owned by any of the regime's opponents that it detained.[49]

Snasp was directly answerable to the Mozambican head of state. A three-man National Security Council chaired by Samora Machel supervised Snasp's activities. Funding of the service came from the Defense Ministry. Personnel drawn from Frelimo's independence war reconnaissance service, Sereco, as well as the Criminal Investigation Police (PIC) staffed Snasp. East Germany's Stasi trained Snasp personnel agents.

In August 1977, there was a major restructuring of the service. The government opted for assistance from Cuba, whose intelligence services replaced Stasi in the training of Snasp personnel. The language and ethnic similarities between the two countries, and the fact that the

Cuban model was more suitable to a Third World country, prevailed in the government's decision.

Colonel Arys Sanchez played a key role in modeling Snasp along the lines of Cuba's intelligence services. Snasp had a total of 19 departments, including the counter-insurgency GLCB unit, a carbon copy of Cuba's Lucha Contra Bandidos (LCB). Afterwards, Snasp created a paramilitary force known as the Special Operative Detachments. These were assigned to the Provincial Military Commands of the Mozambique Armed Forces. A Military Counter-Intelligence (CIM) branch was established. Some of the country's re-education camps fell under CIM's jurisdiction. But it was Snasp's Operations Brigade, the infamous BO, as well as the Investigations Technical Brigade, BTI, which contributed to the notorious reputation of the political police.

In April 1980, Snasp acquired the status of a Security Ministry, retaining its original designation. Jacinto Veloso was put in charge of the ministry. Salésio Nalyambipano, with Frelimo's Security Department since the independence war, became his deputy. CIM came under the command of Lagos Lidimo, another independence war veteran who served in the Security Department. Like Nalyambipano, he was associated with the establishment of Ruarua, one of the country's most notorious re-education camps.

There was rivalry between Nalyambipano and his minister over the appointment of non-black Mozambicans to the various Snasp departments. The vice minister and the CIM chief often complained about the 'settlers' sons' having been given precedence over independence war veterans. The two would see to it that the situation was rectified, even if it meant disrupting the ministry's operational branch.

Jacinto Veloso acknowledged the role of the service as a political police in the service of the Frelimo government, saying that 'Snasp's task is essentially a political one because it is an instrument of the Frelimo Party's political and ideological line'.[50] And expanding on that, President Machel said Snasp's 'principal target should fundamentally be the ideological and political enemies of our revolution and of socialism'.[51]

To conduct its activities, Snasp relied on an extensive network of informers. The People's Vigilance Groups, GVP, established during the transitional government, became part of Snasp's Department of People's Vigilance and Collaborators Groups, the DCE-GVP. By August 1978, in the Province of Maputo alone, Snasp relied on the services of about 550 GVPs involving more than 17 000 informers.[52] In December the following year, President Machel disclosed that the GVP network of informers for the whole country exceeded 150 000 members. And according to

Veloso, Snasp's overall informer network in October 1980 was more than 300 000-strong, deployed in residential areas and at workplaces throughout the country.[53]

Snasp also made use of front companies to gather intelligence both domestically and abroad. Among them was the Sociedade Comercial e Industrial Moçambicana, Socimo. The company branched out into areas as diverse as data processing, investment, management and manufacturing. Its sister company, Socimo Internacional, conducted its external operations. Following the government's decision to ban private clubs, Snasp was put in charge of the former Indo-Português sports club, traditionally consisting of Asians of Goanese extract. The club was renamed Estrela Vermelha or Red Star, and used for intelligence gathering. The club gained the status of a business company known as ADEV or Associação Desportiva Estrela Vermelha, its shareholders including Frelimo Political Bureau members and other senior party officials. ADEV is listed as a shareholder in Interface, a data processing and management company established by Snasp.

In addition to Snasp, the Frelimo government relied on the party's own network of informers. Known as the Serviço de Informação Interna do Partido, SIIP (Frelimo), this network operated under the Central Committee with Jorge Rebelo as its chief. To draft its five-page weekly intelligence reports for the President's Office, the SIIP relied on Frelimo cells at workplaces, residential areas and government administrative structures at central, provincial and district levels, as well as on casual informers.[54]

The PIC was another arm of the Frelimo government's security apparatus. It replaced the colonial Judiciary Police and was given additional powers, often operating in tandem with Snasp. Raposo Pereira, a lawyer active with the Democratas de Moçambique, whose chambers had just been shut down following the government's ban on law practitioners, was appointed PIC director-general. One of his immediate challenges was to fill the posts vacated by the departing Portuguese. Pereira relied extensively on Frelimo military personnel with neither the qualifications nor the experience for the type of service they were required to perform. But what brought Pereira into the limelight was his decision to appoint José Daniel Rocha as a PIC inspector. Rocha, also known as Zeca Ruço, had been sentenced in early 1973 to a 15-year jail sentence for armed robbery, and at the time of his arrest by the Portuguese he was being sought by the South African police after escaping from jail. The PIC assigned Rocha to the city of Beira as chief inspector. Here Rocha unleashed a reign of terror among its residents, arbitrarily conducting arrests, particularly of businessmen of the local Chinese and Indian communities. He showed a keen interest in their jewelry, which he extorted in exchange for their release from detention.

In the same month that it was established, Snasp saw action in a joint operation co-ordinated by the Ministry of the Interior. The PIC, the Mozambique Police Corps and the Armed Forces also took part in the operation, which resulted in the arrest of scores of people in several parts of the country in a matter of hours. A communiqué issued by Interior Minister Armando Guebuza revealed that some 3000 people had been arrested in five provincial capitals between the night of 30 October and the early hours of the following day. The communiqué described those caught in the police swoop as 'thieves, drunkards, vagrants, prostitutes and drug addicts'.[55]

Guebuza's communiqué was misleading. Among those arrested were married couples leaving cinema houses or restaurants, who, failing to produce identification papers, were put in army trucks strategically parked nearby so as to prevent people from escaping the police net. Husbands who did not carry an identity card at the time were taken in as vagrants, and their wives allowed to go free because they happened to have some sort of identification on them. But the reverse was also the case, and in such instances married women were arrested as prostitutes. Also taken in as prostitutes were housewives who had left home to visit a neighbour or to go to a nearby shop during the police raid. Requests for permission to go home and fetch the required identification documents, even accompanied by security personnel, were turned down. There were instances in which children were left unattended at home after their mothers' arrest. Others were luckier if the overzealous policemen demanding identification happened to be illiterate. One citizen reportedly produced the registration of his Honda motorcycle instead of his identity card, only to be told, 'You may proceed, Mr Honda'.

Arbitrary arrests continued unabated in the following years with the various branches of the security system virtually operating with *carte blanche*. People were also arrested on religious and political grounds, but the justification invariably was that the targets were the reactionaries. The city of Beira, regarded by the Frelimo government as the hotbed of resistance, heard President Machel admitting during a political rally in early 1977 that the police had targeted even students:

That is what we did here in Beira with a number of reactionaries: We sent them to re-education camps, for forced labour. Some of them have vanished from schools.[56]

This particular incident refers to high school students who had protested against the government's decision to interrupt their studies and select them randomly for training in Cuba regardless of whether they wanted to pursue a specific career chosen on their behalf by the government or even wished to leave for Cuba. They were instead sent to the Sacudzo re-education camp.

6
Re-education

The arbitrary arrests carried out during the transition to independence and afterwards, coupled with the breakdown of the judicial system, led to an overcrowding of jails. By 1978, the Machava security prison near the Mozambican capital had 1500 people in the cells, three times more than its capacity. According to Jorge Costa, a former Snasp official, many of the prisoners at Machava had not been tried, let alone charged. He said he had

> found people at Machava who didn't even have a police file opened in their name. Some of them had been there for years. They had been put in by the army or the police on the spur of the moment and when the policeman or soldier responsible was transferred elsewhere he left behind these kinds of people, innocent but in prison.

As a solution to jail overcrowding, said Costa, 'the police were told to go out and arrest criminals to populate the re-education camps'.[57]

Frelimo viewed re-education as a means of creating a 'new man' free of all vestiges of the old order, and of eliminating, as Interior Minister Guebuza put it, 'the rotten values of the colonial bourgeoisie that had been assimilated by Mozambicans'.[58] Ultimately, a 'new man', attuned to Frelimo's ideals, would come out of the 'laboratories for the transformation of man', as President Machel used to call the camps, and as

> conscientious and programmed elements, organized patriots who know their role in society, and who have embodied the news values of the revolution.[59]

Although the Ministry of the Interior, through its National Re-education Services Directorate, had jurisdiction over the camps, some of them were under the control of Snasp, and military personnel were often put in charge of various re-education camps. The judiciary, according to Mozambican chief justice Mário Mangaze, had no say either in the arrest or in the dispatch of people to the camps, nor in the actual re-education of prisoners. Mangaze noted that the Office of the Attorney General and Public Prosecutor had access to the camps barred.[60] The judiciary had no say as to how long re-education would last, and the government had no precise idea about it either. Marcelino dos Santos told inmates at the Sacudzo camp that 're-education had no fixed time'.[61]

The exact number of camps established after independence is not known. Based on testimonies by former inmates as well as Mozambican law enforcement officials, it could be fairly estimated that until the disbanding of the re-education system in the late 1980s, there were at least 23 camps. Most of them were in Niassa.

Mozambique's largest but least populated province, Niassa has enormous agricultural potential, but lacks the human resources to ensure a sustainable development. Niassa saw a major drain in its population during the slave trade masterminded by the Sultan of Zanzibar in the 18th century, and continued later by the European colonialists.[62]

Frelimo's approach to the Niassa population deficit was like trying to put things right with a second wrong. The forced relocation of Mozambicans from other parts of the country to Niassa, which to all intents and purposes became a penal colony, was a new slave trade in reverse. Machel saw Niassa as 'a great school for outlaws', where they would 'work, build their houses, produce, be taught, and transformed into dignified, useful and working citizens'.[63]

What happened, not only at the camps in Niassa but in other provinces as well, differed radically from the image that government promoted of the re-education program. Conditions at the camps were certainly unsuitable for the drug addicts and drunkards the authorities had admittedly interned there, about whom the primary concern should have been rehabilitation under medical supervision – not re-education by untrained military personnel. Accounts by former camp inmates and even government officials prove beyond question that the camps did not produce the 'conscientious and programmed' Mozambicans that Machel had paradoxically talked about. Those who did not perish in the camps came out either physically and psychologically damaged, or loathing Frelimo more than when they were sent in.

Table II.6.1. Re-education Camps per Province

Niassa Province:	Zambézia Province:
Chiputo	Carico
Macaloje	
Majune	**Sofala Province:**
Messuruce	Canda
M'telela	Nhangau
M'Swaíze	Sacudzo
Naisseko	
Ilumba	**Inhambane Province:**
Unango	Inhangele
	Inhassune
Cabo Delgado Province:	
Bilibiza	**Maputo Province:**
Chaimite	Banganhane
Ruarua	Chia
	Jafar
Nampula Province:	Mutatele
Itoculo	
Muneia	

The first inmates of the camps bore the brunt of the re-education system in that they were the ones who had to create minimum living conditions. They were literally dumped in thick bush areas and then forced to build the camps' infrastructures from scratch. Such was the situation at M'sawíze, a camp earmarked for alleged prostitutes, although members of the Jehovah's Witnesses sect could be counted among the inmates. M'swaíze started off with just over 500 inmates, including children. They had to fell trees and clear the bush to build a trail linking the camp to a former Frelimo guerrilla Central Base in the province. The inmates also built the camp's installations and opened farms.

Life at M'swaíze fitted into the same pattern as other camps. People had to get up at half past four in the morning. They then cleaned the camp and after breakfast would work in the fields, breaking for a midday meal.

In August 1976, M'swaíze's political commissar painted a grim picture of life in the camp, saying that often the inmates went without eating. 'At the beginning we starved', said the commissar, adding that there had been many cases of anaemia. 'Right now', he said, 'we only have food in stock for another meal. Food is of poor quality. Usually it is only beans and flour.'[64]

The political commissar said M'swaíze was short of clothing and that there were no blankets for the prisoners, despite the pavilions in which they slept being unprotected on the sides. Like most of Niassa's re-education camps, M'swaíze was located in the province's highlands with an altitude of over 5000 feet. In the cold months, temperature is invariably recorded in single digits. Many prisoners are known to have died of exposure.

Health conditions at M'swaíze 'were also very bad', according to the political commissar, who reported that:

> Women at the camp were carriers of many venereal diseases, but the camp lacks medicines. Syphilis cases are referred to the Central Hospital, but it lacks conditions to treat them. We have no malaria tablets, and as a result many of the inmates have been taken ill. Scabs is rampant due to unhygienic conditions. [...] There have been mass desertions because people could not bear the living conditions here.[65]

Jorge Costa, who admitted having 'signed many thousands of warrants' while in the service of the Security Ministry-Snasp, dispatching people to the re-education camps, revealed that the worst thing about them 'was the treatment from the guards'. If you were a woman, he said, 'you slept with the guards and liked it. If you were a man you did what they told you and liked it.'[66]

Fanuel Mahluza, Coremo's defense secretary, was sent for re-education at Ruarua, a camp established primarily for former Frelimo guerrillas who had defected from Frelimo during the independence war. Mahluza spoke of 'an underground cell' at the Ruarua complex, recalling that he had once seen

> two prisoners who had been kept in the underground cell. They looked like walking skeletons, apathetic. The guards used to burn green leaves near the entrance to the cell. Many prisoners suffocated to death.[67]

Concurring with Mahluza, Atanásio Kantelu, a Makonde guerrilla commander who defected from Frelimo in 1967, added that

> Prisoners were forced to work nine hours a day in farms, felling trees, building houses for the guards. We had only one meal a day, consisting of manganhola or boiled maize. Medical care was non-existent.

Kantelu claimed that the guards regularly beat up prisoners, 'invariably twice a day, with whips and sticks'. Prisoners sentenced to die, according to Kantelu,

> would be taken to a nearby tree which had a rope tightened to a branch. A prisoner was made to stand on a table, the rope around his neck. If a prisoner denied an accusation during questioning time, a guard would kick the table. The prisoner would move his arms as if signaling to his henchmen that he was willing to confess anything. All he wanted was to avoid an agonizing death.[68]

António Isaac Maria, a Mozambican in his early 20s, was sent to the Ilumba re-education camp as a vagrant. He was arrested outside a cinema in the Mozambican capital in late 1975 for not carrying identification. He and other prisoners were taken to Niassa in army trucks, covered with canvas. 'During the journey', said Isaac, 'nine of the prisoners died, probably of suffocation and exhaustion'.

Conditions at Ilumba 'were bad', according to Isaac.

> We slept six in a hut. One of the things they did was to keep all the prisoners' clothes and let us sleep only with our underpants on to prevent us from escaping at night. At four o'clock in the morning, the guards woke us up. We went straight to work. We were told to chop trees down, but soon it became unbearable as we had had nothing to eat.

Isaac noted that the only meal, usually cooked flour and beans, was served at two in the afternoon, adding:

> We had to use our shovels as there were no plates to serve the food. The food was cooked in the morning and left in the open with flies and insects at it. Many prisoners suffered from diarrhoea. Four of them died.

In April 1976, Interior Minister Guebuza visited Ilumba and was told by the camp commander that several prisoners had escaped. According to Isaac, Guebuza instructed the guards to shoot any prisoner attempting to escape. In May that year, about 20 prisoners fled from the camp. One of them was captured and sent back to Ilumba.

> We were all asked to attend his trial and execution. A guard shot him in the chest, and another finished him off with bayonet stabs.[69]

7
M'telela – The Last Goodbye

After the April 1975 Nachingwea show trial, more than 300 prisoners sentenced to re-education were sent back to Mozambique. Selected from among them was the so-called 'reactionary group', which included Uria Simango, Gumane, Semião, Kavandame, Casal Ribeiro and several others. The group was taken in Tanzanian Army trucks to Lake Nyasa, then by frigate to the Mozambican navy base at Metangula on the shores of the lake. Boarding trucks once more, the group was taken inland to M'telela. Gwenjere joined the group afterwards.

As Ruarua, the M'telela re-education camp was operated by the Security Ministry-Snasp. It formed part of an old Portuguese Army barracks situated in what was known before independence as Nova Viseu. The camp's commanding officer was Afonso Mambole, an independence war veteran, notorious for his role in the rampant executions that plagued Frelimo after Magaia's death.

Those in the 'reactionary group' were kept in individual cells at the barracks. Unlike other prisoners, the quality of their food is said to have been good and the diet varied regularly. They were allowed to leave their cells for two hours twice a week for exercises. On Sundays, married prisoners received 15-minute visits from their wives, but always in the presence of guards. The prisoners were allowed to write to their families, but not all the letters reached their destination. Simango's children, for instance, received only two letters throughout the lifetime of their parents at the camp. Letters were censored in the provincial capital, Lichinga. The prisoners were told not to give any indication as to the whereabouts of the camp, merely starting their letters with 're-education centre', followed by the date. Guards and prisoners in general were ordered not to look the 'reactionaries' in the eyes. Should they ever come across any of the prisoners, they had to turn their faces. Failure to comply with this bizarre regulation was met with severe punishment.

In October 1979, a motorcade carrying senior government and Snasp officials arrived at M'telela amid a great security apparatus. Simango, Gumane, Gwenjere, Semião, Casal Ribeiro, Kavandame and three other prisoners were told that they were about to be transferred to the Mozambican capital as a prelude to their release from detention. Prisoners with families in the camp were not, according to one of Casal Ribeiro's daughters, allowed to say farewell. 'I managed to see my father', she said, 'smiling and waving at us from inside the jeep, the window closed, as the motorcade, surrounded by armed soldiers on foot, slowly drove away from the camp. It was the last time I would say goodbye to him. The jeeps came back a second and a third time, I think, to fetch other prisoners.'[70]

Not far from the camp, the motorcade came to a halt on the road to Chiputo, east of M'telela. According to Abel Assikala, Snasp's political commissar, the prisoners were told to alight from the vehicles and after walking a short distance away from the road were summarily executed.[71]

Unaware of the executions, human rights organizations and a few Western countries, notably Sweden, acting on behalf of the families of some of the political prisoners, continued to put pressure on the Mozambique government for information about the detainees. In mid-1980, the Frelimo government decided to concoct a writ to legalize the extrajudicial executions. To forestall adverse domestic and international reaction, it was decided that the executions would be explained as a 'revolutionary decision, not as a judicial act'.[72] To accomplish this, a committee headed by Frelimo security chief Sérgio Vieira was instructed to compile a dossier 'stating the complete criminal history of the individuals in question, as well as their confessions to the elements of the Frelimo's Defence and Internal Security Departments who interrogated them, statements by witnesses and deeds of trial and sentence'.[73]

Codenamed *Namuli*, the dossier received input from Costa, Matias Xavier, Snasp's Operations Brigade chief, as well as party stalwarts like Óscar Monteiro and José Júlio de Andrade. Hermenegildo Gamito, a jurist representing the Mozambican government in a number of joint ventures, was seconded to the committee as its legal adviser.

The government, however, opted not to publicize the 1979 executions. Instead, it embarked on an 'offensive on the legality front', the primary goal of which was to blame 'opportunists that had infiltrated the police and other law enforcement agencies' for the human rights violations that the government publicly acknowledged were taking place in the country. Attention would, in the process, be diverted from the fate of the political prisoners. President Machel toured a number of re-education camps allegedly to investigate the situation. Commenting on what he had heard at Ruarua, he said, 'it was as if someone had stacked hay in our stomachs – we cannot digest that'.[74] The highlight of the 'offensive' was a mammoth rally addressed by Machel in Maputo in November 1981. He was at pains to shift elsewhere the blame for the gross human rights violations that had been committed under his government. 'We have noticed systematic violations of legality', he said, adding:

> two principal aspects characterize the present situation: Crimes, abuses and arbitrariness committed by enemy agents that have infiltrated the Defence and Security Forces; and the persistence of values and practices of the colonial-capitalist and tribal-feudal societies.[75]

In the wake of the 'offensive', security personnel were either dismissed or detained. But the key figures in the security establishment, directly responsible for documented cases of human rights violations, were not only left untouched, but proceeded to climb the Frelimo hierarchical ladder. Salésio Nalyambipano, who had set up the Ruarua re-education camp, remained as vice-minister of security for as long as Snasp was in place. Less than a year after the offensive, Parliament awarded medals to Nalyambipano, as well as Lagos Lidimo, Snasp's Military Counter-Intelligence chief, and Abel Assikala.[76] In 1986, Lidimo was appointed commander of the Maputo Military Garrison, and of Zambézia Province Military Command the following year. He also served in the Military Revolutionary Tribunal as one of its presiding judges. M'telela's commanding officer was promoted to supervisor of Snasp's Operations Brigade in Maputo.

In June 1982, less than a year after the launching of the 'offensive', the Frelimo government ordered the executions of Casal Ribeiro's and Simango's wives. Before leaving the camp, the two women were told they were going to live with their husbands.[77]

The Mozambique government never informed the families of those it had executed in 1979 and 1992. Instead, it continued to give them hope that one day they would all be reunited. In 1984, Casal Ribeiro's children were told that their mother and Celina Simango were living in Tete, and their husbands in Cabo Delgado.[78]

In October 1988, the government told a visiting Amnesty International delegation that relatives of some of the prisoners had received full answers to their inquiries. Other relatives would be contacted were they to submit their questions to government.[79] Paulo Gumane's wife, Priscilla, did write to the Mozambican head of state in February 1988, asking him to provide information about the fate of her husband, and to release him if he was still alive.[80] Neither the newly appointed Mozambican president nor any of his government officials cared to answer Mrs Gumane's letter.

Sérgio Vieira, perhaps the Frelimo official best documented on the fate of the country's political prisoners, told Mozambican exiles in the United States in 1988 that the prisoners had been killed in a Renamo raid on the re-education camp at which they were being held.[81] No anti-government insurgency had, however, been reported in the M'telela region of Niassa in 1979. In any event, Renamo only began operating in the province in 1983.

Consistent with this pattern, Afonso Mambole told Judite Casal Ribeiro in Lichinga in 1989 that her mother and Celina Simango were then working as teachers, but he was not certain exactly where.[82]

Frelimo never questioned the validity of the whole concept of the re-education system, even during the 'offensive on the legality front'. Despite the gross human rights violations associated with the system right from the days of its inception, Frelimo continued to believe in the system well after the Mozambican political dissidents had been executed and scores of other citizens perished in the camps. 'The re-education policy is correct', Machel told the fourth Frelimo Congress in April 1984, stressing that

the foundations of that policy rest on the enhancement of the human being and on the belief of his capacity for transformation – these are the fundamental elements of the political line of our Party'[83]

8
Coup Attempt

Disregard for human rights during the transition to independence and afterwards came under criticism from within Frelimo. A documented case was that of Francisco Ndeio, Frelimo's chief of operations for Manica and Sofala during the independence war, who had since been appointed the deputy defense chief for Sofala.

In October 1975, Ndeio accused troops and militiamen in Beira of having taken the law onto their own hands and in the process 'betraying the people and Frelimo's political and ideological line' not only in the city, but in the province as a whole. He took them and the police to task for having arbitrarily imposed a night curfew. Anyone found on streets after hours, particularly women, were arrested as prostitutes. Under the guise of the fight against prostitution, Ndeio complained, the security forces entered houses and arrested entire families. The same fate was reserved for couples at leisure in beaches or strolling in parks.[84]

Afterwards at the Dondo barracks, Ndeio charged the military with gross human rights violations. He spoke of people who had been arbitrarily arrested and of others who had either been disabled for life as a result of torture, or summarily executed. By Ndeio's own admission, Frelimo had in 12 months of governance proportionally tortured and executed more people than the Portuguese in 500 years of colonial rule. On the same day Dondo and Beira residents, including Frelimo armed forces personnel, demonstrated in support of Ndeio. Loyal troops intervened to disperse the demonstrators, arresting civilians and soldiers. Some of the demonstrators were said to have been executed.

Fearing that Ndeio's continued presence in Sofala could serve as a rallying point for the dissatisfied residents, government removed him and his assistant, José Caniço, from the scene. Two years later, they were publicly executed in Cabo Delgado as 'enemy agents'.[85]

The events in Beira were not the only signs of discontent afflicting the Armed Forces. There were in fact serious grievances within the ranks dating back to the days of the independence struggle. The foiled military coup staged in the Mozambican capital some six months after independence reflected that.

On 17 December 1975, a 400-strong Frelimo battalion, consisting mainly of Makonde troops, blocked roads leading to the capital and occupied key military installations. The rebels, who planned to seize the Army and Frelimo headquarters, as well as the airport, the national radio and power station, appeared to have become disorientated when they could not find President Machel upon entering the presidential palace. They were unaware that he was out of the country. In the ensuing confusion, loyal troops regained control of the situation two days after the coup attempt. In addition to most of the rebel troops, at least 300 other Mozambicans were detained for their alleged involvement in the rebellion.

The government's immediate concern was to deny that the coup plotters had been politically inspired. As in the days when it operated from Tanzania, Frelimo continued to deny the existence of genuine grievances in its midst. As if rejecting the much-publicized victory over the 'reactionary' tendency within the organization in the late 1960s, those involved in the coup attempt were presented as 'reactionary elements'. The coup plotters were said to be opposed to recently introduced measures to curb 'corruption, abuse of power, parasitism, disregard for hierarchical structures, alcoholism, use of drugs, pimping, harassment of civilians and theft'.[86] The only sign of the coup plot being political was that it had been inspired by 'imperialism' which had 'mobilized its long-standing agents still camouflaged in our midst'.[87]

Privately, the government saw how volatile the political situation was within the Armed Forces. For that reason, it did not appeal to other military units to rescue it from 'reactionary' or 'corrupt and confused elements', but to 'repel a South African invading force', as stated in marching orders issued to the Armed Forces in Sofala. Had the truth been stated, it is doubtful whether other Armed Forces units would respond favourably to the call. At least in the Dondo barracks, the troops commented openly that had they known that a *coup d'état* was in progress, they would have refused to march southwards.[88]

In August 1975, the Armed Forces had either expelled or suspended nearly 30 senior independence war veterans. Junior armed forces personnel were arrested and sent for re-education. In most cases, the decision had been prompted by 'political incompatibility', a generic term that could include both undisciplined soldiers and those unwilling to endorse government's policies.

There was a sense of betrayal among the war veterans. They realized that the pledges for compensation Frelimo leadership had made during the independence war were nothing but empty promises. In the transition to independence, Machel had actually made it clear that militants and soldiers 'should, like in the past, renounce material benefits, namely salaries'.[89] The measure did not apply to the higher Frelimo echelons who became the new elite with free housing in plush suburbs, chauffeur-driven limousines, access to special shops that were out of bounds to ordinary citizens, a regular monthly income far higher than the average salary of workers, traveling allowances and other perks. What made matters worse was that the new elite included people who had played no part in the independence war, and of necessity were viewed as opportunists jumping on the bandwagon.

For the armed forces the prospects of reaping the benefits of independence were virtually nil. Their horizons were restricted to an unattractive life in army barracks, with no say in political matters. They were expected to endure further hardships in the years to come, including intervening militarily in Angola to prop up the MPLA government in its dispute with UNITA and the FNLA. As the Armed Forces General Staff had told them, the task of the Army was not to 'interfere in the running of party and state affairs, but to support the party and the state in the fulfillment of their mission'. No Army official, let alone a combatant, stated the General Staff, should be authorized to issue orders to the party and state structures.[90]

Government not only refused to compensate the veterans, but saw to it that they would not find alternative sources to change their lifestyle, especially if the option was the fostering of a relationship between the veterans and the white community – the colonial bourgeoisie as Frelimo saw it – already earmarked for destruction. An alliance between the two was inconceivable, not only on ideological grounds, but because Frelimo saw it as a threat and had decided that Mozambique's 'aspiring bourgeoisie' would have to be nipped in the bud.

By and large, the white community was more interested in being in the good books of Frelimo than in being perceived as potential enemies. Whites were genuinely prepared to enter into partnerships with any Frelimo members or even welcome them into their circle of friends. For the reasons already stated, Frelimo could not allow this to happen for it saw moves in that direction as 'sugar-coated bullets fired by imperialism' to kill the revolution.

Attentive to the development of a relationship between the whites and its military personnel, the government recalled from their posts those Frelimo officials whom it felt were capable of fraternising with the 'class enemy'. A well-known case was that of Commander Johan Jehova, in charge of Manica's defense and security. Jehova established a good rapport with local businessmen and the farming community, mostly whites. He had personally intervened to secure the release of people who had been arbitrarily arrested.

Jehova was removed from the scene. In his place, Frelimo assigned security personnel of a completely different calibre. From Maputo, it sent police inspector Enoque, who, on arrival boasted of his intention to 'put the house in order'. White farmers and businessmen began to be harassed. Arrests followed, including the confiscation of property under the guise of a campaign against reactionary forces plotting to undermine the government, and economic saboteurs.

The cases of indiscipline and abuse of power in the Armed Forces, to which the government alluded in the aftermath of the coup plot, were authentic. These, however, were primarily of Frelimo's own making. As Portuguese troops began withdrawing to the main port cities in a phased withdrawal to be completed before independence, Frelimo was expected to deploy its own forces in the areas being vacated. In reality Frelimo lacked military personnel for that. As a solution, it embarked on a massive recruitment of men among the country's unemployed and youngsters roaming the streets. In the process, the new Mozambican army was swamped with a large number of unseasoned and ill-disciplined elements. After a brief and rudimentary training, they were given the responsibility of upholding law and order throughout the territory. The abuses of power, of which the Armed Forces would subsequently be accused, were only the tip of the iceberg of what had had actually taken place. The abuses were in fact sanctioned at the highest level because they served Frelimo's immediate goal of staving off any action likely to be contemplated by quarters opposed to Frelimo before and after independence.

9
Destroying the Sequels

For Frelimo, the attainment of independence was the fulfillment of the stage of national democratic revolution. Its ultimate goal was to reach the socialist revolution stage.[91] To accomplish that, Frelimo followed what Lenin had theorized as the non-capitalist way. With the aid of the proletariat of the advanced countries, Lenin wrote, 'backward countries could go over to the Soviet system and, through certain stages of development, to communism, without having to pass through the capitalist stage.'[92]

According to the Frelimo programme, the people's democratic revolution was one of such transitional stages. Going beyond what Lenin had advocated, Frelimo said that it entailed the wholesale destruction of what had been inherited from the colonial period. In terms of what was decided by the first session of the Mozambique cabinet in July 1975, Frelimo announced that

> all vestiges of colonialism and imperialism would be destroyed with a view to eliminating the system of exploitation of man by man, and to erecting the political, material, ideological, cultural and social basis of the new society.[93]

This goal was restated in more clearly defined ideological terms at the Frelimo congress in 1977. Frelimo saw then the stage of the people's democratic revolution as the 'historic period in which the process of destruction of all forms of foreign domination of our fatherland, especially economic domination', and 'the process of eliminating all sequels of the traditional-feudal and colonial-capitalist societies would be deepened'.[94]

This proved to be a recipe for disaster. Frelimo did not have a viable alternative to what it had set out to destroy, except for the overrated 'rich experiences' of the liberated areas it wanted to apply to the rest of the country. The validity of these experiences was, to say the least, negligible. None of the Mozambique cabinet members could give a first hand account of what those experiences were, let alone bear testimony to life in the so-called liberated areas, for they had all lived in Tanzania or under Portuguese rule during the war for independence. Indeed, President Machel's triumphant journey to the Mozambican capital a month before independence did not start in any of such areas, but in Dar es Salaam where Frelimo's headquarters was based throughout the war. A 'utopia' was how a Mozambican historian viewed the liberated areas, noting that once the independence war was over, peasants who had lived in Frelimo-controlled areas of Cabo Delgado Province refused to continue living there and began returning to their places of origin.[95]

The Frelimo government dealt first with the 'colonial bourgeoisie', effectively destroying its socio-economic powerbase. A month after independence, government confiscated private schools, hospitals, doctors' practices, legal chambers and even funeral parlours. Overnight, the private exercise of law, medicine and education became a criminal offense subject to imprisonment without the option of a fine. A few months later, private houses were also confiscated.

As a result of these measures, coupled with the sense of insecurity stemming from arbitrary police action since the transition to independence, the exodus of whites gained momentum. The country would steadily be deprived of experts, artisans, teachers, medical and paramedic personnel, managers, small-scale businessmen and others who formed the backbone of the Mozambican economy. Mozambicans who were entitled to do so obtained dual citizenship from Portugal. In response, the Frelimo government ordered in early 1977 their expulsion from the country and the confiscation of their property.

Among those who left the country during this period were former members of the Democratas de Moçambique, including Carlos Adrião Rodrigues who had been appointed vice governor of the central bank. In his letter of resignation to President Machel, Rodrigues based his decision on the government's policy of driving members of the white minority community out of Mozambique. Instead of using their skills, said Rodrigues,

it was decided to torment them. Arbitrary arrests, verbal abuse and disregard for private property increased double fold. Men that were absolutely irreplaceable at the onset, and who were prepared to stay under different circumstances, were chased out of the country.[96]

A June 1977 UN Economic and Social Council report on the impact of the exodus, indicated that the manpower position in Mozambique was serious and affecting both the public and private sectors.[97] Nonetheless, the government went ahead with its policy of destroying the 'sequels', this time targeting the civil service. The minister for state administration, Óscar Monteiro, oversaw the 'shattering to pieces' of the civil service, pledging to replace it with one that would serve 'the people's democratic dictatorship'. Elaborating on this, Machel said the new civil service's 'best positions would be filled by party members'. In promotions, he added, 'priority would be given to party members, and in admission tests for the civil service, the first to be taken on board would also be party members'.[98]

Four years after it had been earmarked for destruction, Machel himself acknowledged that the civil service was riddled with incompetence and sloppiness. In the civil service, he said,

There is indiscipline, theft, alcoholism, and lack of punctuality. And all this is considered the norm. Laziness, vagrancy and destruction are considered virtues. There is no hygiene and cleanliness. There is no courtesy. There is corruption and insubordination.[99]

An equally bleak picture emerged from the health, education, and housing sectors. The Mozambican leader again personally acknowledged a marked decline in the standard of services provided at state-run hospitals. After touring a number of provincial and district hospitals, Machel identified 'an endless chain of anomalies'.[100] The quality of the health service was such that even party and government officials preferred to be treated abroad, notably in South Africa.

The credibility of the educational system was undermined by widespread corruption. Exam papers could be purchased on the black market, and students could be exempted from exams in exchange for a bribe.

An immediate consequence of the ban imposed on private ownership of houses was the collapse of the building industry. Less than two decades later, the country faced a backlog of two million dwellings yet to be built.[101] Buildings rapidly decayed as the state housing board, APIE, lacked the resources to attend to each and every unit of the gigantic infrastructure that had suddenly been created. 'What used to be perfect buildings, are now ruins',[102] admitted Machel ten years after the state had confiscated them. Partly to blame, though, were government departments, which failed to pay rental, owing over 62 billion meticais in rental arrears by the end of 1991.[103]

Frelimo's call for the destruction of foreign 'economic domination' in reality meant a realignment of the country's traditional links with the Western economic system. The goal, according to Machel, was to 'rapidly complement the political and ideological unity already established with the socialist world, with economic unity.'[104] Marcelino dos Santos, the Frelimo Politburo member in charge of economic policy, would in vain work tirelessly for Mozambique's integration in Comecon. 'One must understand', said Santos, 'that Mozambique's participation in an organization like Comecon is a natural development in the socio-economic process of the People's Republic of Mozambique, it is part of Comecon's natural growth.'[105]

In his endeavour, Santos relied on the dedication of Mário Machungo, a Lisbon-trained Mozambican economist rather eager to erase his past flirtation with the colonial power. 'Our fatherland', announced Machungo, 'shall be the tomb of capitalism.'[106]

The Soviet Union, however, already burdened with the Cuban, Mongolian and Vietnamese membership of Comecon, barred Mozambique's entry into the economic community, despite the ideological commitment of its leaders.

Having also banned private ownership of land, the government declared agriculture as the foundation upon which Mozambique's economy would develop. Huge state enterprises were established out of what used to be viable commercial farms. The bulk of government investment was channeled to the state sector of agriculture. Subsistence farmers were neglected.

The Angónia and Limpopo state enterprises, intended to be the showcases of Frelimo's centralized planning, proved to be a fiasco. Established in 1976, the Limpopo Agroindustrial Complex, CAIL, for instance, never succeeded in equaling the annual rice yield of 70 000 tonnes, or 80 per cent of Mozambique's requirements, previously attained by the Limpopo valley's commercial farmers. Rice production dropped to 46 000 tonnes in 1976, and to 30 000 tonnes the following year. In 1981, the downward trend continued with the all-time low of 25 000 tonnes.[107]

Several factors contributed to CAIL's failure. Bank credit to Mozambique's state farms, notes a report prepared by the African Studies Center in Maputo, was treated as a subsidy and as such not to be paid back.

Those employed in state farms neither planned nor had any real control over production.[108]

Despite the lack of skilled manpower on the Limpopo valley, resulting from the ongoing exodus, the government decided that CAIL should be a fully mechanized agricultural project, allocating huge sums for the importation of agricultural machinery from Eastern bloc countries. In 1978, heavy equipment for state farms, particularly CAIL, consumed $25 million of the $38.5 million budgeted for agricultural development.[109] One by one, however, the combine harvesters, lorries and tractors began to lie idle as there were no mechanics to maintain them. The lack of spare parts, an inevitable situation faced by importers of Eastern European machinery, led to the cannibalization of the brand new equipment. Of CAIL's 200 tractors for the 1979–80 season, 130 did not run.[110] And in the 1981 harvest, 25 per cent of the combines and 75 percent of the tractors were inoperative.[111] Fertilizers, pesticides and fuel often did not reach CAIL on time.[112]

The disincentives faced by CAIL's workers, particularly casual labour employed for the harvest season, were yet another factor that contributed to the collapse of the project. Each year it became more difficult to recruit casual labour, especially from nearby communal villages. In 1978, CAIL managed to recruit 10 000 casual workers, but in 1979 and 1980 the figure was just over 6000 workers. And in the following year, the complex only managed to recruit 4300 workers.[113] Visibly irritated with the peasants' lack of interest in working for CAIL under unattractive conditions, President Machel did not mince his words, publicly describing as monkeys the peasants of the Primeiro de Maio Communal Village during a visit to the Limpopo valley in 1979.

By focusing its attention on state farming, the Frelimo government overlooked the important role that peasant farmers played in the country's economy. Figures for 1973 revealed that peasant farmers contributed with 70 per cent of Mozambique's agricultural production consumed domestically. Yet, between 1978 and 1982, 90 per cent of the government's expenditure in agriculture was channeled to state enterprises. A mere 2 per cent was earmarked for the co-operative sector. Individual peasant farmers were simply ignored. As a result, peasant farmers were soon faced with an acute shortage of farming tools, seeds and fertilizers.[114]

The government's neglect of both individual peasant farmers and agricultural co-operatives was also reflected in its decision to expropriate land from both of them for state farms on the Limpopo valley. But in the end, notes the African Studies Center report, the land was not put to good use because of the state farms' inability to develop it.[115]

The role of peasant farmers was further eroded by the government's disruption of the rural trade network in the hands of the *cantineiros*. These were small-scale shop owners, predominantly Portuguese and Asian, who operated in remote parts of the country. They formed an important component of the Mozambican economy, ensuring the supply of a wide range of basic commodities to the rural population. The *cantineiros* often supplied the commodities on credit, and assured subsistence farmers of a gateway for their crops. The *cantineiros* did have a reputation for indulging in malpractices such as overpricing their goods or fiddling with weights when buying from peasant farmers. But it was more the exception than the rule, and the situation could have been easily corrected. The government, however, opted for a more drastic solution.

In line with recommendations made at the first national agricultural seminar on the eve of independence, the government decided that subsistence farmers would sell their crops exclusively to state-owned marketing companies.[116] In yet another move to undercut the *cantineiros*, the government established People's Shops throughout the country. In what was seen as unfair competition, the People's Shops, unlike the *cantineiros*, paid no rental, and were exempt from business licenses or any form of taxation. Having secured the monopoly in the importation of consumer goods, the government distributed these unevenly, with the bulk going to state-owned outlets, including the People's Shops. The amounts allocated to the private sector were insignificant and did not justify them staying open. This, in addition to the freeze on bank credits to the *cantineiros*, was a key factor in them eventually winding up their activities.

The People's Shops were an unsuccessful venture. They often sold goods at prices higher than the former *cantineiros*. They were staffed with unqualified personnel with no managerial experience. Says José da Silva, the head of the Matola Inter-cooperative's Trading Department:

> The workers employed by the People's Shops were irresponsible. This led to the bankruptcy of the People's Shops. A worker was given a job for which he had no motivation. His only concern was to distribute goods at random to friends and relatives...[117]

People's Shops were either understocked or supplied with the wrong commodities for the rural areas, such as electrical appliances or Indian spices. If torches, for instance, were on sale, batteries would be unobtainable. They became debt-ridden enterprises unable to pay for the commodities ordered from factories and wholesalers. Peasant farmers felt discouraged, questioning the purpose of producing more than they needed for their own subsistence if they could not buy essential commodities with what they earned.

Another disincentive experienced by peasant farmers was the method employed by the state agricultural marketing company, Agricom. The state company fixed crop prices at levels that were unattractive to peasant farmers. These, however, had no option but to sell their crops to Agricom when the state enterprise adopted arm-twisting tactics by barring the sale of consumer goods to peasants who did not turn in their farm products at its buying posts. The measure led to the emergence of a black market. Farmers sold their products privately to informal traders who in turn ferried the goods to towns and cities faced with acute food shortages. Farmers living along border areas smuggled cash crops to neighbouring countries where they fetched higher prices. To curb the situation, the government erected checkpoints on provincial boundaries to confiscate any farm products leaving one province for another. The aim was to force farmers to sell their products to state buying agencies within their own provinces only. In the process, many peasant farmers preferred to let their crops rot than to sell them to Agricom. Production declined further as in subsequent crop seasons farmers only planted the essential to ensure their subsistence and to guard against possible crop failures.

The shortage of staple foodstuffs worsened throughout the country. Money ceased to be a medium of exchange in the rural areas. A barter system was introduced, whereby at the end of each agricultural season Agricom exchanged consumer goods for crops. This was a period marked by unfair dealings on the part of the state enterprise, further discouraging farmers. In times of drought, Gapecom, the state company that marketed livestock and hides, employed methods that did not differ much from what Agricom pursued in the agricultural sector. In the drought-stricken area of Chókwè, Gaza Province, in July 1986, Gapecom bartered two bags of maize for a cow from peasants in dire straits.[118]

In the face of the peasant farmers' apathy, the government adopted a policy that was reminiscent of the old colonial days. Gaspar Dzimba, the governor of the northern province of Nampula, provides a case in point. Dzimba, a party appointee from southern Mozambique, reintroduced forced labour in all of the province's districts that had been adversely affected by manpower shortages during harvesting. In the province's

Mecubúri District child labour had been used to make up for manpower shortages, but that had not solved the problem. As a local official noted, children's output was low, even though they represented 50 per cent of the labour force.[119] Dzimba ruled that each peasant family should prepare four hectares of land and compulsorily sow specific crops. Peasant families were allocated daily quotas to work in the fields, from where they could only return after sunset. Traveling within the province during the agricultural season was restricted. A *guia de marcha* was required for traveling, but would only be issued to those who could prove that they had met their daily quotas, paid their taxes, and done their military service.[120]

10
Revolutionaries and Traditionalists

Having dealt swiftly with the 'colonial bourgeoisie', the Frelimo government proceeded to destroy the 'sequels of the traditional-feudal society'. In the former's case, the main goal had been the control over the means of production, distribution and exchange; in the latter, the goal was the paving of the way for a centralized form of government whereby traditional authority in the rural areas would be eradicated. In doing so, Frelimo believed that its rural development program would be implemented without hindrance or challenge.

The alliance Frelimo fostered with traditional chiefs during its campaign for independence had been to all intents and purposes a matter of expediency. Once in power, Frelimo saw no need to honor its pledges that the long-standing grievances of Mozambican peasants would be addressed after liberation. In fact, the Frelimo government took stern measures against traditional chiefs that dared to challenge its policies. Some were interned in re-education camps and later executed.

At independence, the government announced that the rural population would be resettled in communal villages. The official view was that it would not be feasible to develop the country socially and economically if the population was scattered: hence the need to relocate peasants from different areas into communal villages.

Although viewed as the model for a new society, communal villages were anathema to the peasant folk. They aimed at radically transforming the peasants' lifestyle, but in the process interfered with centuries-old customs and beliefs, and material expectations. The conditions under which transformation began to take place were the negation of the benefits proclaimed in the resettlement program.

The program entailed 'the combat against obscurantist, traditional-feudal and capitalist practices' as regards to the rural areas.[121] These practices included religious and spiritual ceremonies, adherence to cultural heritage, succession rights, ownership of land and livestock, and trading. They were all viewed as incompatible with the tenets of a revolutionary society.

By relocating families from their traditional homesteads, government disregarded sacrosanct values such as graveyards where ancestors were laid to rest, shrines to which headmen retired to communicate privately with the spirits, or the spiritual value attributed to landmarks in a given village. In an head-on collision with peasant tradition, government expected families to renounce their own identity and deeply rooted sense of privacy, and move into communal villages where, by virtue of their physical planning, they would have to share their lives with neither a relation nor an acquaintance, something unheard of in most of Mozambique's rural societies. The resettlement program impacted negatively on matrilineal societies where it is customary for newly married couples to move in with the bride's family. In doing so, families are enlarged, their prestige and importance within the community enhanced. The larger the number of daughters a family had, the greater the sense of prosperity they conferred to it. Communal life disrupted this long-standing tradition.

The first communal villages were created out of the *aldeamentos* (strategic hamlets) the Portuguese army had built as a counter-insurgency measure. In Cabo Delgado, about 70 per cent of the communal villages were former *aldeamentos*.[122] Resettlement land included holdings expropriated from peasant farmers and co-operatives.

The way resettlement was conducted led to the disruption of household agricultural production, and in some instances to land scarcity. Often there were more families than communal villages could accommodate. Soil degradation was noticeable in areas surrounding communal villages.

Resistance to the resettlement program is known to have taken place wherever it was introduced. Interior Minister Armando Guebuza once threatened to use 'retaliatory measures' against peasants in the Limpopo valley who refused to be relocated. Subsequent floods in the valley came as a blessing in disguise to the government for it seized the opportunity to move peasant families to 'safer grounds'. Similarly, the government used the 1976 and 1977 floods of the Zambeze River to speed up its resettlement program in Tete and Sofala. In Manica, after several attempts to relocate peasants from a Rotanda village to a designated communal area had failed, the government resorted to deception. A local army unit, pretending to be from the Rhodesian armed forces, simulated an attack on the village in 1976, putting the villagers to flight. They were subsequently regrouped in a communal village.[123] In Tete, peasants were reluctant to move into communal villages because they knew they would be leaving fertile and irrigated land on the banks of the Zambeze, Chire and Ziu-Ziu Rivers for less productive areas.[124] In Cabo Delgado's Mueda highlands, resistance to the resettlement program stemmed in part from the sharp contrast between traditional Makonde villages and the communal concept. The location of the communal villages and the way people were relocated also played a role.[125] In 1977, ten peasants from the Cabo Delgado's Namaua region were sent to a re-education camp for opposing resettlement.[126] An official report acknowledged that there was resistance to the program not only in those provinces, but in Niassa as well. Yet, resistance was interpreted as the peasants' dislike of 'the new values of collective life and work that reject obscurantist and traditional-feudal practices'.[127]

Six years after the resettlement program was introduced, 19.8 per cent of the Mozambican rural population, or 1 808 693 people had been relocated from their traditional homes to 1360 communal villages.[128] The government forecasted that by 1990, ten million peasants would be living in communal villages.[129] So much for the concern President Machel expressed in his inaugural speech, when he took Portugal to task for having 'displaced entire families from their places of origin, forcing them to abandon ancestral lands, livestock, houses and their meager belongings'.[130]

As peasants began to abandon communal villages, the government retaliated by not only denying them access to health and educational facilities, but also burning their houses as a means of forcing them to return.[131] In times of drought, the government used relief aid to force peasants into communal villages in that no food would be provided to those wishing to remain in their traditional areas.

Life in communal villages followed the pattern that the government had introduced elsewhere. Frelimo ruled that each communal village should have a party organ, an assembly composed of party-designated members, mass democratic organizations, and the standard security services.[132] Frelimo's Ideological Department through its News Media Institute, ICS, controlled access to domestic and international news. The ICS was responsible for the installation and operation of sound systems that relayed exclusively the national radio for collective listening. The ICS' *Jornal do Povo*, a wall newspaper reflecting the party's standpoint, was replaced by an audio version in view of the high illiteracy rate in rural areas.

The resettlement program had the opposite effect to what it intended to achieve. Rural Mozambicans became even more entrenched in their traditions, and developed an even greater sense of hostility towards Frelimo. The decision to appoint party officials from southern Mozambique to be in charge of the central and northern areas of the country previously administered by or under the influence of traditional rulers only served to alienate further the rural population. By disregarding their interests, Frelimo reawoke in the peasants the quiescent ethnic hostility between northerners and southerners, weakened its incipient power base and ultimately exposed itself to forces that would seize the opportunity to subvert the established order. What came as a surprise was the fact that the proponents of the resettlement program included a large number of Mozambicans of rural extract, the last people one would expect to be so insensitive to the impact that the program would necessarily have among the peasant population.

11
Frelimo and Religion

For Frelimo, religion was yet another 'obscurantist manifestation that served to deceive, trick and divide the people'.[133] As such, it was subjected to the same treatment of other sequels of the colonial and traditional societies.

Frelimo banned religious teaching from all government schools during the transition to independence. Restrictions were also imposed on church activity in general. As Machel ruled, nobody would be 'allowed to go from village to village to preach religion because only Frelimo can mobilize, unite, organize and lead' the people.[134] Church officials were required to carry a *guia de marcha* to be able to travel within the country.[135]

The ban on private educational and health establishments after independence adversely affected all churches since they operated mission schools, seminaries and clinics. Frelimo justified the confiscation of these church establishments on the grounds that they symbolized racial discrimination by catering essentially for black Mozambicans. However, the bulk of the establishments were in the rural areas, where over 85 per cent of the Mozambican population lived. Attendance of necessity had to reflect that environment.

Church-operated educational and health facilities reverted to party and state institutions, including the Armed Forces. The government froze the bank accounts of dioceses, missions, church institutions and even missionaries.

Churches saw their activities further restricted in 1978. The government told churches not to build new places of worship as priority had to be given to the construction of health and educational establishments as well as factories. Publishing and distribution of religious literature were also curtailed, with churches having to rely on the state-run

National Book and Record Institute, INLD, for the publication, importation and distribution of all their materials. Educational materials would, however, take precedence over religious ones.

A ban was imposed on church associations catering for the youth since they already had an organization fully equipped to deal with their affairs – the party's Mozambican Youth Organization, OJM.

The government also curbed the enrollment of students at seminaries. Students could only attend seminaries if they were older than 18 and had complied with their military obligations. In the case of applicants who had studied in government schools, they first had to work for a number of years in state institutions before enrolling at a seminary.[136]

In the first year of independence more than 600 missionaries left the country because they found it difficult to operate under the new conditions; others were ordered to leave the country.[137] The exodus of church personnel continued in the following years. Early in 1979, the authorities in Cabo Delgado ordered missionaries to leave all the districts in which they operated.[138] The measure was taken in view of Frelimo's concern over the presence of churchmen in areas that had been designated for the construction of communal villages where only the ruling party was allowed to operate.

Particularly affected by the official policy on religion was the Catholic Church. By virtue of the colonial power being predominantly a Catholic nation, the church had a strong influence in Mozambique that surpassed other Christian denominations, though not that of Islam. Given the close relationship that members of the Catholic hierarchy had with the colonial regime, Frelimo sought to, and to a certain extent succeeded in, presenting its anti-religious stance as a dispute with the Catholic Church only. In reality, government policy affected all religious groups, Christian and non-Christian alike.

According to a circular issued right after independence by Interior Minister Guebuza in his capacity as Frelimo's national political commissar, churches as a whole were 'banners of imperialism, against whom it is necessary to start an organized popular combat'. The circular warned Mozambicans to be on guard against 'the enemy who is acting through foreign and several Mozambican missionaries and evangelists', adding:

People must be told that to attend those denominations or to spread the word of missionaries is like working against Mozambique and serving the imperialist powers which resort to any method to achieve their goals.[139]

Prior to the issuing of the circular in October 1975, it had been reported that Nazarene Church and Assembly of God Church missionaries had been arrested in July and August. It was also reported that 150 missionaries and church workers were being held without charge in Maputo and Beira prisons.[140] Subsequently, members of the 12 Apostles Church were rounded up in Maputo for, according to a government daily, 'having been caught spreading their faith'.[141]

Several other church officials were subjected to a smear campaign so as to explain the action that the Frelimo government had taken against them. In most cases, the allegations included sexual intercourse with minors and married women, and corruption. In the case of the Good Pastor Church leader, Fernando Magaia, the media labeled him a 'charlatan' and a 'criminal in cassock', allegedly for promoting use of drugs, among other charges.[142]

The Jehovah's Witnesses, described in the circular as 'a sect founded in imperialist America and whose main source of income originates in that country', perhaps could be said to have suffered the brunt of the government's drive against religion. For openly refusing to be resettled in communal villages, the Jehovah's Witnesses forced President Machel to intervene personally in the matter. While on a tour of his home province of Gaza, Machel announced the Jehovah's Witnesses would be given a 'final destination', and that they 'should be immediately arrested'.[143]

According to *Awake!*, the official publication of the Jehovah's Witnesses, in that same month 'almost all of the 7000 witnesses of Jehovah in Mozambique had been imprisoned'. A house-to-house hunt was launched to find and arrest men, women and children. Men were arrested at their places of work without being able to contact their families. In many cases, says *Awake!*, the arrests were accompanied by 'brutal beatings'. Referring specifically to events in Gaza, *Awake!* reported the imprisonment of two small congregations of Jehovah's Witnesses ordered by the provincial governor who had them beaten. The magazine mentioned an incident in the town of Magude, where 'thirteen Witnesses were arrested, beaten and forced to dig up trees with their fingers. Then their legs and arms were tied and they were rolled around like drums.'[144]

One of the 'final destinations' where the Jehovah's Witnesses were sent was the Naisseko re-education camp in Niassa. The treatment meted out to them at the camp was the subject of a government weekly editorial, which said that the witnesses 'were tortured, their arms tied with ropes soaked in salt'. Many of the Witnesses 'were crippled for life'.[145]

In addition to the Naisseko, some of the Jehovah's Witnesses were sent to the M'swaíze re-education camp as well as refugee camps in Zambézia, built by the Portuguese to accommodate Witnesses fleeing persecution by the Malawian regime of Kamuzu Banda.

Part III

Resistance

1
The Conflict with Malawi and Rhodesia

The Mozambique government's foreign policy was consistent with the trend that prevailed within Frelimo from 1969 onwards. Until the death of Eduardo Mondlane, Frelimo had maintained channels opened to both Western and Eastern countries, though ideologically independent from the latter. Under Mondlane, Frelimo publicly condemned the USSR invasion of Czechoslovakia in 1968.

With the rise to power of the Machel-Dos Santos alliance in late 1969, Frelimo adopted a pro-Eastern stance. This was more openly stated after independence, with the Frelimo government referring to the socialist bloc countries as its 'natural ally', with both forming part of the 'liberated zone of mankind'.[1] 'Ideologically, politically, diplomatically, economically and socially', said President Machel about Mozambique's new allies, 'we defend the same cause and struggle for the same goals'.[2] In the Sino-Soviet dispute, Mozambique took Moscow's side.[3] Within the Non-aligned Movement, Mozambique supported Cuba's redefinition of non-alignment, whereby the socialist bloc was viewed as an integral part of the Movement.

In tandem with this stance, the Mozambique government pledged support for the liberation movements fighting for the independence of Namibia and Zimbabwe. Active assistance was subsequently given to the African National Congress of South Africa in its campaign against the apartheid regime. Mozambique also supported opponents of President Kamuzu Banda of Malawi. As Frelimo saw it, this support fitted in the context of the struggle against Western imperialism.[4]

If the Frelimo government's domestic policy had sowed the seeds of discontent amongst Mozambicans in general, its foreign policy would prompt the neighbouring countries to retaliate, either directly or through forces opposed to Frelimo.

In retrospect, as a former Mozambican first lady admitted, Machel had 'failed to realize that the forces that opposed our so clearly defined stance and our personality could effectively hit back'. Frelimo, she said, 'had misread its own capacities'.[5] It appears that if Mondlane had held the reins of power when Mozambique became independent, he would have pursued a moderate foreign policy. According to his widow, he would not have 'sacrificed' Mozambique's interests at the expense of a non-colonial and non-racist Southern Africa.[6]

Regarding Malawi, the Mozambican government, with the active support of Tanzania through Southern Africa's Revolutionary Council, made a concerted effort to steer President Kamuzu Banda away from white-ruled Rhodesia and South Africa. The methods employed varied from political persuasion to economic and military pressure. Attempts were made, with different degrees of success, to enlist the support of the Malawian youth and the armed forces through cultural and co-operation exchanges. The promotion of domestic unrest was another option taken into consideration.

Mozambique not only gave shelter to opponents of Banda's regime, but also safe passage to Malawian guerrillas wanting to infiltrate their country from bases in Tanzania. They were said to enter Malawi through the Mozambican provinces of Niassa, Zambézia and Tete as corridors. Others entered Malawi directly from Tanzania.

The autocratic Banda regime, notorious for its repression of any signs of dissent, was prepared to go to great lengths to silence its opponents wherever they could be found. The attempt on the life of the League of Socialist Malawi leader, Dr Attati Mpakati, in the Mozambican capital in February 1979 bore the mark of the Malawian Special Branch. Given Mozambique's hostile policy toward Banda, the Malawian government decided to assist Mozambicans that had long been at loggerheads with Frelimo in their campaign against Machel.

Amós Sumane, the former Frelimo member who had been living in Malawi since mid-1965, established the Partido Revolucionário de Moçambique (PRM) in June 1976. In view of his long association with the Mozambican community in Malawi, Sumane was able to draw into his fold those fleeing the Frelimo government, including Mozambicans willing to militarily challenge a regime that they regarded as having reneged on its pledge to a free country. At the onset, the PRM advocated the use of arms to bring about a political change in Mozambique. According to the PRM, 'Frelimo had brought communism and a tribal government to the country instead of true independence, democracy, development, freedom of worship for which Mozambicans had died, suffered and striven'.[7]

The PRM, according to Gimo Phiri, the organization's political commissar at the time, launched its armed campaign against the Frelimo government on 8 August 1978. Describing the PRM's first armed attack, Phiri said that 'a group of 10 ill-equipped men, but dedicated to the national cause, began the armed struggle by raiding an enemy base in the Jalasse area of Zambézia'. Similar operations, but with slightly larger and better equipped groups, continued in the following years with the PRM extending its operations into Niassa, in 1979, and Tete in 1982.[8] Prior to the August 1978 incidents as reported by Phiri, the PRM had, however, made claims of attacks inside Mozambique the previous year.

Apprehensive about the PRM's activities, the Mozambican government decided to bolster its counter-insurgency measures with harsh punishment of captured members of the organization. In February 1981, the Revolutionary Military Tribunal tried 32 PRM members, sentencing four of them to death by firing squad, and the remainder to jail sentences ranging from eight to 14 years. The indictments revealed the extent of the PRM's network in Zambézia, its mobilization of the rural population and traditional chiefs in areas as far afield as Mopeia, the presence of civilians in the movement's military bases, the infiltration of PRM female members into Frelimo's women's league, and the travelling of PRM members to Malawi to meet its 'ringleaders'.

It was disclosed during the proceedings that Amós Sumane was in detention in Mozambique, awaiting trial.[9] He would be summarily executed shortly afterwards. It appears that he had been abducted from Blantyre around 1980. After the arrest of Sumane, the PRM's political and military wings came under the overall command of Gimo Phiri. Sumane's demise had little or no impact on the movement's military campaign since it had for a long time been the responsibility of those in the field.

In fact, PRM's insurgency activity continued. About three months after the February 1981 trials, guerrilla attacks were reported in the Milange district, with a raid on the Mônguè communal village. In June, PRM activity was reported in the same area. The guerrillas spread their presence inland, with small-scale attacks conducted in the Gurué, Namarrói and Lugela Districts of Zambézia. Operations continued in Niassa's Mecanhelas region ever since it was activated in 1979. The PRM was also reported to have used land mines in Zambézia.[10]

In June 1982, the Revolutionary Military Tribunal sentenced seven Mozambicans to death for subversion. Two of the accused, Matias Tenda and Joaquim Veleia, were PRM members. Tenda had joined Frelimo in 1963 and rose to administrative secretary at its Mbeya hospital in Tanzania. He left Frelimo in 1967 to join Coremo. Veleia was a former Frelimo political commissar in Zambézia, becoming a deputy in Gurué District's assembly in 1977. Two years later he began collaborating with the PRM.[11] But, like the February 1981 executions, those did not deter the PRM from pursuing its goals. In August 1982, its operations were extended to Amaramba in Niassa, Ile in Zambézia, and Mutarara in Tete.

Mozambique's direct involvement with those fighting to oust Ian Smith's white minority regime was to have far more serious repercussions than the skirmishes near the border with Malawi. The Rhodesian government's determination to hold on to power had dire consequences for internal stability in Mozambique, as a result not only of Rhodesia's direct attacks on insurgent bases in the Mozambican territory, but also of its support for opponents of the Frelimo government.

While the Portuguese still ruled in Mozambique, in mid-1970 Frelimo gave safe passage to Zimbabwean guerrillas wanting to infiltrate their country through Tete. The Rhodesians sought permission from Lisbon to operate against ZANU guerrillas before they could cross the border. When it became clear that Mozambique would become independent with a Frelimo government in power, the Rhodesians opted for a policy of coexistence, hoping that their neighbours would follow suit.

Advised by the Central Intelligence Organization, CIO, the Smith regime reasoned that Frelimo would not enter into confrontation with Rhodesia for purely economic reasons. Mozambique's economy depended to a large extent on Rhodesia, and, through it, on Zambia and Zaire for their use of the Mozambican ports. The fragile economy that Frelimo would inherit from Portugal, the CIO insisted much to the annoyance of sectors of the Rhodesian military, was in itself proof that no government in Mozambique could possibly entertain the idea of provoking hostilities with any of its neighbours. Indeed, the CIO argued that Zimbabwean guerrillas still inside Frelimo bases in Mozambique from the days of the war against Portugal should be left alone. As a CIO intelligence officer advised, 'The Frelimo want peace and we must be careful not to upset them, otherwise we will lose the port facilities of Mozambique'.[12]

The Rhodesians appeared convinced that friendly relations could be established with independent Mozambique. Steps in that direction were taken right after the Frelimo-led transition government was inaugurated. In the wake of the cyclical floods that hit southern Mozambique in late 1974, the Rhodesians dispatched food aid for displaced persons in the Limpopo valley. As food shortages were reported in central Mozambique, Rhodesia sent 40 tonnes of flour to Manica early in 1975.[13]

As reports of food shortages continued to emerge from Mozambique, a Foreign Ministry spokesman announced in Salisbury in February 1975 that Rhodesia would 'give sympathetic consideration' to any request by the Mozambican government for help to ease the critical food shortages. In the wake of this pledge, the first five trucks of a train of 18 laden with Rhodesian maize meal arrived in Beira on 11 February.[14]

These, however, were fruitless efforts. By March 1975, some three months before Mozambique was due to become independent, the Rhodesian armed forces finally received clearance to mount an attack on a ZANU staging post in Tete. Stringent conditions were laid down. Specifically, no air-support, except for very serious casualty evacuations, would be given. The attack had to be carried out in such a manner that no finger could be pointed out at the Rhodesians.[15] In August 1975, as large-scale ZANU guerrilla incursions from Mozambique continued, the Rhodesian armed forces were allowed 'to take out and generally harass known ZANLA staging posts within Mozambique, though strict limitations still applied'.[16] Accordingly, the Rhodesian armed forces were forbidden to strike any target more than five kilometres from the Rhodesian border and, at all costs, avoid attacks on Frelimo. If ZANLA and Frelimo occupied jointly any staging posts, these should be left alone. The initial restrictions on air support remained in force.

In a further attempt aimed at preventing Mozambique from assisting the Zimbabwean guerrillas, the Rhodesian defense minister, Pieter van der Byl, said publicly that it was his 'government's aim to maintain the spirit of friendship and co-operation with all her neighbours'. Speaking in parliament upon the inauguration of President Machel, Van der Byl added:

> I would like to take this opportunity of congratulating President Machel on his appointment as President of the new Republic of Mozambique. I take this opportunity of assuring him, his government and the people of Mozambique, that we offer nothing but goodwill towards them. In all ways we are prepared to assist in the solution of any mutual problem, and to co-operate in the development of our two countries.[17]

But that was wishful thinking on the part of the Rhodesians. The build up of Zimbabwe nationalist forces in Mozambique led the Rhodesian armed forces to step up military operations against ZANLA positions from January 1976 onwards, including air-backed raids in Gaza and Tete. It was against this backdrop that on 3 March 1976 the Mozambique government announced the closure of its border with Rhodesia in compliance with UN sanctions. The Frelimo government reiterated its fully-fledged support for Zimbabwe's independence war. On the same day, the official Mozambican radio began 'Voice of Zimbabwe' broadcasts on behalf of the Zimbabwean independence movement.

Frelimo believed that its support for the Zimbabwean cause would be short-lived and that a settlement of the Rhodesian dispute would be reached before long. It was not until late 1979, after Mozambique had suffered dearly in view of its direct involvement with the Zimbabwe independence war, that a cease-fire finally put an end to the conflict. Nonetheless, the British-brokered cease-fire accord had no impact on the civil war that meanwhile had broken out in Mozambique, for which the beleaguered Ian Smith regime provided key support.

2
The *Magaia* Pamphlet

In addition to full-scale military action against Zimbabwe guerrilla bases inside Mozambique, the Rhodesians embarked on a political campaign aimed at the Frelimo government. The Rhodesian Broadcasting Corporation (RBC) began transmissions in Portuguese to Mozambique in April 1976. Ostensibly for Mozambican migrant workers in Rhodesia, the programs were markedly anti-Frelimo. A Portuguese national employed by the recently created Branch of Special Duties (BOSD) of the Rhodesian Information Ministry, produced them.

Much to the delight of the Mozambican authorities, the radio programs had a racial bias and appealed to colonial nostalgists. In one of its transmissions, the service claimed that Mozambicans were an 'uncultured people'. Playing with the Portuguese word for culture, which also means crop, it was stated that the 'only culture Vasco da Gama had found when he landed in Mozambique was that of cassava'. In another transmission, Mozambicans were told that 'if today they do not live in trees, know how to read and write, and dress as humans they should be thankful to white colonizers'.

Surprised by the radio broadcasts was Orlando Cristina, an old Frelimo foe who had been living in Rhodesia since late 1974. Backed by several Mozambican exiles, including two former Frelimo members who had fled to Rhodesia a month before the closure of the border, Cristina manoeuvred to seize control of the radio service and rearrange its content so as to serve a more tenable purpose.

Cristina was born in Portugal in 1927. He lived briefly in Mozambique when his father, a non-commissioned officer in the Portuguese army, served in the colony and later retired there. He returned to Portugal when his parents separated, the father remaining in Mozambique where he lived with a Yao woman in Niassa.

As a law student at the University of Lisbon, Cristina joined the youth wing of the Democratic Union Movement, a Portuguese Communist Party front organisation.[18] Cristina's mother, who years later became a Communist Party militant, was warned that her son was about to be arrested due to his political activities. She decided to send him back to Mozambique to live with his father.[19]

Not long after his return to Mozambique, Cristina was conscripted into the Portuguese army in 1948. Upon his discharge from military service, Cristina began working with his father in Niassa, mainly as a big game hunter. His exposure to traditional African lifestyle led him to embrace the Yao, learning their language and customs, going through their rituals. Following his father's steps, Cristina married an Islamized Yao woman, the daughter of a local traditional chief.

In anticipation of insurgency activity in Mozambique, the Portuguese Armed Forces invited big game hunters active on the border areas to assist their Military Intelligence Service in providing information on underground activity. Cristina began working for the service in November 1962, submitting weekly situation reports to the General Staff of Intelligence in Nampula. In his reports, so Cristina claimed, he repeatedly stressed that unless efforts were made to address the social problems he identified among the rural population, any insurgent movement would be able to subvert the established order.

In 1963, Cristina crossed the border into Tanzania to join Frelimo. It is not clear whether his defection was genuine. Cristina said he was dissatisfied with the Portuguese and believed in Frelimo as an alternative to the colonial regime. As for his subsequent return to Mozambique in 1964, Cristina attributed this to his equal dissatisfaction with what he saw in Dar es Salaam: racial and ethnic disputes afflicting a movement purporting to free Mozambique. Other quarters, however, say Cristina faced heavy fines for hunting without a license, and was about to be prosecuted. It has also been claimed that he went to Tanzania on a PIDE mission, but this does not tally with his connection with the Portuguese military intelligence, and the fact that he informed Tanzanian police about Mozambicans he had seen with Frelimo in Dar es Salaam, but who he knew were working for the Portuguese. What is even more intriguing is that, upon his return to Mozambique, Cristina was promptly arrested. The PIDE would have treated an agent differently. His release from detention, thus avoiding being court-martialed by the Portuguese Armed Forces, was due to Jorge Jardim's interference in the matter.

According to Cristina, Jardim visited him in jail and told him that he 'understood his motives in searching for Frelimo, but that there were other ways of resolving the Mozambican problem'. Jardim told Cristina that he could arrange for his release as long as he was 'prepared to join him in his plan and ask no questions if he felt puzzled by what he would eventually come to realize'. Cristina was not only surprised by the visit, but also equally astonished when he found out who Jardim was and what he represented in Mozambique. The ensuing relationship between the two was to last until Jardim's death some 20 years later.

Cristina was put on Lusalite's payroll as the man responsible for maintaining the security of the company and the employees' compound at Dondo. Cristina's real job, however, was to be part of the plan that Jardim envisaged for an independent Mozambique. Cristina stressed to Jardim that his plan could only succeed if a genuinely Mozambican military force was in place for sooner or later the Portuguese would wash their hands of their colonial quagmire. Mozambicans, both black and white, opposed to a Frelimo take-over, Cristina reasoned, would be powerless without an army of their own.

Without the resources and the justification for creating such a force, both Cristina and Jardim had no option but to rely on the Portuguese administration to bring it to fruition. The force, which became known as the Grupos Especiais, or the GE, came into being in January 1971. Costa Campos, a colonel who was not from the Jardim camp, was appointed its commanding officer. Jardim succeeded in having Cristina involved in the recruitment and political education of the GEs. But his role with the unit was short-lived. He left the GE after disagreeing with Campos over the issue of the command of the unit. Jardim reacted bitterly when Cristina broke the news to him. 'You should have stayed regardless of your differences with Costa Campos', said Jardim, adding: 'At least we would have someone within the unit, now we have none'. When the unit's airborne version, the Grupos Especiais Pára-quedistas (GEP) was established in late 1971, Jardim had one of his daughters serving as paratroops instructor.

Cristina had been very enthusiastic about the GE concept. He used to go to the heartland of the Makua in Zambézia as well to the Makua enclave of Mecanhelas, in the southern tip of Niassa, to meet local traditional chiefs and through them recruit members for the GE. 'I am here to gather volunteers for a new army – neither Portuguese nor Frelimo – but a truly Mozambican one', was how Cristina introduced himself in village after village. In his behind-closed door sessions with the recruits, Cristina often startled them with his views of a distinctly non-Portuguese, independent Mozambique, though opposed to

Frelimo, whose leaders, he told them, were seeking to replace Portugal and impose a new form of domination.

Cristina was involved in the training of the Malawi Young Pioneers, the youth wing of the ruling Malawian party. He also played a leading role in the so-called Mecanhelas Self-Defense System. According to Cristina, the system effectively prevented the infiltration of Frelimo guerrillas into Zambézia from their bases in Niassa. For this, Cristina counted on two factors – the terrain and the ethnicity of the area. The Amaramba, Chirwa and Chiuta Lakes along the Malawian border with Niassa forced Frelimo guerrillas to march through Mecanhelas before they could cross the Lúrio River and enter Zambézia. Cristina exploited the differences between the Islamized Yao and the Makua living in the Mecanhelas enclave, which stemmed from the slave trade of the 18th and 19th centuries. Frelimo's alternative was to by-pass the lakes, using Malawi as a corridor. But this exposed Frelimo guerrillas to the Malawi authorities who were opposed to their territory being used as a conduit for incursions into Mozambique.

At Jardim's request, Cristina conducted an investigation into the attempt on the life of Brás da Costa, a Portuguese businessman living in Niassa. In 1971 Brás da Costa had his hands blown off as he opened a parcel-bomb, said to have been posted to him by Frelimo. As Frelimo guerrillas began calling at Costa's network of rural shops in the Lichinga area for food supplies and medicines, he approached Cristina and told him of his dilemma: if he reported the matter to the Portuguese authorities Frelimo would eventually retaliate by at least destroying his shops; and if he kept quiet, the Portuguese would soon find out and accuse him of collaborating with Frelimo. Cristina assured Costa that he should continue supplying the guerrillas and nothing would happen to him or his business. In exchange, Cristina would covertly gather information about the presence of Frelimo guerrillas in the area, their infiltration routes from Tanzania and their plans once inside Mozambique.

Unaware of this arrangement, the PIDE assumed that the military were either deliberately turning a blind eye to the matter or had entered into a deal with Frelimo so as not to come under attack. Cristina had strong reasons to believe that Frelimo had not been behind the parcel-bomb. His unofficial investigations revealed that the parcel-bomb had been assembled by the PIDE in Beira and posted from Tete. As the PIDE learned of Cristina's moves, they warned him 'not to underestimate PIDE's methods'. Cristina backed off. Costa underwent extensive surgery, and was fitted with artificial limbs. After independence Frelimo awarded him a medal in recognition of his services.

Cristina had grown disillusioned with Jardim and with his ideas on how to settle the dispute in Mozambique. As he confided to a French correspondent visiting Mecanhelas, time was running out. Jardim, he said, 'knows it, but wants to be the president of Mozambique and yet is forced to rely on the army for support'.[20]

Of all Jardim's associates, Cristina was the only one to flatly reject any action in support of the September 1974 settler uprising in Lourenço Marques in protest against the peace accord Portugal signed with Frelimo. For Cristina, that would be an affront to the independence Mozambicans had just gained. Most probably Cristina realized that to join the settler movement served no purpose since none of them had the means to sustain any revolt against the independence deal. 'All we can do', Cristina reasoned, 'is to wait for Frelimo to get into power for it is bound to create dissatisfaction among the people and that will be the rallying point for any hypothetical action'.

In the wake of the independence accord, Cristina left for Malawi but was imprisoned shortly afterwards. It appears that he wanted to cross the border into Mozambique and be with the 800 or so Makua militiamen of the Mecanhelas self-defense system. Cristina's arrest is said to have been masterminded by none other than Jardim himself. Jardim wanted to avoid at all costs any action that could be interpreted as hostile to Frelimo because he believed Machel would invite him to serve as prime minister after independence.

Jardim and Cristina were briefly reunited in Salisbury in December 1974. Jardim went to live in Las Palmas, and Cristina opted to stay in Rhodesia. Manuel Abecassis, one of Lusalite's owners living in Portugal, agreed to Cristina's request to keep him on the company's payroll for another year.

In September 1975, Cristina began circulating clandestinely inside Mozambique an anti-Frelimo pamphlet which he called 'Magaia – A Voz Livre do Povo Moçambicano'. Named after Filipe Magaia, the pamphlet was aimed at the Mozambique armed forces, particularly independence war veterans loyal to the late Frelimo defense chief. The pamphlet sought to drive a wedge within the armed forces, claiming that Machel's government had disavowed the initial Frelimo program of action by establishing a dictatorial regime. The mimeographed pamphlet was posted from within Mozambique and from Malawi, Swaziland and South Africa, as well as Europe and Brazil to specific addresses in Mozambique. Publication ceased in mid-1979, the last issue being devoted to the transfer to Mozambique of the remains of Filipe Magaia who had since been given national hero status by the Frelimo government.

The pamphlet did not influence the December 1975 military coup attempt in Mozambique. The coup attempt, staged barely three months after the pamphlet began its restricted circulation, was an inevitable occurrence, whose origins are to be found within Frelimo as a liberation movement, not as a government.

But what the 1975 events signified to Cristina, as if what he had told Jardim and his followers had been correctly predicted, was that the situation in Mozambique was not entirely favourable to the Frelimo government. Thus Cristina decided that he should continue in Rhodesia longer than he anticipated. Yet, this posed a problem in that Manuel Abecassis' offer to maintain Cristina would no longer apply if he remained in Rhodesia after December 1975. Cristina secured financial assistance through Peter Burt, a CIO officer seconded to the Rhodesia mission in Lisbon who had recently been relocated to Salisbury to work for the Mozambique Desk of the CIO's Operations Department.

3
The Voz da África Livre

Among those Frelimo arrested during the transition to independence were Jacob Chinhara and Janota Luís. Chinhara, from Niassa, had joined Frelimo in 1965. Dissatisfied with conditions prevailing within Frelimo in the wake of Magaia's assassination, Chinhara defected to the Portuguese in 1967. Luís was from Sofala and had joined Frelimo in 1968 at the age of 18. He was wounded and taken prisoner by the Portuguese during a clash in Tete. They were both sent to the former GE barracks at Dondo, which had since been transformed into a Frelimo political and military training centre.

The two escaped to Rhodesia in January 1976. After being briefly detained by the Rhodesians as 'prohibited immigrants', Chinhara and Luís met Orlando Cristina in Salisbury through the CIO and became involved in the Portuguese radio broadcasts to Mozambique.

Having secured a foothold in the radio transmissions, Cristina then impressed on the CIO the need for a more effective campaign over the air waves. Ideally, he wanted an independent radio service with more clearly defined objectives whose links to Rhodesia would not be so obvious. Cristina had, however, to reconcile his interests with the Rhodesians'. To talk in terms of a radio station serving as the mouthpiece of an exiled movement opposed to the Frelimo government was too advanced for the prevailing Rhodesian way of thinking. Rhodesia would prefer to be in control of events. If any action needed to be taken against Mozambique, they would prefer to do it themselves, taking advantage of whatever resources at their disposal, Mozambican included. Aware of this situation, Cristina and those working closely with him realized that they had no option but to accept the reality, hoping that in the future they would gain more leverage. The alternative, as Cristina repeatedly stated in reference to exiled politicians, 'would be for us to engage in sterile conversations around restaurant tables in Lisbon or Johannesburg and conjecture about the best way of toppling Machel'.[21]

As a first step, Cristina forged listeners' letters addressed to the 'Portuguese Service' of the RBC, praising the initiative, while stressing the importance of having longer air time on a single slot, instead of the existing three. The same network of collaborators that disseminated the *Magaia* pamphlet was used to post the letters. Cristina succeeded in convincing the Rhodesians. Two months after the first RBC broadcasts had gone on air, they approved a budget to pay for the hiring of an independent transmitter.

The naming of the new radio service as the Voz da África Livre was a compromise reached between the Portuguese man responsible for the initial RBC radio broadcasts and Chinhara. The former wanted to simply call it the Rádio Moçambique Livre. Chinhara argued that this would be reminiscent of the September 1974 uprising, generally viewed as being opposed to Mozambique's independence. 'We shall be playing into Frelimo's hands and expose ourselves to well founded criticism if we adopt that name', Chinhara argued.

The Voz da África Livre began 60-minute daily transmissions on 5 July 1976. The service used a powerful medium wave transmitter that the Rhodesian government had acquired in 1966 to jam British broadcasts from Botswana, opposing Ian Smith's UDI regime. Big Bertha, as the transmitter was called, could cover the whole of Mozambique. The radio programs were produced in Salisbury and then sent by land line to the transmitter site at Guinea Fowl in the Midlands, from where the signal was beamed to Mozambique. The station broadcast in the main native languages of Mozambique as well as in Portuguese, English and kiSwahili.

By the end of August 1976, Cristina's camp had editorial control of the station. In addition to the two former Frelimo members, a couple of younger generation Mozambicans had joined Cristina, lending to the station a clearly distinct anti-colonial stance rooted on genuinely democratic values developed right from their student days. They all agreed that the broadcasts should adopt a more coherent outlook than the ones initially broadcast by the RBC. Primarily, the broadcasts should not deny Mozambique's independence, but instead uphold Frelimo's struggle for the country's sovereignty and in particular the initial Frelimo program of action to which most of those in the station had in the past adhered to. Colonialism and any form of racism should be rejected outright, and under no circumstances could the station align itself with the Rhodesian or South African regimes, but condemn them whenever possible. In a nutshell, the radio broadcasts should campaign for the establishment of a democratic order in Mozambique through free, multiparty elections.

This and particularly the station's claimed allegiance to the views espoused by Frelimo during Mondlane's tenure, was interpreted by observers as an opportunistic stance designed to justify a nationalistic legitimacy that did not exist. But the Mozambicans in the Voz da África Livre, regardless of the fact that most of them had a history of either direct association with or sympathy for Frelimo in the years preceding independence, saw no reason why they should not state their allegiance to what a fellow Mozambican had advocated to their own country and which was in sharp contradiction with what Frelimo pursued after independence. They argued that the Frelimo government's policies in no way reflected the program of action the liberation movement announced at its inception, notably its pledge, *inter alia*, for the establishment of a democratic order, in which all Mozambicans would be equal before the law and with the same rights and duties; the formation of a government of the people, by the people and for the people; and the upholding of the Universal Declaration of Human Rights.[22]

The Voz da África Livre opposed the Frelimo government on the account of the latter's domestic and foreign policies. Domestically, it berated the government's human rights record and its control of the judiciary and the legislature. A dominant factor in the station's tirade against Frelimo was its economic program, in particular the forced relocation of peasants from their ancestral lands that it entailed. State farms were often compared to colonial plantations.

The Voz da África Livre scored also on the close links Mozambique developed with the former USSR despite the non-aligned stance pursued by the Frelimo government. The station made extensive use of New China News Agency material as well as Chinese Communist Party literature in its effort to discredit 'Frelimo's social imperialist allies'. A theme often played whenever the question of non-alignment surfaced was the Soviet Union's annexation of European and Asian territories after World War II, and the invasions of Czechoslovakia in 1968 and Afghanistan in 1979. Mozambique's voting at the UN General Assembly, alongside the USSR, against resolutions calling for the Soviet withdrawal from Afghanistan was used as an example to prove the Voz da África Livre's depiction of Samora Machel as a 'Moscow stooge' bent on transforming Mozambique into 'a Soviet Bantustan'.[23] The warming of relations between Mozambique and the West, particularly the United States in the early 1980s, prompted the Voz da África Livre temporarily to scale down its anti-Soviet stance, centering its criticism on 'capitalist imperialism' and on 'the new allies Machel has found in Washington'. On American linkage of Namibia's independence to the withdrawal of Cuban troops from Angola, the station accused the United States of 'having created an impasse in Namibia by claiming that independence for the occupied territory must be achieved by interfering in Angola's internal affairs'.[24]

The Mozambique government portrayed the Voz da África Livre as the 'voice of the hyena'. In a series of lengthy statements, the government claimed that the station was 'subsidised by the CIA-created and Swiss-based Free Africa Organisation, religious sects and anti-Communist movements'. Conceding that the Voz da África Livre used 'highly perfected propaganda methods', the government explained that this was because 'American, South African and West German propaganda experts connected to the CIA and reactionary radio stations like the so-called "Free Europe" and "Radio Liberty" worked for the voice of the hyena'.[25]

Despite the rhetoric, the underlying fact was that the Frelimo government was being openly challenged by a medium beyond its control. At best, the government could only attempt to jam the station's broadcasts, but these proved to be ineffectual. Although registered as having an output of 100 KW, the real capacity of the Big Bertha transmitter was four times higher than that, though it never operated at more than 250 KW.

The station never had more than eight permanent staff members in its service at any one time. None had any previous journalistic or radio experience. 'We were no propaganda experts and had none assisting us', says a former Voz da África Livre member, who noted that:

> I think the Voice of Free Africa's role ought to be put in the right perspective. In a country whose news media was saturated with government propaganda and revolutionary hymns, surely you couldn't go wrong if you touched on the regime's sore points and presented an alternative to the existing order.[26]

There were two distinct phases in the lifetime of the radio service. The first was when the station, while maintaining its own editorial line, sought to operate as a medium through which exiled groups opposed to the government in Mozambique could air their views. It gave air time to organizations like the Fumo party of Domingos Arouca and Monamo of Máximo Dias. In this phase, the station pressed for a change in the country's political system, whereby Mozambicans should be free to elect a democratic form of government.

After the emergence of a military opposition to Frelimo in the form of the Resistência Nacional Moçambicana, Renamo, the station identified itself with the goals set out by the armed group. But like the station earlier on, Renamo's initial agenda did not include the seizing of political power in the country. Renamo's ultimate goal then, as portrayed in Voz da África Livre's broadcasts, was merely to create, through military means, conditions for the holding of elections and the establishment of a democratic order in the country. As the Renamo leadership became aware of its political clout, the station too developed a political agenda fitting the new situation.

4
Renamo, the Early Days

There was no-one in the Voz da África Livre who even remotely thought that their campaign over the airwaves would evolve into an armed movement capable of challenging the regime in power in Mozambique. At best, they believed the broadcasts could encourage a civilian uprising in the main urban centres. In their view, the Armed Forces would support the uprising and bring down the government. It was based on this assumption that the station included a weekly program specifically addressed to the Armed Forces, impressing on them the need 'to distance themselves from a government that has betrayed the ideals of independence by bringing about new forms of oppression and exploitation'.[27]

If the defection to Rhodesia in October 1976 of André Mathadi Matsangaice Dyuwayo, a former independence war fighter, did not prove the Voz da África Livre's perception entirely wrong, it nonetheless took them by surprise. André Matsangaice told Cristina that he did not believe it would be possible to change the political situation in Mozambique through a radio campaign. The only way of achieving that, he said, was by the force of arms. 'And that is what I intend to do. People are ready to follow me', added André Matsangaice, pointing out that all he needed was assistance from whoever was ready to provide it.[28]

The CIO dismissed André Matsangaice's idea as unrealistic, not warranting the support he was looking for. What the Rhodesians had in mind was the formation of a commando unit, not a genuine opposition movement. The latter entailed aspects that the CIO did not want to concern themselves with, namely a political agenda, a strategy of its own, and allegiance to an indigenous leader rather than to the Rhodesian security establishment. A CIO officer told Cristina privately that unless he could come up with his own money to fund a genuine resistance movement he would always be at the mercy of the Rhode-sians. 'People in the CIO are old-fashioned', said the officer, 'and as your chances of raising money are very slim, I strongly advise you to start a new life elsewhere.'[29] And CIO's Peter Burt could not have been more straightforward when he told André Matsangaice that if things were as easy as he had claimed them to be, he should return to Mozambique, gather his followers and take them back to Rhodesia where the govern-ment would then consider his request.

André Matsangaice Dyuwayo was born in Chirara, Manica, in 1950. His great grandfather, Saugweme Dyuwayo, fought with the Nguni in their thrust into eastern Zimbabwe. As a reward, Saugweme was given land in the Chimanimani region. Saugweme Dyuwayo's grandson, Mat-sangaice, fought alongside the Mutassa in their land dispute with Makone, and in reward was given land in the Penhalonga region. André Matsangaice studied at a Catholic mission school in Jécua, and afterwards in Rhodesia to where his father had emigrated. He joined Frelimo in 1970 and after independence served with the Army's engi-neering corps in Beira.

In September 1975, he was arrested for allegedly stealing Army prop-erty. According to his brother, Luís, the arrest and internment in the Sacudzo re-education camp was due to André Matsangaice's objection to the government's confiscation of the family-owned school as well as their land, itself a source of prestige among the Dyuwayos. Luís recalls that his brother once told him that he would challenge Frelimo's deci-sion to take their property, even if he had to 'resort to violence'.[30]

About two months after his arrival in Rhodesia, André Matsangaice returned to Mozambique to try to prove to the CIO the viability of his plan. Alone and armed only with a pistol, he intended to raid the Sacudzo re-education camp and set free its inmates with whom he would then form the core of the force he wanted to lead against the Frelimo government. The raid was planned for Christmas Eve. In November, Cristina announced over the Voz da África Livre that condi-tions had been created to wage a military campaign against Frelimo in the form of Resistência Nacional Moçambicana.

There has been a great deal of speculation about the movement's name and its origins. The name owes its existence to a Voz da África Livre listener in Maputo, whose brief missives to the station invariably ended with 'Viva a Resistência!'. The Voz da África Livre adopted the slogan and used it whenever the question of domestic opposition to the Frelimo government was raised. For the radio station, the slogan epitomized the underground resistance to Frelimo it believed existed in Mozambique. Examination of scripts broadcast by the station show that the movement was consistently referred to in its original designation in Portuguese or its initials, RNM, and afterwards by the acronym, Renamo, both standing for its original name. The foreign media referred to the movement in English as Mozambique National Resistance, coining the initials, MNR. It would have been nonsensical for Renamo to identify itself to a Mozambican audience in any medium other than Portuguese.

The December 1976 raid on Sacudzo was a failure. André Matsangaice was detained for being absent from the camp without permission, but managed to escape once again to Rhodesia. For their part, the Rhodesians went ahead with their own plan and formed a small commando unit to operate in Mozambique. The unit's primary task was to gather intelligence for the Rhodesian war effort, and launch selective attacks on key Mozambican installations. Its members included former members of the Portuguese armed forces, who had moved to Rhodesia after the political changes in Mozambique. The unit called itself the Resistência Moçambicana, or Remo, but there was no connection with the Voz da África Livre or even the RNM. In fact, Cristina disliked the Remo concept and those involved with it. The dislike was mutual. Remo members realized that Cristina was opposed to their presence. The Voz da África Livre's anti-colonial stance contributed to a worsening of relations between the two. An individualist, Cristina saw Remo as a nuisance to his personal agenda. For him, the presence of whites in a group that had the necessary ingredients to become a genuine indigenous movement could only complicate matters. The movement's credibility among the rural population would be questioned. Moreover, André Matsangaice would not be willing to be led by anyone, especially whites, and neither were the latter prepared to operate under the command of a black. In an attempt to have the Rhodesians review their policy toward Remo, Cristina impressed these aspects on Peter Burt, pointing out to him that whites, however harsh their training might have been, lacked the stamina to endure the hardships Africans were accustomed to by virtue of their upbringing.

The Rhodesians reconsidered the viability of Remo in view of the fiasco of an operation launched in January 1977. Remo blamed the CIO for the setback and felt that the Rhodesians used that as an excuse to disband the unit. Remo member Aires de Oliveira claimed that the CIO misled those involved in the planning of the operation, feeding them wrong information.[31] Without realizing it, the eight-man Remo unit walked at night into a Zimbabwe guerrilla base inside Mozambique. A book[32] published by Remo members in Portugal mentions an exchange of fire with the Zimbabweans the day after the group infiltrated Mozambique. Oliveira sustained light wounds, but another member, only identified as the 'game ranger', was seriously wounded in one leg, and was left behind by his comrades in disarray. He was captured and subsequently identified as Rui Silva, a Mozambican of mixed race, holding Portuguese citizenship. With the introduction of the death penalty three years later, Silva was among the first ten prisoners to be executed by firing squad. Once back in Rhodesia, the surviving Remo members were banned from engaging in further operations. Some left for Portugal and others for Brazil.

André Matsangaice still had to assert his position and show the CIO that he was a viable proposition. On 6 May 1977, he carried out yet another raid on the Sacudzo re-education camp. This time he was accompanied by Manuel Mutambara and Marcos Amade, both former Mozambique government soldiers who had defected to Rhodesia before André Matsangaice and had since joined him. As the three armed men entered the camp, they saw a group of about 50 prisoners being escorted by Frelimo soldiers. The prisoners included high school students whom President Machel had alluded to in his March 1977 speech in Beira. The soldiers were disarmed and André Matsangaice identified himself as being from the África Livre. He deliberately failed to mention Renamo by name for he realized that it was a nonentity at the time, the radio station being more widely known by Mozambicans. André Matsangaice told the prisoners that he had come to free them. 'If you want to join me in the struggle against Frelimo', he said, 'you should be prepared to walk from here on foot for the next two days until we reach our base'.[33] The prisoners agreed to follow him, and from there they headed to the Rhodesian border. André Matsangaice stopped at his home village in Chirara, where his younger brother, Oliver, joined the group. After enduring a number of attacks, the group crossed the border after sunset on 7 May.

Of the initial group, only 28 made it to Odzi, an old farm near the border town of Mutare, where the first Renamo base was located. In addition to those killed during Frelimo's counter-attacks, others got lost or decided to part ways.

At Odzi, military training was given by Special Air Forces, SAS, instructors seconded to the CIO. The Rhodesians saw it appropriate to transfer from Odzi a couple of former Portuguese military men serving as instructors because André Matsangaice resented their presence.

After the raid on Sacudzo, the Voz da África Livre promoted Renamo domestically. The station created among its listeners the impression that Renamo was a well organized force and that the military campaign against the Mozambican government was irreversible. As a result of this, Mozambicans began to arrive in Rhodesia in search of Renamo. In June, three families, consisting of 19 people, fled to Rhodesia from Beira. They included a nurse and a light aircraft pilot who thought they could serve in Renamo's non-existent medical corps and air force. Three others wanted to receive military training and start fighting. To their disappointment, the Rhodesians treated them as illegal immigrants, keeping them in Salisbury's remand prison pending their deportation.

For the CIO, the three families did not fit into its concept of a 'small and manageable' unit, particularly because of the logistics involved in catering for the education of children and the provision of more suitable accommodation for the married women. After negotiations between the Voz da África Livre and a Rhodesian Foreign Affairs Ministry official, the group was allowed to stay in the country on an exceptional basis. The radio station agreed that it would not encourage people to flee to Rhodesia.

Nonetheless, more Mozambicans continued to arrive in Rhodesia. One of them would play a prominent role in Renamo – Afonso Dhlakama, the 24-year-old son of a Ndau traditional leader from Sofala. Dhlakama had been with Frelimo since the transition to independence and at the time of his defection served in the Armed Forces' logistics department in Beira. As with André Matsangaice, the Mozambique government media alleged that Dhlakama had been disciplined for corruption. Dhlakama denied this, claiming that he felt discriminated against on ethnic grounds, and that he had even obtained the necessary travel documents from the local party committee before traveling to the border area with Rhodesia. 'I could not have done this if I were guilty of misconduct.'[34]

By the time Dhlakama arrived in Rhodesia in July 1977, Renamo's strength was made up of just over two platoons. Orlando Macamo, a former Criminal Investigation Police officer who had defected to Rhodesia, served as André Matsangaice's deputy. Among the early Renamo members was João Fombe, a Manyika like André Matsangaice, who had fought with Frelimo in the independence war.

In less than six months, Dhlakama established himself as a leader, replacing Macamo as Renamo's second in command. He led the raid on the town of Machaze in southern Manica, and made Renamo's presence felt, near the north-south highway in Sofala Province.

5
The Quest for Autonomy

There was an anti-climax after the raid on Sacudzo in that it was not followed by regular reports of Renamo activity. The Voz da África Livre, which had capitalized on the raid, could add nothing substantial to the military campaign that it promised against the Frelimo government. It could hardly be expected otherwise. By September 1977 Renamo only had 76 men, the majority of whom still undergoing military training.

Yet, the radio station continued to build up the image of Renamo, presenting it as the embodiment of nationwide resistance to the Frelimo regime. To protect Renamo's image, the station stopped broadcasting military communiqués that the PRM continued to send from Malawi. Military incidents that had taken place in areas where Renamo was not active were presented to listeners as evidence of resistance against Frelimo. Although Renamo and the PRM only merged in August 1982, it appears that the two organizations had agreed on the concept of a broader resistance. A Renamo communiqué issued in September 1978, reported that 'Resistance forces' operating in the Milange area of Zambézia had reached Mutarara in Tete.[35]

Renamo's low level of activity was also a matter of concern to André Matsangaice. In September 1977, Cristina met Matsangaice at the Odzi camp to discuss what the Renamo leader viewed as 'the difficulties created by the Rhodesians in the recruitment of more members for the Resistance'. According to Cristina, 'André had to turn back many volunteers who wanted to fight with the RNM because the Rhodesians only wanted a certain number of fighters'. This, Matsangaice complained, prevented him from establishing Renamo permanently in Mozambique's rural areas and expanding its operations to other parts of the country. At stake, Matsangaice argued, was Renamo's credibility among the people who were willing to accept the movement in their

midst. 'Once we establish a relationship with the people', said Matsangaice, 'we cannot just abandon them because they will feel betrayed,
especially in the face of Frelimo reprisals for having assisted us.'[36]
CIO's reluctance to meet Matsangaice's demands was due to an
alleged lack of funds to equip a larger Renamo contingent. In subsequent discussions with the CIO, Cristina was once again told that if he
wanted something different from what was in place, he would have to
find the means himself. The Rhodesians insisted that their resources
were limited, a situation that suited their idea of a small, purely military
unit that could, in the words of the former CIO director general, 'provide the eyes-and-ears of our Intelligence in Mozambique'. This did not
require Renamo to be permanently based inside Mozambique. And
rather than having Renamo expand its operations beyond the strip of
land in Manica Province running along Zimbabwe's eastern border, the
Rhodesians preferred that the movement concentrated its operations in
that area. This would help to create a buffer zone, making it more
difficult for Zimbabwe guerrillas to infiltrate Rhodesia from bases inside
Mozambique.

In the wake of the September 1977 meeting, Cristina renewed efforts to
raise money not only to fund Renamo's activities, but also to give it the
autonomy that he had envisioned at the outset. Estimates had put at
US$1 million annually the amount necessary to maintain a 500-strong
guerrilla army. Until then, such efforts had proved fruitless. Not even
Jorge Jardim, allegedly a man with immense economic power who had
claimed to have arms caches in Mozambique for an 'emergency plan'
against a Frelimo takeover in 1974, had been able to come to Cristina's
rescue. He told Cristina that 'his resources were nearly depleted', and that

> we should not go any further nor shall we be blamed for not attempt-
> ing to do something for which no one wanted to help us. It would be
> preferable to intelligently accept defeat than to deceive others and
> ourselves with utopian dreams even if these are worthy and just.[37]

Jardim had in fact become a nonentity after the collapse of the Portuguese colonial administration. Ironically, it was the Frelimo government
that promoted his image as Mozambique's public enemy No. 1. The CIO
doubted Jardim's influence in Mozambique and the impression that he
created of being the rallying point of all Frelimo opponents, real or
imaginary. An internal CIO report drafted by Peter Burt in the second
half of 1976 questioned 'the so-called "good, permanent and safe"
contacts Jardim claims he has with the people fighting against Frelimo

inside Mozambique'. The report dismissed as 'mostly propaganda' the publicity surrounding the Liberation Front of Cabo Delgado, the guerrilla activity by the Popular Front of Zambézia, and the claim that Fumo was 'strongly organized' in southern Mozambique, pointing out that 'it would be surprising if Jardim's Portuguese sources have avoided the national characteristics of vanity and boasting'. Viewing Jardim's suggestion that a 'a rebellion is in full swing' as 'a gross exaggeration', Burt summed up by saying that 'Jardim appears to fall into the Portuguese trap of stating the situation, evaluating and reaching certain conclusions, but without providing the answer'.[38]

Aware of his irrelevance among the CIO and the importance of playing to an African gallery, Jardim would years later expose in book form how the oil embargo on Rhodesia had been circumvented. The Rhodesians made no effort to prevent a Salisbury house from publishing it.

For his part, Cristina already had indirectly approached the US Government for assistance. Using a language that he thought would appeal to the United States, Cristina's conduit sought help for 'an anti-Communist struggle' against a 'Soviet puppet regime' in power in Mozambique. Cristina was taken aback by the Americans' response. While agreeing that the Frelimo government was rabidly anti-capitalist and anti-West, the United States saw no need to back any campaign against the Mozambican government. Washington reasoned that within the next seven to ten years, Frelimo would be knocking at the West's doors, asking for help and showing desire to develop relations with the capitalist world. Cristina concluded that 'if we do not change the political situation in Mozambique within the next 10 years, the country shall fall under the influence of American imperialism and we would have less chances of succeeding'.[39]

Cristina also approached France for aid. A French diplomat told Cristina that France had 'burned its fingers' in Africa a number of times and was not keen to be embarrassed one more time. Cristina could not make the diplomat change his mind when he retorted that the way France was perceived in Africa would not be altered whether Paris supported Renamo or not.[40]

Initially, Renamo ruled out South Africa as a source of assistance in view of Pretoria's commitment to regional stability. In 1976, the South Africans were working closely with the United States to force the Rhodesian government to reach an internal settlement. They could hardly be expected to show sympathy for Renamo. Nonetheless, Cristina sought funding for Renamo among the large Portuguese community in South Africa. Estimated to be in the region of 600 000 people, it was assumed that if each member of the community contributed monthly with one Rand, then roughly on par with the American dollar, there would be a budget of R600 000 per month, or R7.2 million annually, which was far in excess of the initial estimate. Appeals were made through the Voz da África Livre, and by means of circulars posted to addresses chosen at random from South African telephone directories. Signed by Mário Salimo, who was identified as Renamo's secretary general, the circulars urged interested people to send crossed cheques in the name of Barros de Sousa, the organization's treasurer, to a postal address in Salisbury. Salimo and Sousa were one and the same person – Orlando Cristina.

The money collected through a network of Renamo sympathizers in the Witwatersrand and Durban areas was far below what had been expected because the bulk of the Portuguese community in South Africa had no affinity to Mozambique. It consisted primarily of people of Madeiran origin and several thousand immigrants from Angola. Though insufficient to maintain a guerrilla force for even a day, the money was enough to pay for Cristina's traveling expenses abroad. This source of income was disrupted when members of the network fell out with Cristina in the last quarter of 1977, as a follow up to the events that led to the creation of Remo.

In yet another attempt to raise funds, Cristina sought help from an Arab country. Juma Abudo, a Mozambican Muslim living in Durban who had been presenting on the Voz da África Livre every Friday religious programs addressed to the Mozambican Muslim community, was sent on a mission to the Middle East in 1978. As head of Renamo's Ethnic and Religious Co-ordination Department, a post created specifically for the mission that he was about to undertake, Abudo was instructed to present the movement's case from a Muslim perspective. He would underline the plight of Islamized Mozambicans who, since the rise of Frelimo to power, had seen their religious rights gradually curtailed. He would also ask for educational assistance to promote the teachings of the Koran in Mozambican mosques.

Cristina never heard from Abudo after he left for the Middle East. Subsequent developments led Cristina to believe that his envoy had been successful in getting the support that Renamo had been looking for so long. Suddenly, the CIO showed signs of having the financial resources to bank roll a larger Renamo campaign. In late 1978, André Matsangaice was finally given the green light to recruit as many people he wanted to beef up his small guerrilla army. Cristina later found out that the CIO had closely monitored his Middle East initiative, and had somehow outmanoeuvred Abudo.[41]

Later, Cristina exposed the CIO cabal, naming its director general, Ken Flower, as the main culprit. In a May 1980 broadcast from South Africa, the Voz da África Livre reported that 'over US$5 million that Renamo had negotiated with a friendly country had been fraudulently diverted by Ken Flower'. To make sure that the broadcast was quoted by foreign correspondents, copies of the radio script were passed on to the editor of a Portuguese language newspaper in Johannesburg from where the story was picked up.

The news caused quite a stir in the South African intelligence community, in particular the Directorate of Military Intelligence. As liaising between the CIO and the South Africans continued after Zimbabwe became independent, there were fears in Pretoria that the link could be severed, thus disrupting a valuable source of information.

Flower, who was still serving as CIO chief under Prime Minister Robert Mugabe when the Voz da África Livre made the claim, reciprocated. In his memoirs, Flower referred to Renamo in a manner that did not differ much from Frelimo's official stand on the guerrilla movement. To prove his point, he even doctored a 'Top Secret' report, claiming that in April 1974 he had discussed in Lisbon with his PIDE counterpart, Major Silva Pais, the formation of Renamo.

The report refers to events that at the time of writing had not as yet taken place. Specifically, Flower spoke of 'the surprising ease with which the Mozambique National Resistance developed [. . .] during the first five years', clearly indicating that Renamo had already been established in 1969. Still according to Flower, Renamo's

> undoubted success [. . .] also signified that Frelimo lacked that essential measure of support that they needed from the population: or the Portuguese had acted too hastily in transferring power to a liberation movement which could not establish popular support through free elections.[42]

The fact was that in April 1974, Mozambique was not yet independent. The Portuguese only transferred power to Frelimo in June 1975. It would be inconceivable to talk in April 1974 about 'the surprising ease with which the Mozambique National Resistance developed [. . .] during the first five years' because neither Renamo nor the conditions that led to its emergence were in place. If Renamo, as Flower suggested, had been established in 1969, he would not have needed to meet Major Pais in April 1974 to discuss its formation.

6
Gorongosa

Renamo had no control over the funds raised on its behalf by the CIO, but its leaders gradually acquired the autonomy that they had long wanted. The CIO could not impose conditions as before, namely the length of Renamo operations and the areas where they could take place. As he asserted himself as leader of the growing number of Renamo guerrillas, André Matsangaice was able to dictate his own terms. He decided where and for how long he could deploy his forces in Mozambique, and eventually establish Renamo permanently in the country.[43]

Renamo's strength increased from 76 men in September 1977 to 288 in early 1978, and to 914 by the end of that year.[44] Renamo instructors began to train new recruits, but for specialized training, for instance in explosives, it relied on the SAS.

Military operations carried out in 1978 continued to be reported primarily in Manica, with raids on Frelimo garrisons and ambushes on the main Chimoio-Tete highway and other roads featuring high in Renamo's communiqués.[45] Operations far from the Rhodesian border region began to be reported from late 1978 onwards. In Sofala, the guerrillas launched ambushes on the Beira–Chimoio highway and railway line, and on the Dondo–Inhaminga and Inchope–Maputo roads. Traffic on all those routes was eventually restricted to daylight hours with the government forced to introduce military escorts. Renamo seized the town of Macossa, near the boundary between Manica and Sofala Provinces in October. In Sofala in 1979, Renamo raided Marínguè. Castro, a Portuguese national from Madeira, was captured during the attack. As he was about to be taken to the border with Rhodesia for release, Castro asked to join Renamo. He fought with Renamo until his death from an illness in the late 1980s.

To the south, Renamo overran the town of Machaze in July 1979, and in October it raided the town of Goy-Goy. Earlier, on 10 April, Renamo raided the Sacudzo re-education camp for the second time, reportedly freeing over 300 prisoners.

In June 1979, Renamo conducted its first major public relations exercise. Foreign correspondents visited a Renamo area close to the border with Rhodesia, where they met Matsangaice and some of his men. As a result of this media campaign, diplomatic missions in Lisbon, where Renamo's sole representative abroad was based, showed a keen interest in the guerrilla movement. Through them, Renamo established links with political parties, foundations and research institutions in various Western capitals. Apart from marking an end to Renamo's international isolation, such links proved to be of great political value to Renamo in the following years.

In late April 1979, Renamo had begun to make arrangements to establish itself permanently inside Mozambique. The Gorongosa region, which Matsangaice knew from his days as a Frelimo guerrilla fighter, was chosen as the movement's central base. This was a turning point in Renamo's *modus operandi*, shaping the manner in which it developed militarily and politically.

Until then, Renamo operations inside Mozambique lasted for 20 days, and afterwards up to two to three months. Whenever necessary, roving units would return to Odzi to collect ammunition and medical and other supplies that Renamo needed. As there were no radio communications available to Renamo at the time, requests for resupplies were recorded on audio cassettes. Military activity reports reached the Voz da África Livre by the same method. All this changed radically with the move to Gorongosa. (See Map 2.)

Under the command of André Matsangaice, a 300-man battalion left Odzi for the Gorongosa Mountain on 21 and 22 August 1979. Upon arrival on 5 September, the battalion was split into three companies of 100 guerrillas each. Matsangaice's company established Renamo's central base on the mountain. The second company was based in Cuzi, southwest of the mountain, under the command of Jorge Sixpence. The third company, led by Zeca Sardinha, was deployed in the Gravata region, east of the mountain. Additional Renamo members began to be recruited in the area. Training of new recruits was given at Matsangaice's base, and afterwards in other bases as Renamo widened its presence further afield.

A second Renamo battalion left Odzi for Manica in October 1979. Once inside Mozambique, the battalion was subdivided into

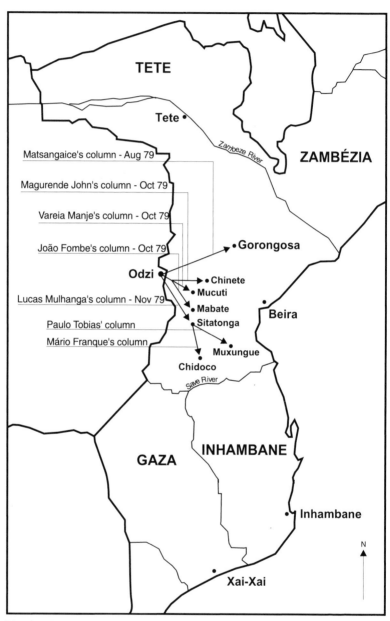

Map 2 — Renamo enters Mozambique from Rhodesia
Designed by Haider-Soft

three companies. The first, under the command of João Fombe, set up a base in the Mabate region, south of the Mussapa River. A second, led by Vareia Manje, was deployed in Mucuti, north of that river. A Sena from Tete, Manje was mistakenly referred to by the Mozambique media as a Portuguese mercenary, apparently because his Christian name sounded like the common Portuguese family name of Varela. He had been with Renamo since May 1977 after Matsangaice freed him from the Sacudzo re-education camp. The third company was based in Chinete, north of the Revué River, under the command of Magurende John.

In November 1979, another 300-strong battalion led by Lucas Muhlanga left Odzi for the Sitatonga Mountain, near the Rhodesian border. Muhlanga was a former People's Militia commander for the Espungabera region who had been with Renamo since February. From Sitatonga, Mário Franque, a Renamo member since 1978, but serving under Muhlanga, moved with 100 men to the south of Manica Province, where he established a base in the Chidoco region. Also at the head of 100-man company, Paulo Tobias headed for Muxungué, to the south of Sofala.[46]

Renamo's strength by November 1979 was in the region of 1 350 men. This number does not include those recruited after the setting up of bases in Sofala and Manica, nor the nearly 200 men that stayed in Odzi after the August–November influx into Mozambique since they had not yet completed training. These men never crossed the border into Mozambique from Rhodesia. Instead, they were taken by air and road to Letaba in South Africa after Zimbabwe's 1980 elections. The Voz da África Livre team also left for South Africa the day after the election results was announced. The station resumed its transmissions on 17 March, using a short wave transmitter at the Waterkloof Air Force Base in Pretoria.

Renamo established a team of radio operators who became the core of a simple but effective telecommunications unit. The central base was connected to all Renamo positions in Sofala and Manica by transceivers powered by hand-driven generators. An SAS radio operator ensured encoded communications between Gorongosa and Odzi. The use of radio communications terminology in English by Renamo operators reflected the source of their training. The practice was subsequently abandoned.

Over the years, Renamo developed a communications system that covered virtually the entire country. Renamo headquarters was equipped with South African-made transceivers with frequency hopping capability, rendering the Mozambique Armed Forces (FAM) detection, location and jamming countermeasures unviable. From the mid-1980s onwards, Renamo was able to monitor most of FAM's communications networks. Renamo's Casa Banana base in the Gorongosa region had a 20-member team of radio operators working round the clock to keep an open watch on all of FAM's communications in the central region, namely Manica, Sofala, and Tete. FAM's communications in the northern region, which included Zambézia, Nampula, Cabo Delgado, and Niassa, were monitored from Renamo's listening post at Alfazema, Zambézia. In the south, Renamo's base at Ngungue, monitored Maputo, Inhambane, and Gaza.

This played an important role in the forecast of government military offensives while in the planning stage. The success of this role was to an extent due to information Rhodesia, and subsequently South Africa, obtained from their monitoring of Mozambique's military communications, which was then passed on to Renamo. The Hammanskraal and Phalaborwa listening posts in South Africa assumed great importance at the height of the war. When Renamo expanded its operations to Niassa and Cabo Delgado, information received from the South African listening posts in the Comoros and Malawi proved equally valuable.

The establishment of Renamo in Mozambique on a permanent basis, which was to last until the end of the war, was unprecedented in the context of southern African guerrilla movements. Reliance on sanctuaries in neighbouring countries was a common feature to Mozambican and Angolan independence guerrilla movements. Similarly, Zimbabwean, South African and Namibian liberation movements campaigned from sanctuaries abroad.

Although supplied with weapons from outside the country, Renamo had nonetheless to depend even more on the rural population for food, shelter, porterage and information than would a movement that relied on safe havens outside the country where it operated. It also meant that Renamo had to sustain on its own every military offensive mounted by government and allied forces, without having the possibility of retreating to friendly territory.

Of necessity, Renamo had to establish an administration to ensure not only the survival of its military infrastructure, but also its continued presence in areas it controlled. The powers that Renamo reinstated on traditional chiefs reflected its social background as well as its dependence on an entity other than military to administer the plantations and health and educational facilities that it felt incapable of running in tandem with its war effort.

Renamo's medical corps consisted of people with a rudimentary knowledge of first aid procedures, but who were expected to attend to critically wounded guerrillas and civilians. They were trained initially in Rhodesia and afterwards by South African Defence Force medical doctors stationed at Renamo's main bases. A Renamo Central Hospital was established at the Inhamasichi base on the foothold of the Gorongosa mountain, where health personnel were also trained.

Schools operated in Renamo areas, but not beyond primary education level. As with its medical corps, schools were by and large staffed with untrained personnel.

Given Renamo's essentially peasant origin, both animist and Western cults enjoyed free rein in its areas of influence where traditional rites were celebrated at will. This stemmed not from a win-hearts-and-minds approach by the Renamo leadership, but from the rank and file's linkage to that social setting. The importance attached to ancestral spirits was patent not only among ordinary guerrilla fighters, but also in Renamo's higher echelons. Before Renamo established a base, permission was as a matter of course sought from the local medium. This was normally arranged through the area's traditional chief. Samatenje, a medium influential in the Gorongosa area, blessed André Matsangaice himself. Traditional chiefs spoke at length about the customs and beliefs of their areas, which were supposed to be strictly adhered to by Renamo's rank and file. John Kupenga, a Renamo guerrilla from Manica, stressed that failure to adhere to local traditions could upset the spirits who then punished the transgressors severely.[47] Expressing his confidence in the successful outcome of the war against Frelimo, Raúl Domingos, then geared to become chief of operations in Renamo's General Staff, believed that the guerrillas were guided by spiritual forces.[48]

7
Matsangaice Killed

While Renamo made preparations to establish bases in the Gorongosa area, Afonso Dhlakama left Odzi for Sofala in June 1979. Leading a 150-strong contingent, Dhlakama's role over the next few months was to divert the Mozambique Armed Forces' (FAM) attention as Renamo consolidated its positions in and around the Gorongosa Mountain. From his Chinete base, south of the Revué River, Dhlakama directed operations that included the disruption of traffic on both the Beira–Machipanda and the great north–south highways. A stretch of the Inchope–Vila Franca do Save road was for the first time closed to traffic.

By September, however, FAM began to strengthen its presence in the town of Gorongosa, most probably because it became aware of Renamo's intentions. According to Renamo, Cuban military personnel was deployed in the town, and Soviet military advisers arrived in Beira to assist FAM in the launching of an offensive on guerrilla positions in the Gorongosa area. This reportedly coincided with the unloading at the port of Beira of combat vehicles, tanks and heavy artillery pieces.

In mid-October, Renamo attacked Morombodze, north of the town of Gorongosa, but met strong resistance. Having gained the upper hand, FAM counter-attacked, forcing Renamo to ask for reinforcements from its central base. In response, André Matsangaice led an attack on government forces, while some of his units mounted ambushes near the town of Gorongosa. FAM was said to have retreated.[49] Against the advice of his lieutenants, Matsangaice decided to raid the town on 17 October. They argued that the town had not as yet been reconnoitred, and the probability of success was, therefore, questionable. Matsangaice's views prevailed.

He mounted a three-pronged attack on the town. Having driven off the first pockets of FAM resistance, Matsangaice climbed on to an army tank, and as he was ready to toss a hand grenade into the turret, a government soldier shot him dead. Several Renamo guerrillas were either killed or captured, but its central base, as well as other positions around the Gorongosa Mountain remained intact.[50]

Matsangaice's fatal raid on Gorongosa was launched ahead of time. The idea was for Renamo to first consolidate its positions in the region, and only then attack and seize the town. This would ensure control over the Beira corridor, and make Renamo's Gorongosa stronghold less vulnerable.

FAM gave a different account of what happened in the Gorongosa area in October 1979. An FAM General Staff communiqué made no reference to Renamo or to Matsangaice. His men were either referred to as 'Rhodesians and mercenaries of various nationalities' or as 'a few Mozambican traitors'.[51] Rather than having been routed from Morombodze, as Renamo claimed, FAM said the opposite had actually happened, noting that 'the Rhodesian contingent suffered heavy casualties and was forced to retreat to their defense lines high on the mountain'. The communiqué does confirm the raid on the town of Gorongosa, and that a few days later FAM 'launched a final attack against the enemy's principal base, flattening it to the ground, occupying it afterwards'. The communiqué claimed that 'the Rhodesians suffered many casualties', putting the overall casualty figure at 'over 100 dead, countless wounded and 22 captured'.

Bernardo Cadeado, a government soldier who took part in the defense of the town of Gorongosa in October 1979, contradicted Renamo's account of how Matsangaice had been killed. Cadeado said that after 'being blown to pieces by a mortar grenade, the bandits managed to carry him, and he was then taken by helicopter'.[52]

Afonso Dhlakama, who had recently returned to Odzi, replaced Matsangaice as Renamo's leader. He was flown by helicopter to Gorongosa mountain to assume leadership of the movement. Although he had already established his credentials in the battlefield as the one most likely to succeed Matsangaice, Dhlakama felt he needed to assert his new position among some of Matsangaice's closest commanders before he could consolidate his leadership. 'Some of the older Renamo commanders objected to my being in the leadership', acknowledged Dhlakama.[53] To placate their fears, he not only retained all of Matsangaice's appointees, but brought others that owed allegiance to the former Renamo leader into the movement's inner circle. João Fombe, Languane Oliveira, John Kupenga, and Mário Franque are some of Renamo's commanders of Manyika extract who remained in the movement, rising to senior positions. But while doing that, Dhlakama also surrounded himself with people whose loyalty to him was beyond question.

An aspect of the Renamo leadership style that intrigued observers was how the powers that be functioned and how Dhlakama related to them. That he did not hold absolute powers within the organization is inferred from remarks that he made that he could not 'merely impose (his) views on Renamo, be it on matters military or political'. He said that he had 'to take other commanders' views into account, and consult them before taking a decision, otherwise I would be putting my own position at stake',[54] meaning that he could be ousted if he led the organization heavy-handedly.

Although Matsangaice's tenure as Renamo leader was short-lived and evolved while the movement was still growing from scratch, it is possible to compare his leadership style with Dhlakama's. Those who served under both men agree that Matsangaice showed himself in the battlefield to be a more daring soldier, without much concern for precaution or his and his men's safety. A myth of Matsangaice's invulnerability to enemy fire developed among not only Renamo guerrillas but also FAM soldiers. Matsangaice made a point of having his men singing Renamo songs as they marched in broad daylight through the bush in central Mozambique. In leading an attack against FAM positions, Matsangaice would often stand up to order his men to move forward. 'He had great powers because bullets just passed his head, whistling, while he saw that we moved step by step to where Frelimo soldiers were', said Roberto Wayne, who served under Matsangaice before joining the Voz da África Livre.[55]

Dhlakama was a more cautious soldier. He would weigh the pros and cons of his decisions before taking any action. Instead of facing FAM with means that he knew were inferior, Dhlakama would simply follow the basic guerrilla tactic of withdrawing. That is not to say that he never allowed the advice from spiritual mediums living near his bases to prevail over the reality of a given situation. FAM's storming of the Renamo central base at Chicarre in Manica in December 1981 was a case in point. The mediums had assured the Renamo General Staff of the inviolability of the base.

The reported power struggle between Dhlakama and Lucas Muhlanga, allegedly over which of the two should succeed Matsangaice, has, according to Renamo, been misrepresented. The two were at odds, but well after Matsangaice's death. Muhlanga had only been with Renamo for about eight months when Matsangaice was killed, and was unlikely to aspire to the movement's leadership. He would have to run not only against Dhlakama, but several others who had been around for much longer and had built a following among their men. The quarrel between the two occurred in the first quarter of 1980, after Dhlakama had succeeded Matsangaice and consolidated his position as Renamo leader.

After Zimbabwe became independent, Dhlakama learned that certain Rhodesians were manoeuvring to retain their influence with Renamo, and through it control Zimbabwe's outlets to the sea. Their conduit was Lucas Muhlanga, a man with whom they had worked closely since his defection from Mozambique's People's Militia. According to an exchange of radio messages between Odzi and Sitatonga, where Muhlanga had been since November 1979, he would move with an SAS team to South Africa to co-ordinate South African logistical assistance to Renamo. A factor that counted in the Rhodesians' option for Muhlanga, instead of the Renamo leader, was that he had a good command of the English language. Once in South Africa, though, the SAS team, including its officer commanding, Major Dudley Coventry, saw their plan thwarted by the South African military. The Rhodesians were welcome to stay in South Africa as long as they joined the South African Defence Force and came under the overall command of Pretoria. Since the stakes were too high for the Rhodesians, they declined the offer and returned to Zimbabwe where Coventry continued to serve under the Mugabe government. Years later, Coventry spearheaded Zimbabwean operations against Renamo in Mozambique, culminating in the raid on Casa Banana in 1985. After being briefly detained at Sitatonga on Dhlakama's orders, Muhlanga was released as the base came under FAM attack in June 1980. After a spell at the Mabate base, where the Renamo contingent that evacuated Sitatonga had regrouped, Muhlanga was dispatched to the south of Manica Province to open the new Renamo headquarters at Chicarre in August 1980. It was in November that year that Muhlanga's fate appears to have been sealed. Dhlakama's decision to demote Muhlanga is something that still needs to be clarified, as do the reasons why he has never been heard since.

8
Cristina Marginalized

Unlike Frelimo in the 1960s, which had to deal with the dual leadership syndrome where politicians and soldiers jockeyed for supremacy, Renamo developed as a military organization with a leadership and objectives of its own, operating independently of exiled political forces. This was consolidated as Renamo became permanently based inside Mozambique, far from the squabbles and intrigue that characterize exile politics. Even those in the Voz da África Livre, who could rightfully be regarded as Renamo's precursors, soon occupied the backstage, serving as the mouthpiece of a cause for which they were the first to campaign. That is not to say that the radio station members, or rather the majority of them, did not accept the reality of the situation. In fact, they saw themselves as being part of the same movement, and went on to serve those directly challenging the Frelimo regime in the battlefield, by furthering Renamo's cause at home and abroad.

But there were others, like Orlando Cristina and a few around him, who had their own agenda. They saw the military in Renamo as a stepping-stone for achieving their goals. Cristina promoted among the circles in which he moved the view that he was the *de facto* Renamo leader, the ultimate decision-maker responsible for every single aspect of the day-to-day running of the organization, including the planning of military operations. In doing so, Cristina can actually be credited for having contributed to the divide between exiled political forces and Renamo, a situation that prevailed throughout the Mozambique conflict and was noticeable after the war ended. Such forces failed to distinguish between myth and fact, overestimating the level of influence that Cristina had among the military. Moreover, Cristina succeeded, though unwittingly, in making the Mozambican authorities regard him as the main cause of the threat that they faced domestically. The misinterpre-

tation continued after Cristina's demise. The Frelimo government treated his successor, Evo Fernandes, as the principal enemy and even had
him assassinated in the belief that without him Renamo would crumble
or at least fall into disarray.

Cristina never came to terms with the fact that Matsangaice and
Dhlakama were not his pawns. The Renamo leadership had, in fact,
grown suspicious of Cristina thanks to a distorted image that was portrayed of him at the time of his dispute with the Portuguese community
in Salisbury and Johannesburg. Members of the Voz da África Livre team
conveyed to the Renamo leaders at Odzi the impression that Cristina
had embezzled funds raised on behalf of the organization. When Cristina's wife left him and went to live with her daughter abroad, this was
presented as proof that she was actually taking the funds to buy property
for the couple.

In an attempt to gain influence within Renamo, Cristina sought the
help of Zeca Caliate, a former Frelimo guerrilla commander who
defected to the Portuguese in 1973. Caliate had been living in Portugal
since the collapse of the colonial administration.[56] To convince Matsangaice, Cristina spoke of Caliate's military experience and his first hand
knowledge of Tete Province. As a native of Zambézia, Cristina reasoned,
Caliate could well pave the way for Renamo expanding its activities into
that province. Privately, Cristina saw this as an opportunity to re-estab-
lish links with those who had been involved with the Mecanhelas Self-
Defence System.

About two weeks after his arrival in Salisbury in March 1978, Caliate
left for Odzi where he started training with a group of 12 Renamo
guerrillas. In a report submitted to Cristina at the end of his mission,
Caliate complained that

> Some people in the group began to publicly show indiscipline.
> Whenever I tried to maintain discipline no one obeyed me. One
> day, when I stressed the importance of discipline in a military organ-
> ization, some of them said I had come from Portugal to become the
> Resistance leader.[57]

Caliate and the group entered Tete Province on 3 May. Indiscipline
prevailed throughout the mission. When the time came to raid the FAM
barracks at Chioco, Caliate literally had to force the men under his
command to follow his orders. It was clear that the men, acting on
orders from none other than Matsangaice himself, were bent on thwarting his mission. Caliate returned to Portugal late that month. After a

spell with Domingos Arouca's Fumo party, Caliate formed a political organisation in Lisbon called the Frente de Salvação de Moçambique, Fresamo.

Rather than being taken aback by Matsangaice's death, Cristina saw it as a blessing in disguise. Although Cristina had no say in Dhlakama's ascent to power, he felt that now he stood a better chance of developing a more intimate relationship with the Renamo guerrillas. Yet, he could not test the new Renamo leader's receptivity since Dhlakama was beyond reach. Cristina, who had last met Dhlakama about a month before Matsangaice died, would only see him again more than a year later.

Arrangements had, meanwhile, to be made to secure Renamo's future in view of the rapid changes in Rhodesia's domestic political situation. The likelihood of the Patriotic Front winning Zimbabwe's independence elections was on the cards, which meant that alternative forms of assisting Renamo needed to be found. South Africa had already indicated its willingness to step in. A delegation of South Africa's Directorate of Military Intelligence (DMI) visited Rhodesia a few weeks before the elections to discuss the mechanisms of channeling aid to Renamo, and of transferring the Voz da África Livre team to Pretoria.

Cristina played no meaningful role in the negotiations, except on matters relating to the radio station. At the outset, Cristina was disliked by DMI. The South Africans were at the time committed to Domingos Arouca and those around him, who happened to be Cristina's foes involved with the bogus Remo movement.

Aware of his predicament, Cristina spread the word that Dhlakama had signed a credential empowering him as the only authorized person to deal with Renamo affairs outside Mozambique. Aimed at both the DMI and Arouca's men in Johannesburg, Cristina's claim proved to be false, and put Dhlakama in an uncomfortable position among his senior commanders. 'I felt awkward about Cristina's claim. I last saw him in September 1979 when Commander André was still alive and could not have gone over his head, especially in matters such as delicate as this.'[58]

9
The Renamo Program

Renamo's ultimate political goal remained essentially the same throughout its campaign against the Frelimo government – the establishment of
a democratic order in Mozambique. Over the years, Renamo reviewed its
ideas about how to accomplish that goal.

The view prevailing in early 1979 was that Renamo should aim at a
political change in Mozambique, but would not assume political power.
This would be left to civilians. As André Matsangaice told Renamo
members in February 1979, 'none of us here are politicians nor have
the political capacity to rule the country'.[59] Matsangaice was willing to
accept exiled political leaders in Renamo's midst and even let them
campaign on its behalf, on condition that 'they spend about six months
in Renamo bases so that they understand who we are and how we live'.
Politicians, said Matsangaice, should not impose themselves on the
military, but treat them as equals. 'I am not afraid of any politician',
Matsangaice told the gathering, 'and am willing to serve them as a
soldier once we bring about a political change in Mozambique.'

The idea of importing an external political figure into Renamo during
the early stages of the organization was viewed as a valid proposition,
and attempts were made to find such a figure. Fumo leader Domingos
Arouca appeared to be a plausible choice. Arouca, working in Lisbon as a
high school principal, cited professional commitments for not agreeing
to Matsangaice's conditions. He wanted a more clearly defined leadership role for himself, and that his party should be at the forefront of the
campaign against Frelimo. Renamo guerrillas would be part of Fumo's
military wing.

Fumo had spelled out these views in a letter to Rhodesian Prime
Minister Ian Smith in February 1977. Signed by Fumo Vice President
Kamati Mahose, the missive stated *inter alia* that Fumo would mobilize

and give military training to Mozambicans, and that all military operations carried out in Mozambique should be attributed to Fumo.[60] Without Matsangaice being consulted about this, Fumo issued a statement in
Lisbon, claiming responsibility for Renamo's April 1977 raid on Sacudzo.

In a letter to the CIO prior to the Sacudzo raid, Arouca called for a
meeting with Rhodesian political and military officials to discuss a
'future strategy' which should exclude 'any groups of Portuguese'.[61]
This was a reference to Cristina and in particular Jorge Jardim with
whom Arouca already was at loggerheads.

Jardim had tried to be the driving force behind Arouca and Fumo, his
conduit being Evo Fernandes, then the party's secretary general. Arouca
objected, among other things, to Jardim's suggestion that Fumo should
adhere to the memorandum that Jardim and Kaunda had drafted in
Lusaka in 1973 and which he wanted to keep alive at all costs. To hit
back at Arouca, Jardim even went as far as trying to undermine Fumo,
creating a bogus splinter group which he called Fussa or Frente Unida do
Sul do Save.

Arouca's tactless approach to Renamo stemmed from his misconception about the real influence that Jardim and Cristina had over the
incipient guerrilla movement. The misconception was such that Arouca
ultimately saw Matsangaice, and thereafter Dhlakama, as people who
might as well come into his fold as they had in relation to what he
viewed as the Jardim camp. For the Fumo leader it was simply a question
of a change of masters.

The Rhodesians treated Fumo's requests with reservations, keeping
Arouca at arm's length. When Arouca renewed efforts with the Rhodesians in March, 'to see if regional co-ordination of any movement within
Rhodesia and Fumo was possible', the CIO's response was that any such
co-ordination

> should be dealt with by FUMO directly with the movements con-
> cerned. Once again, our Government should not admit its associa-
> tion with any Mozambican liberation group.[62]

Arouca saw it necessary to keep open his channels to Cristina. In
March 1977, Arouca appointed his brother-in-law, Pinto Fernandes,
who lived in Johannesburg, as Fumo's sole Africa representative,
empowering him to maintain contacts with Renamo.[63] After all, it was
through Cristina that Arouca and Fumo could be heard in Mozambique
through the Voz da África Livre. An agreement to that effect gave airtime
to Arouca and his party on the radio service. The station would carry

statements on behalf of Fumo, and on occasions recorded speeches by Arouca. In return, Cristina hoped that with Arouca on board, he could raise funds through an influential member of the House of Lords in Britain to support Renamo's activities. This never materialized.

In the wake of the February 1979 Renamo meeting, the movement released its first formal program of action. Included in a statutes booklet, the program reflected what the Voz da África Livre had until then been advocating. It called for the eradication of Frelimo's 'oppressive regime' and its centrally planned economy, and an end to the communal village system. As an alternative, Renamo said it would establish a multiparty democracy and uphold the religious and traditional rights of Mozambicans. The establishment of a free enterprise system was seen as a means of transforming Mozambique into an economically independent and developed country. Renamo pledged to abolish the re-education camps and all 'partisan forces' – namely the Mozambique Armed Forces, the People's Militia, the Vigilance Groups, and Snasp – replacing them with a 'National Defence Force free of racial, ethnic or political discrimination'.[64]

Reflecting Matsangaice's views, the program stated that Renamo was not a political party through which political systems could be imposed against the will of Mozambicans. Instead, Renamo saw itself as a political and military organization seeking unity among all Mozambicans to wage a national struggle that would ultimately 'enable Mozambicans to freely and conscientiously choose their political future through parties to be organized after the liberation of the people of Mozambique'.[65]

Fumo, and subsequently other political parties, followed their own paths. Individual Mozambicans in exile, notably in Kenya, remained committed to Renamo, playing an active role in furthering its goals.

Fumo did not desist from the idea of being in the forefront of the political and military campaign against the Frelimo government. Following the Rhodesian internal settlement of March 1978, Arouca sought permission from Abel Muzorewa's government to open a Fumo delegation in Salisbury as a matter of 'urgency'. This, said Arouca, would make it easier for Fumo to expand its military and political efforts against the Mozambican government.[66] Arouca had no intention of accomplishing this through Renamo. He saw his party 'as the only real African movement in the struggle against Samora Machel' and Renamo a 'masquerade' that had been 'deceiving even the new Rhodesian government'.[67]

Arouca's initiative bore no fruit. Disillusioned with Arouca, Renamo thought of Reverend Uria Simango as an alternative. A plan was devised in 1978 to raid the re-education camp where the former Frelimo vice president was thought to be held. A Renamo commando team was trained for a rescue mission, but as it was about to be flown to Malawi from where it would be deployed in Niassa, the operation was called off. At the last minute, Renamo learnt that Simango had been transferred to another camp.[68] The Frelimo government appeared to have learned of Renamo's plan and decided to kill Simango and other detainees. As Marcelino dos Santos explained, Frelimo wanted to deprive 'the enemy of dissatisfied Mozambican elements, notably those that could be useful to it'.[69]

The idea of Renamo co-opting an external political figure gradually faded away. As the movement became aware of what it was capable of achieving with its own resources, it developed its own political structure and set out a more comprehensive political agenda.

10
Renamo Survives the Wind of Change

With the Rhodesian dispute settled, the Frelimo government breathed a sigh of relief. There would be no more military incursions into Mozambique, and logistical assistance to Renamo would cease.

In spite of its support for the ANC's struggle against apartheid, Mozambique believed that South Africa would not in return assist Renamo. 'I am sure', said President Machel, 'that South Africa does not want war in this region and is not going to serve as the reactionaries' base against the People's Republic of Mozambique'.[70]

The elimination of the Renamo menace in central Mozambique thus became not only a matter of priority, but also something that the Frelimo government believed could be easily accomplished. The build-up of FAM forces in the Gorongosa area from September 1979 marked the start of a major military offensive against Renamo positions. In tandem with this, the government declared an amnesty, urging Renamo guerrillas to surrender with their weapons. In exchange, they would be reintegrated into society and face no reprisals.

Although in October 1979 FAM claimed to have 'flattened to the ground' the Renamo central base on the Gorongosa Mountain, major military operations occurred in the area afterwards. From January 1980, FAM launched a three-pronged attack on Renamo's central base complex on the Gorongosa Mountain from Muanza in the east. Units of FAM's 2nd, 3rd, 4th, 5th, 7th and 8th Brigades took part in the operations. Soviet military advisers based at FAM's 5th Brigade Headquarters in Beira assisted in planning the operation.

Undoubtedly, Renamo was facing its most difficult period ever. The operations came as Renamo was busy consolidating positions it had established after the move from Odzi. Personally, Dhlakama needed to assert his own position since his rise to power. Logistical supply lines that had been negotiated with South Africa were still to be opened. Instead of facing FAM's offensive, Renamo vacated its Gorongosa central base. FAM ceased operations in the area at the end of February, and began to withdraw on 5 March.

Renamo, meanwhile, learned from the South Africans that they could not air drop military supplies in the Gorongosa area because of the long distance from South Africa. The South Africans argued that FAM could easily down their cargo planes. Given the arms embargo on South Africa, they said they could not afford to lose any aircraft.

Not entirely clear to Dhlakama was that the South Africans were merely using that as an excuse. Their intention was to have Renamo near the South African border from where it would be easier to supply Renamo by means of logistical trails leading to guerrilla bases. Ultimately, Pretoria wanted Renamo to operate as close to Maputo as possible so as to bring more pressure to bear on the Frelimo government.

Without consulting Dhlakama, the South Africans had even co-opted Domingos Arouca as the politician who, 'in a matter of six months, would replace Samora Machel as a result of Renamo's effort around Maputo', reasoned a DMI officer. The South Africans had even began preparations for a meeting between Arouca and Dhlakama in Pretoria.

Dhlakama was reluctant to embark on the South African plan for a number of reasons. He realized that the northern area of Gaza, bordering South Africa, was sparsely populated and the terrain unsuitable for guerrilla warfare. In Gaza – in the whole of southern Mozambique for that matter – Renamo would face one of the best defense systems in the country. Since independence, the Frelimo government had invested heavily in the protection of a wide area around the capital. This was something Dhlakama preferred to avoid for the time being, particularly in view of the recent setbacks Renamo had suffered. For Dhlakama, a move southwards would be tantamount to Renamo turning its back on the peasant population that had seen the movement grow and given it shelter. If he did that, he felt he would lose the confidence that Renamo had built among the local population and that it would be difficult to return to the area and expect to be welcomed again without reservations. As for the envisaged meeting with the Fumo leader, Dhlakama told the South Africans that he was not interested in meeting Arouca. 'I don't even know him', said Dhlakama in a radio message to the South Africans.

Pretoria used arm-twisting tactics on Dhlakama to make him change his views on Arouca. In April, they temporarily discontinued Voz da África Livre transmissions. Logistical supplies for Renamo were delayed.[71]

In April, Dhlakama ordered Renamo forces deployed north of the Beira corridor to move to Sitatonga. Guerrilla units operating close to the south bank of the Zambeze River were left to their own devices as they could not be reached by radio to be told of the move. Several Renamo members opted to remain in the Gorongosa area, mingling with the rural population. As they moved southwards, the guerrillas established arms caches that would prove useful when Renamo returned in force to the area in December 1981.

The transfer to Sitatonga occurred in the midst of FAM's Operation Leopard. The operation covered an area bound roughly by the Save River to the south, and the Beira corridor to the north. FAM's 8th Brigade deployed two of its battalions along the south bank of the Save River to prevent Renamo guerrillas from fleeing southwards. Units of the 4th and 5th Brigades were deployed along the north bank of the river. In an attempt to bar guerrilla contact with the rural population, peasants were relocated to communal villages. To ensure that communication lines remained opened, FAM planted anti-personnel land mines near road and railway bridges in the central provinces. The Air Force was extensively used in the bombing of suspected concentrations of Renamo guerrillas.

Operation Leopard culminated with the storming of the Sitatonga base in June 1980. The attack was co-ordinated from Chibabava, serving as the forward headquarters of FAM's 5th Brigade. Units of the 2nd Brigade advanced from the south, and of the 3rd and 4th Brigades from Dombe in the northeast.

Zimbabwe, which had become independent in April, gave tactical support to FAM's attack on Sitatonga. Zimbabwean forces were deployed along the border with Mozambique overlooking Sitatonga to stop Renamo guerrillas trying to retreat into Zimbabwe.[72] During a meeting of Zimbabwean and Mozambican defense and security chiefs in Salisbury before the attack, CIO Director General Ken Flower reportedly exchanged information with his Mozambican counterpart on the precise location of the base, access routes and Renamo strengths at Sitatonga.[73] Permission was given to FAM forces to enter Zimbabwe from where they could reach the south of Sitatonga via Espungabera and Goy-Goy.

Cuban military personnel played both an advisory and combat role in the attack. Soviet military advisers were reportedly present in Beira throughout the operation.

Frelimo artillery, including BM-21 multiple rocket launchers, pounded the Sitatonga mountain for several days from the south bank of the Lucite River. From Machaze, FAM forces moved towards the Búzi River, mounting ambushes on both banks of the river to where they believed Renamo guerrillas, fleeing to the south of Sitatonga, would head. Following sorties by MiG-17 fighter-bombers, FAM's final assault was launched from Chibabava along the north bank of the Búzi River. Fire was exchanged from early in the morning until late at night on 30 June.

Renamo attempted to halt FAM's advance on Sitatonga with Evelino Bote firing the guerrillas' only B-10 recoilless gun from the top of the mountain. Renamo, however, was forced to vacate the base at 22.00. Left behind, was a substantial portion of the 16-tonne ammunition supplies that South African C-130 Air Force planes had dropped over the base on 20 June. As they could not flee westwards into Zimbabwe, and to avoid the largest FAM concentration to the south and east of Sitatonga, Renamo headed north towards the Lucite River to where Vareia's forces had since been sent to assist the beleaguered guerrillas. Renamo forces eventually regrouped further north, in Mabate, after crossing the Mussapa River. To take pressure off the fleeing guerrillas, Mário Franque sent reinforcements from Chidoco to engage FAM forces deployed around Sitatonga.[74]

FAM claimed to have killed 272 Renamo guerrillas and captured 300 others, but made no mention of its own casualties. FAM radio messages intercepted in June and July gave a glimpse of government losses. In mid-July, FAM's 5th Brigade headquarters in Beira informed the General Staff in Maputo that 18 wounded Cuban soldiers and the corpses of eight others had arrived on a flight from Chibabava. In another message, Beira reported the arrival from Espungabera and Chibabava of 20 wounded soldiers, six of whom were Cuban. The Voz da África Livre made use of this piece of information more than a month later. In an attempt not to reveal the source, the station broadcast a news item datelined Havana, reporting that the bodies of eight Cubans killed in clashes with Renamo in June had arrived in Cuba.[75]

Renamo claimed to have suffered only two wounded during the shelling of Sitatonga. According to Renamo, it was after the fall of Sitatonga that FAM suffered most of its casualties as a result of ambushes by Vareia's and Franque's men.

As in previous offensives, Operation Leopard showed that FAM's handling of the insurgency war fell short of what was expected. FAM was able to harass and disrupt Renamo's infrastructure, but not deal a final blow on the rebel movement. Renamo activity continued to be reported not only near the Sitatonga area, but also in other parts of

Manica as well as Sofala. The government was still unable to exert its full authority over large areas of central Mozambique. The 1980 population census failed to cover parts of the two provinces because census teams were unable to move freely. FAM convoys were regularly ambushed and their movements further restricted as a result of sabotage of road bridges. Machaze, southeast of Sitatonga, was until mid-1981 besieged by Renamo guerrillas, with logistical supplies reaching that town only by air. Traffic ground to a halt on the stretch of the main north–south highway that crossed Sofala.

USSR training of FAM had since independence been geared towards conventional warfare. In addition to lacking in counter-insurgency capability, FAM had neither the mobility nor the equipment to fight a guerrilla war, far less the means to deliver such equipment and logistical supplies to its forces in the field. In operations against Renamo, FAM often relied on civilians for porterage, compromising at the onset the secrecy of its plans as some of the porters were bound to be Renamo informers. Combat rations issued to FAM forces involved in operations lasted only for three days. Logistical supplies to ground force were erratic.

Renamo only faced a real counter-insurgency threat when the Zimbabwe National Army (ZNA) intervened directly in the conflict. Unlike FAM, which was built from scratch but called to play a major combat role right after independence, the ZNA retained battle-hardened Rhodesian forces, notably the counter-insurgency capability that the SAS had gained in the fight against Zimbabwean guerrillas. FAM's strength by the end of 1980 was estimated to be in the region of 48 000 men. In the first five years of independence, FAM grew not only faster than the government had originally planned, but also under abnormal conditions in view of the need to deal with the conflict with Rhodesia and the domestic guerrilla problem. This, the government acknowledged, posed serious logistical, organizational, financial and administrative problems to FAM, a situation worsened by the country's deteriorating economic situation.[76]

Unhappy with the training provided by the USSR, the Frelimo government tried to remedy the situation through Tanzania. In May 1981, President Machel asked his Tanzanian counterpart to revamp FAM because, according to him, the USSR had failed to instill administrative and logistical knowledge into the Mozambican Armed Forces.[77]

In the face of yet another setback and taking into account his logistical needs, Dhlakama decided to move his headquarters further to the south, though not to Gaza as the South Africans wished. Lucas

Muhlanga was sent ahead to reconnoitre a suitable area, opting for Chicarre. Otherwise referred to as Garágua by FAM, the Chicarre base was located on a 416-metre high hill, 26 km east of the Zimbabwean border. Some 50 km to the south lay the Save River, marking the boundary between Manica and Gaza Provinces.

In the third quarter of 1980, Renamo forces were concentrated in an area limited to the north by the Beira corridor, the Save River to the South, the Zimbabwe border to the West, and to the East the vertical line from Nhamatanda to Vila Franca do Save. Renamo's army at this time was put at 14 battalions of 428 men each. Theoretically, this represented nearly 6000 men in arms. Some of the battalions were, however, under strength, considering the casualties the movement had recently sustained, as well as the desertions that are known to have occurred as a result of renewed FAM offensives coupled with the uncertainty created by the political changes in Rhodesia. Nonetheless, Renamo's higher echelons stayed put and were to remain loyal to their cause over the next 12 years that the war was to last.

Part IV
The Turning Point

1
South Africa Backs Renamo

For South Africa it was obvious that the April 1974 coup in Lisbon would pave the way to the independence of the Portuguese colonies. Pretoria moved quickly to ensure that an independent Mozambique would not pose a threat to the apartheid regime.

With Zambia's backing, South African Prime Minister John Vorster sought a stable southern African region where economic co-operation, rather than military confrontation, would prevail. For that, he was prepared to go to great lengths: bring about a solution to the Rhodesian dispute, which included sacrificing Ian Smith, settle the Namibian problem, and recognize the independence of Mozambique with Frelimo in power. Zambia, for its part, undertook that there would be no ANC or other insurgent activities directed against South Africa from either Zambia, Mozambique, Botswana or Rhodesia.[1]

The South African and Zambian initiative bore no significant results simply because they had no mandate from the other parties concerned. Frelimo was, perhaps, the main beneficiary in that it felt assured that Pretoria would not prevent it from taking over the government in Mozambique.

Despite Frelimo's stand on apartheid and its publicly stated 'political and diplomatic support' for the ANC, South Africa felt comfortable to have a Frelimo-ruled Mozambique as its neighbour. Pretoria believed that economic factors would determine the relations between the two countries. South Africa not only allowed bilateral economic relations to continue, but encouraged them to develop. Kobus Loubser, the general manager of the South African Railways (SAR), was among those who were instrumental in furthering that goal. In 1975, he took a delegation of South African businessmen to Mozambique, urging them to make full and effective use of Maputo's railway and port facilities if, as he put it, 'an export drive has to get out of South Africa'.[2]

Frelimo, it appears, resisted Pretoria's overtures. It was as a result of the Frelimo government's policies that economic relations between Mozambique and South Africa deteriorated after independence. A case in point was the decline in the number of Mozambican migrant workers employed in South Africa, primarily in the mining sector. Mozambique imposed restrictions on the hiring of its workers by the South African labour bureau, Wenela. It ordered the bureau to close down 17 of its 21 recruiting offices in Mozambique.[3] Potential migrant workers were prevented from leaving the country because the Mozambican government was reluctant to issue them with travel documents.[4]

In the last year of Portuguese rule there were 113 405 Mozambicans employed in various South African mines. The number dropped to 32 496 in 1976, rising slightly in 1977 to 36 433, and to 37 904 in 1978. There was a marked decline in 1979 to 25 090, with no increases above the 1978 mark recorded until 1983.[5] Financially, this represented a major loss to Mozambique.

Under the Mozambique Convention of 1909, 60 per cent of the workers' earnings was retained in South Africa. Portugal, and Mozambique after independence, paid that percentage in Mozambican currency to the miners back home. The workers could draw 40 per cent of their salaries at the mines, which then lodged the deferred pay with the South African Reserve Bank. Roughly every quarter, the pay was converted into gold at the official South African price, and subsequently sold by Mozambique at the market price. In April 1975, for instance, the deferred pay amounted to 33 million rands, or US$37.95 million at the then rate of exchange. At the official US$42 gold price, that bought 903 571 ounces of the metal, compared with 246 428 ounces if it had been bought at the market price of US$154 per ounce.[6]

South Africa's use of the port of Maputo also declined after independence. The port, which in 1975 handled 18 per cent of South African freight, contributed 30 per cent of Mozambique's total foreign earnings. In view of a drop in productivity caused by the departure of Portuguese skilled personnel, freight volumes moving from South Africa to Maputo plummeted in the early months of 1976 from 25 000 to 18 000 tonnes a day.[7] It went down further from June 1977 onwards as most of the remaining Portuguese personnel at the Maputo port and railways did not renew their contracts.

Nonetheless, South Africa remained committed to using the port of Maputo. SAR spent 70 million rands electrifying and upgrading the

Witwatersrand–Komatipoort railway line linking the port of Maputo. SAR assisted its Mozambique counterpart in doubling the 31 km section of the line between Moamba and Machava, thus eliminating the last single-line bottleneck on the 600 km route.[8]

South Africa reviewed its attitude towards Mozambique when it became aware that Frelimo's degree of involvement with the ANC was beyond acceptable levels. As a sign of its change of heart, Pretoria decided in 1978 to stop exchanging the earnings of Mozambican migrant workers for gold at the official price, selling it instead at world market prices. The year before, South Africa announced its intention to build a strategic air force base at Hoedspruit near the border with Mozambique. There was a complete reappraisal of the relations between the two countries when P W Botha, who served as Vorster's defense minister, replaced him in September 1978. From then on, the military would gain the upper hand in the running of South Africa.

P W Botha viewed Mozambique's support for the ANC as part of a well-devised strategy to subvert the prevailing political order in South Africa. The ANC had for some time been using Mozambique as a transit point to infiltrate its guerrillas into South Africa. Some of them entered the country's rural areas with the assistance of the Mozambican Border Guard Troops, TGF. Trained as a reconnaissance unit by USSR's Spetsnaz instructors, the TGF had an operational radius of 50 km beyond Mozambique's borders. Posing as migrant workers, other ANC guerrillas entered their country with forged travel documents issued by the Mozambican government.[9] Arms for the ANC were shipped directly from the USSR to Maputo. Joe Slovo, the deputy head of the ANC's armed wing, was transferred from Lusaka to Maputo with responsibility for operations in the South African provinces bordering Mozambique.[10]

In response to this, South Africa decided to assist Renamo: first, through Rhodesia, and then directly, after the Rhodesian settlement of 1979. The group of about 200 Renamo recruits still at the Odzi camp during Rhodesia's transition to independence was transferred to South Africa and accommodated in a camp at Letaba, near the Mozambican border. A radio communications centre was established at the camp, enabling contact with the Renamo headquarters and other bases in Mozambique. To prevent detection by surveillance satellites believed to be hovering in the South African skies, Renamo personnel at the camp were told to wear SADF fatigues, and those entitled to carry arms were issued with weapons from the local armoury.

Upon completing training given by Renamo instructors, the group was airlifted in South African Air Force Super Frelon helicopters and deployed just south of the Save River, Gaza, on 20 October 1980. A DC-4 Skymaster plane fitted with electronic surveillance equipment remained airborne throughout the airlift operation to monitor any FAM ground or air response. The Renamo contingent was led by Lucas Kwambirwa and included several senior commanders, notably Calisto Meque, Raúl Luís Dique and Francisco Girmoio, a nephew of Afonso Dhlakama.

Although the South Africans had succeeded in convincing Dhlakama to activate Gaza, the newly trained group was forced to cross the river and join the Renamo headquarters at Chicarre after a number of set-backs, including the death of Kwambirwa on 26 December. The contingent suffered a substantial number of casualties while trying to cross the flooded Save River into Manica. Some of the survivors found their way into Zimbabwe, mingling with the local population. The South Africans would later deploy in Gaza a commando unit consisting of Mozambicans serving with the SADF. FAM claimed to have wiped out most of the unit not long after its deployment inside Mozambique.

South Africa's backing of Renamo had a clear-cut political agenda: the replacement of the Frelimo government with one that would not threaten Pretoria's domestic interests. The DMI was given the responsibility to assist Renamo not only militarily, but also politically. From the onset, Pretoria linked its logistical assistance to Renamo to the proviso that the movement represented a viable political alternative to Frelimo.

Prior to South Africa's direct involvement with Renamo, the DMI's Department of Covert Collection had been cultivating a relationship with Domingos Arouca. The DMI felt that Renamo lacked a credible leader, one who would be representative of Mozambique's intelligentsia, never mind the fact that the guerrilla movement was essentially rural. Arouca fitted squarely with DMI's perception of what a leader should be. It took a while before the DMI realized that it was impractical to transplant a politician exiled in Europe into an existing organization with a leadership and dynamics of its own.

In April 1980, the DMI brought Arouca to South Africa. Much to DMI's embarrassment, Dhlakama refused to meet the Fumo leader in Pretoria. Earlier, the DMI had agreed in principle to the first point on Arouca's agenda, which called for the removal of Cristina from the scene. Arouca told his hosts that 'the second point on the agenda would only be placed on the table pending the approval of the first one'.[11]

With an empty-handed Arouca back in Lisbon, where he later claimed to have 'visited Mozambique, crisscrossing the liberated areas at will',[12] the DMI realized that it had to deal solely with Dhlakama. The irony of the DMI–Arouca scheme was that it ultimately benefited the man whom they both wanted out of the way – Cristina. Gradually, the South Africans began to liaise with him.

In November 1980, Cristina met Dhlakama at the Letaba camp. He impressed on the Renamo leader the need to drum up international support for the organization, particularly since the South Africans were not keen to go it alone. Cristina recommended that Renamo should make its political goals clearly known outside Mozambique. He stressed that since Renamo's leadership was based in Mozambique, a fully-fledged external wing would have to be established so as to further those goals. Someone whom the Renamo leadership could trust would guarantee the link between the domestic and external wings. Cristina saw himself as the right person for the job.[13]

On 4 November, Dhlakama called a meeting attended by his immediate advisers and a few junior military commanders who had traveled with him from Chicarre, as well as Cristina. Dhlakama opened the meeting which dealt with the creation of an external wing and the appointment of someone who would liaise between the central base and that wing. The Renamo leader briefed those present about Cristina's role in the Voz da África Livre over the past four years, adding that the time had come to review Cristina's status in the organization.

During the course of the meeting, Manuel Domingos, one of Dhlakama's personal secretaries sitting on his right, asked Cristina about his links with Jorge Jardim. Domingos then raised objections to the formation of an external political wing, which he saw as unviable since its members would operate detached from the Renamo leadership.

Cristina saw Manuel Domingos as a nuisance, failing to realize that Domingos' questions not only had been cleared by Dhlakama, but also fitted the Renamo leader's style of having others raise the questions he did not want to ask personally. Domingos' objection to the idea of an external wing in fact reflected the Renamo's leadership uneasiness about a body beyond their immediate control.

Cristina told Domingos he had parted ways with Jardim in 1974, but were still friends. He went on to reiterate what he had discussed with Dhlakama the day before, stressing that since a Renamo delegation would soon travel to Europe, a decision needed to be made on what was under discussion.

The meeting continued in the afternoon without Cristina. Seeing Mozambique from the angle of their rural environs, Dhlakama and his men decided that no external political wing would be formed. They remained committed to their 1979 program of action, which envisaged for Renamo the role of creating conditions that would enable political parties to establish a democratic order in Mozambique. Dhlakama agreed to designate Cristina as Renamo's secretary general, arguing with his advisers and junior commanders that it would be preferable to have someone like Cristina, despite the embarrassment that his colonial past posed to Renamo, rather than an unknown exiled figure. Cristina, reasoned Dhlakama, would keep at bay the squabbles and the intrigues of exiled politics, without letting them spill over into the organization. The Renamo leader felt that this arrangement would leave intact his own domestic structure which, at the time, consisted of a 14–man National Council.[14]

Table IV.1.1 Renamo National Council (Members' ethnic group in brackets)[15]

1	Afonso Dhlakama, commander in chief and president of Renamo (Ndau)
2	João Macia Fombe, deputy commander in chief and 1st Battalion commander (Manyika)
3	Vareia Manje Languane, 2nd Battalion commander (Sena)
4	José Domingos Cuanai Calção, secretary in the National Defense Department (Manyika)
5	José Luís João, 9th Battalion commander (Sena)
6	Raúl Manuel Domingos, secretary in the National Defense Department (Sena)
7	José Marques Francisco, head of the Training Department (Sena)
8	José Manuel Alfinete, head of the Telecommunications Battalion (Lomwè)
9	Mário Franque, 3rd Battalion commander (Manyika)
10	Joaquim Rui de Figueiredo Paulo, deputy battalion commander (Shangaan)
11	Henriques Ernesto Samuel, deputy battalion commander (Chope)
12	Ossufo Momade, deputy battalion commander (Makua)
13	Olímpio Osório Caisse Cambona, head of the telecommunications department (Yao)
14	Albino Chavago, head of the health department (Ronga)

2
Renamo Reviews the 1979 Program

In the wake of Cristina's appointment as secretary general, Renamo organized a trip to Europe for 18–27 November 1980. The delegation included Dhlakama, Manuel Domingos, Raúl Domingos and Cristina. Evo Fernandes, the Renamo representative for Europe, joined them in Lisbon.

Despite having been questioned about his links with Jardim, Cristina went ahead and informed his old friend of the visit, leaving it for Fernandes to arrange a meeting between Dhlakama and Jardim in Lisbon. Dhlakama told his European representative that he did not wish to see Jardim. About a year later, Jardim hit back. He told a correspondent that he did not believe that Renamo, like any other guerrilla movement, would defeat the government militarily, but could bring about a change within the regime itself.[16] Jardim's message was clear: it would be the politicians, such as himself – not the soldiers, that is, Dhlakama – who would play a role in the aftermath of Renamo's military campaign.

Nonetheless, scheduled meetings went ahead in Portugal. The Renamo delegation met officials of the ruling Social Democratic Party, Catholic Church representatives, and other dignitaries. Pledges of varied assistance came from all those quarters.

In addition to Portugal, the delegation visited France and Germany. In Paris, the delegation held an informal three-hour meeting with an official from the office of the French president. Jardim had arranged the meeting. The French official pledged to open diplomatic channels to Renamo in Francophone Africa, and encouraged Dhlakama to appoint a permanent representative in Paris.

In Bonn, the Renamo delegation met parliamentary officials representing two German foundations. The visit to Germany was the culmination of contacts Fernandes had established with the German

Embassy in Lisbon through André Thomashausen, a German who had been raised and educated in Portugal. In Lisbon, Thomashausen befriended Wolfgang Richter, the German Embassy's chief intelligence officer, whom he introduced to Fernandes. This paved the way to close links between Renamo and Germany's Christian Democratic Union, notably in CDU's stronghold in Bavaria.

As a whole, the tour was very promising for Renamo, considering that it was the first time that its leader had been exposed to foreign politicians. Renamo saw that it not only enjoyed sympathy in the European capitals visited, but that it could also draw political support from various quarters, which, in turn, could channel the movement to even more influential circles. A lesson that Dhlakama personally learnt from the meetings he held was that European politicians expected Renamo to have more concrete political goals, rather than being primarily concerned with bringing about a political change in Mozambique whilst leaving to unknown political forces the task of democratizing the country. As Cristina noted, the Renamo president and his two aides

> have come to the conclusion that politics is a business and that no one would be willing to invest in a movement which does not offer guarantees that dividends would be paid later.[17]

Dhlakama reviewed his views on Renamo's political role. He instructed Cristina to bring in other Mozambicans who would form the core of a shadow cabinet. Dhlakama would chair the cabinet, but could delegate powers to a prime minister. The cabinet would run the country during a transitional period until elections were held.

It was clear to Renamo that from now on it should go its own way, independently from the exiled political parties. From Fumo could be expected only the same tactless approach that it had shown before. When Fumo members suggested, not long after Renamo's European tour, that all exiled groups should unite, Arouca's position was that 'any unity talks should imperatively be held with South African officials'[18] because he did not want Cristina to be part of a deal.

Departing from the views outlined at its February 1979 meeting, Renamo decided to accord itself a more direct role in the running of the country. In a program of action drafted with Thomashausen's assistance in 1981, Renamo called for the establishment of a government of national concord with Frelimo. The government would, 'in a spirit of national reconciliation', pacify the country and establish a democratic order. Frelimo would have to abandon its centralized economy to give way to the private sector, which would play a leading role in the development of Mozambique.[19]

As an immediate step, Renamo began preparations for the formation of its external wing. An envoy was sent to Nairobi in early 1982 to meet the exiled Mozambican community with whom the movement had been in touch since 1976. Through Khembo dos Santos, the Renamo representative in Nairobi, the envoy met other exiled Mozambicans, outlining to them Renamo's intentions. They agreed with the Renamo plan, but with reservations. Santos in particular felt disturbed about Cristina and suspected that he merely wanted to use the Mozambicans in Kenya for personal gain. Santos' attitude stemmed from the fact that ever since his first meeting with Cristina in 1977 no progress was made in furthering Renamo's cause, particularly in Africa. The Mozambicans believed that as an African movement, Renamo should enter the international scene through an African door, not via Europe. They complained that Cristina had left them in the dark about developments within Renamo.

Nonetheless, a meeting between the Renamo leadership and representatives of the Mozambicans from Kenya was arranged for May. The Voz da África Livre compound north of Pretoria served as the venue. In addition to Santos, the Nairobi delegation included Fanuel Mahluza, the former Coremo defense secretary, Vicente Ululu, a Makonde from Cabo Delgado, and Nota Moisés, employed by the BBC's monitoring unit at Karen. Like Ululu, Moisés was a former student at the Instituto Moçambicano in Dar es Salaam. From Lisbon came Evo Fernandes.

Just in time for the meeting, Cristina and Fernandes worked hard to encourage Dhlakama to bring into Renamo's fold the two Bomba brothers. Adriano Bomba, the Mozambique People's Air Force flight lieutenant, had defected to South Africa in July 1981. His brother, Boaventura, who had been living in Johannesburg for quite some time, was part of the Remo circle of friends and the one who planned Adriano's defection with the DMI's Department of Covert Collection. Cristina's rationale in coopting the Bomba brothers, particularly the pilot, was to prevent Remo from using them as a trump card in its political endeavour. After all, Remo viewed the two as 'the most viable solution that satisfies all sides regarding the formation of the desired political wing'. Through the Bomba brothers, Remo argued, 'new cadres, even some from Frelimo, would soon emerge for the formation of a political structure that seconds the RNM's military activity'.[20]

Dhlakama, and more so Raúl Domingos, felt that the Bombas were of no use to Renamo since their image, particularly Adriano's, had been tarnished for having openly associated themselves with the South Africans. Cristina succeeded in persuading Dhlakama to change his mind, pointing out to him that by bringing the two on board, the rug would be pulled from under the feet of the Johannesburg group, thus finishing them off once and for all. In fact, the opposite happened. Through Boaventura, the Portuguese from Johannesburg finally succeeded in establishing the long desired foothold in the Renamo camp.

The meeting decided that a government of national conciliation would assume power over a two-year period during which conditions would be created to establish a multiparty democracy in the country. A more clearly defined commitment was made regarding the reinstatement of traditional rulers whom the Frelimo government had disbanded after independence. In essence, the participants endorsed the revised 1981 program of action.[21]

In the distribution of posts in the newly created departments that functioned under the Renamo secretariat-general, Mahluza was put in charge of political and external affairs. Santos and Ululu were appointed Mahluza's deputies, though Santos remained based in Nairobi as Renamo's Africa representative. In addition to retaining his European representative post, Fernandes became co-ordinator of the Political and External Affairs Department. Raúl Domingos became head of the Defense and Security Department, keeping his post as Renamo's chief of staff planning. Adriano Bomba was given the post of information chief, and his brother was appointed national political commissar.

3
Cristina Killed

Fanuel Mahluza's immediate task was to establish official contacts with exiled Mozambicans in Europe and the United States. In July 1982, Mahluza left Pretoria for Germany. Through Horácio Nunes, whom he had appointed Renamo representative in Germany, Mahluza met a group of Mozambicans living in various European countries, and succeeded in bringing them into the organization. He designated Renamo representatives to Germany, Canada and the United States. While in Germany, Mahluza attended a three-week international summer course on national security. The course was organized by the Political Science Institute of Kiel's Christian Albrechts University. The prime minister of the state of Schleswig Holstein hosted Mahluza, and other participants.

Giving an account of his visit to Germany, Mahluza told the Voz da África Livre that he had met representatives of political parties and cultural groups 'with great influence in the government circles of their countries', and some of them had pledged 'material assistance to the anti-Communist cause'. Mahluza noted that the representative of one of the parties had promised to do 'his best to mobilize authorities in his country for an effective support for the activities carried out by our combatants'.[22]

Around the same time, Cristina was feeling the consequences of his hasty decision to integrate the Bomba brothers in Renamo's political wing. Almost immediately after the 22–23 May meeting, Boaventura Bomba began drumming up support to have a National Council session in November, specifically designed to discuss the replacement of Cristina as secretary general. Instead of a National Council session, Cristina summoned Bomba for a meeting in August with other newly appointed department chiefs and senior military personnel. Bomba came under a barrage of accusations and was said to have broken down during the proceedings. The issue of Cristina being replaced was not even put to discussion.[23] The secretary general had won the first round in a power struggle he was unwittingly being drawn into by someone whom he had only met recently and yet had felt confident to appoint as Renamo's national political commissar. For the second and final round, Boaventura Bomba was better prepared and determined to win.

Afterwards, Cristina made a series of other blunders, splitting his own camp down the middle and pushing aside the last of the few remaining trusted collaborators he could still count on. He demoted Evo Fernandes from the post of co-ordinator of the Political and External Relations Department. Although he remained Renamo's European representative, Fernandes was left in the dark about developments within the organization.

In March 1983, Cristina went to Germany for a meeting with exiled Mozambicans that Mahluza had brought into Renamo. In Kiel, Cristina reshuffled the newly created political wing. He removed Mahluza from the external relations department and appointed Artur Vilankulu, a Mozambican living in the United States, in his place. Adriano Bomba suffered a similar fate, his information portfolio being taken over by Antero Machado, a Mozambican artist living in Johannesburg where he owned an advertising firm. Horácio Nunes was dismissed as the organization's representative in Germany, and Rajabo da Costa given the post. As if to compensate Fernandes for the loss of responsibilities in the foreign relations department, Cristina designated him to head a studies department created there and then.

The reservations Khembo dos Santos had voiced to the Renamo envoy in Nairobi the year before proved correct. For Fernandes, the only plausible explanation for the unprecedented behavior of the secretary general was that Cristina had become drunk with power in the wake of Jardim's death in Gabon in December 1982. While Jardim was still alive, Cristina kept a low profile out of consideration for the man who had saved him from imprisonment in 1963. The loyalty phenomenon was now repeating itself: like Jardim, who felt free to break his colonial vows and jockey for political power after Salazar's death, Cristina saw himself entitled to be in the forefront of equally pointless political games of no consequence to Mozambique's domestic situation.

Still bitter about the humiliation he suffered at the hands of Cristina during the August 1982 meeting, and spurred by the news that his brother had been dismissed as information secretary, Boaventura Bomba decided to strike back. Most probably, he weighed in his favour the prevailing mood of dissatisfaction towards Cristina from amongst other Renamo members, not only Mahluza, but also Dhlakama himself who felt disappointed with both Cristina and the outcome of the Kiel meeting. Relations between Cristina and the Renamo leadership, notably with General Staff members, had reached a low ebb around July 1982. They resented him for meddling in Renamo's military affairs, especially for wanting Boaventura Bomba to lead the Renamo contingent that would enter Zambézia and then merge with the PRM. 'I couldn't allow that', said Dhlakama. Bomba, he added,

> is a non-entity among the military and would certainly be a source of discontent among the Renamo rank and file, particularly those who have been around for some time. They would feel as if I was being inconsiderate to them.[24]

In the evening of 17 April 1983, Bomba drove off from the Voz da África Livre compound, returning minutes later with four men whom he had picked up nearby. Before crossing the compound's gate, the four alighted from the vehicle and walked to a field where they hid under cover of darkness. As soon as the compound's generator was switched off, plunging the compound into darkness, the four men walked briskly towards the house where Cristina lived. One of the men stopped by the radio station's mobile studio, while the others proceeded to the window of Cristina's bedroom. Alerted to the presence of strangers in the precinct, Cristina's dogs began barking, making Cristina draw the curtains and look outside. At once, one of the men fired a single shot from a 9–mm Uzi rifle, hitting Cristina in the neck. He was rushed to a Pretoria hospital, but was certified dead on arrival.[25]

The extent of Bomba's plot remains a matter of speculation. It was obvious that people linked to Remo were involved in the assassination. Some of the hit men were in the group of young Mozambicans forming in Remo's youth wing, the Juventude Moçambicana, or Jumo, whom Bomba had brought along to Renamo with Cristina's approval. The man who waited by the mobile studio was not Mozambican, and was heard swearing in English at the barking dogs. This suggests the involvement of the South African security establishment, not necessarily the DMI branch directly involved with Renamo.

South Africa's motive in eliminating Cristina, using Remo as a smoke-screen, was, according to his friends, because he had spread his wings too wide for Pretoria's taste. A Portuguese military intelligence officer, who was at Cristina's house the night he died, believes that the Renamo secretary general had become much of a nuisance for the South

Africans.[26] That view is shared by a former DMI officer who feels that the South Africans had grown concerned about Cristina's connections with the United States. After their experience with UNITA, where the United States prevailed on Savimbi to the detriment of Pretoria, the South Africans feared that Renamo could follow the same course, thus jeopardizing their plans for Mozambique.[27] Others in Cristina's camp believe that the Bomba brothers had from the outset been on a Frelimo mission. The defection of Adriano Bomba was merely to divert attention from Frelimo's ultimate goal, namely to infiltrate Renamo. Boaventura Bomba and four of his associates died while under police interrogation. Adriano Bomba, who was at Renamo's Gorongosa base when the assassination took place, was said to have been killed in an ambush.

4
Heading for Maputo

Renamo launched a number of military attacks to coincide with its European tour of November 1980. On 22 November, the Beira–Mutare oil pipeline was sabotaged, and eight days later the town of Dombe was occupied. The town of Espungabera came under Renamo attack on 2 December, and a week later FAM's garrison at Magomburi met the same fate.

On 27 November, Renamo sabotaged for the first time the Cahora Bassa transmission lines running through Manica. In addition to the propaganda value of the operation, Renamo wanted the owners of the hydroelectric complex to agree to pay a fixed sum in exchange for allowing the flow of Cahora Bassa energy. Pressured by both the Portuguese and South African authorities, the owners never struck a deal with Renamo, in the end losing far in excess of what the guerrillas wanted. By sabotaging the power lines, Renamo wanted also to make a political statement in light of the widely held view that it was serving the interests of South Africa, by then the sole consumer of Cahora Bassa energy.

Renamo's November operations showed that FAM still had difficulty in controlling central Mozambique despite the April–July 1980 offensive that culminated in the storming of the Sitatonga stronghold. In January 1981, the Mozambican government found it necessary to sign a security pact with Zimbabwe, paving the way for joint military operations against Renamo. The overconfident Zimbabweans believed that they could end the conflict and that the demise of Renamo, as an editorial in the Zimbabwean government daily put it, was 'bound to come sooner rather than later'.[28] In the end, they became bogged down in the Mozambican bush for more than a decade, with Renamo literally laying down the terms for their withdrawal from the country.

FAM's strategy from mid-1981 onwards revealed a greater emphasis on depriving Renamo of contact with the rural population. FAM launched operations specifically designed to drive peasant families from their land in an attempt to disrupt food supplies to Renamo bases, and dismantle the network of informers the insurgents had been building up around their bases. It was reported in June 1981 that 1200 peasants had fled into eastern Zimbabwe as a result of FAM operations in the Espungabera region.[29] There were similar population movements in Mozambique itself, with the government seemingly unconcerned that district capitals received an unexpected influx of people.

With the same goal in mind, the government boosted the construction of communal villages in central Mozambique. The villagization program was rapidly becoming a military rather than an economic strategy. Peasant families resisting resettlement in communal villages saw their houses and belongings destroyed. In times of drought, the government relief agency, the DPCCN, used food as a weapon, refusing to distribute it to peasants resisting the resettlement program.

The depopulation of the rural areas worsened agricultural output. Until then the war had disrupted road communications, preventing the flow of produce from the countryside to the main urban centres; now the fields were being emptied of peasant farmers with the result that agricultural activity declined dramatically. A new cycle of food shortages ensued, plunging the country into greater food aid dependence from the international community. With their involvement in Mozambique, governmental and non-governmental relief agencies from a number of Western countries contributed to the protracting of the war in that they strengthened the government's position by making up for the food shortages.

While it continued to operate in the region bound by the Beira corridor in the north, and the Save River in the south, Renamo was busy planning to expand its operations beyond those boundaries. The intention to head southwards had been envisaged for early 1980, but the setbacks suffered as a result of Matsangaice's death as well as FAM's concerted effort to eradicate Renamo from central Mozambique in the wake of the disruption of Renamo's logistical supply lines from Rhodesia, aborted the guerrillas' plans. By mid-1981, however, Renamo was able to revive them.

On 4 July 1981, Vareia Manje, at the head of a 300–strong Renamo battalion, left the Chicarre central base to open the Inhambane front (see Map 3). In view of heavy FAM presence along both banks of the Save River to prevent Renamo from taking its war further south, Vareia had to

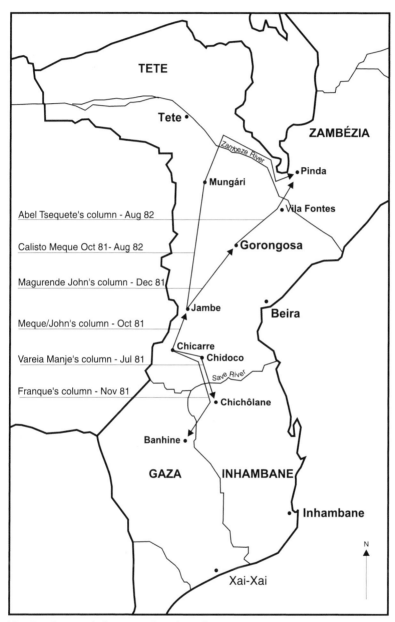

Map 3 — Renamo's thrust south and north
Designed by Haider-Soft

follow a zigzag course from the day he left Chicarre until he crossed the river in the Chidoco region to finally enter Inhambane. As a decoy tactic, the Renamo column did not proceed in a single file. Instead, it was spread over the widest possible area, making an effort to leave no sign of its presence behind. Nonetheless, clashes occurred almost daily until Vareia was able to enter the thick bush of the Zinave National Park to the south of the Save River, establishing a base near the Chichôlane swamps. Before he could consolidate his position in northern Inhambane, Vareia's forces had an average of five clashes with FAM daily. By September 1981, pressure from government forces subsided in view of the considerable losses they began to sustain whenever they ventured into the bush area harbouring the guerrillas.

FAM Chief of Staff Sebastião Mabote's personal endeavor to prevent Renamo from even crossing the Save River had been in vain. In vain also were the recommendations for the same purpose made by Colonel Domingos Fondo, commander of FAM's 2nd Brigade deployed south of the river, to his tactical commander, Major Manuel Manjichi. 'You are to kill all the bandits', he said, and 'when captured, make them suffer as much as possible and then kill them in the presence of the people so as to intimidate them not to help the bandits'.[30]

During this period, air force planes dropped thousands of leaflets over the area of Inhambane where Renamo was active, urging the guerrillas to surrender, and Vareia in particular to join the government. Dhlakama, so the leaflets claimed, had been captured.

As in other regions of Mozambique, in Inhambane Renamo sought counseling from traditional chiefs as it established its bases. Among the traditionalists in the province, who had been sidelined and even antagonized by Frelimo after independence, Renamo guerrillas were seen as the 'Mulunguisse', or the ones who are coming to straighten things up.

In November 1981, Mário Franque left Chicarre to link up with Vareia's forces in the Chichôlane area (see Map 3). Franque's mission was to activate Gaza. Following the same path that Vareia's column had taken in July, Franque's contingent of 300 men called at Chichôlane and after a brief stay, it moved southwards, then crossing into Gaza. The column came to a halt in the Banhine National Park where it set up camp.

The Renamo contingents in Inhambane and Gaza included members of the Female Detachment. Created in 1980, the detachment assigned its members primarily to artillery units where they served as nurses, radio operators and even instructors. Politically trained members of the unit served in Renamo's Department of Internal Administration, as well as with the intelligence, personnel, logistics and operations branches of the General Staff.[31]

Both Vareia's and Franque's forces soon began operating in the two provinces, expanding their activities to the south. Inhambane and Gaza became known as Military Regions 2 and 3, respectively. Renamo divided the country into six military regions, the first being Maputo Province. Military Region 4 included the southern area of Manica and Sofala Provinces, Military Region 5 the central area of the two provinces. The northern part of these two provinces formed Military Region 6. Each region was subdivided into three sectors.

The thrust southwards was carried out quite rapidly. Less than a year after Inhambane had been activated, military activity was reported on the southern tip of the province. Road traffic on the main south–north highway that ran through Inhambane, namely between the city of Inhambane and the Save River, came under constant attack, forcing FAM to introduce military escorts. Sections of the highway were subsequently closed to traffic until the end of the war. The railway line between Inhambane and Inharrime was frequently sabotaged. The town of Inharrime came under attack in August 1982, and again the following month, with Renamo claiming to have seized large quantities of weapons from the FAM barracks.

Vareia's forces were in September 1982 reinforced with a group of some 100 men, parachuted from South African Air Force C-130 planes over the Renamo provincial base at Tome. The newly arrived group was part of a contingent of 200 men whom José Marques, a former FAM member, had gathered from several Renamo bases in Inhambane and Gaza and taken across the border into South Africa in March that year. They received specialized training at an SADF facility near Phalaborwa, forming the core of Renamo's commando unit that in future could be deployed in any part of the country and even engage in urban guerrilla warfare. The second part of the group was parachuted into the Búzi area of Sofala at the same time as the first.

In Gaza, the spread to the south was even quicker. By January 1982, barely two months after the province had been activated, Renamo had reached the northern bank of the Limpopo River. The railway line linking the port of Maputo to Zimbabwe, which ran along the river, came under regular attack, first in the Combumune region, and afterwards further down in the Mabalane and Caniçado areas. The railway line and road between the provincial capital of Xai-Xai and Manjacaze were also targeted, as was the stretch of the main south–north highway running through Gaza.[32]

Initially, Renamo ambushes on the south-north highway, as on other routes, were by means of roadblocks. Passengers from civilian vehicles, usually buses, were ordered to alight with their belongings. Other cargo was usually confiscated and taken to the nearest Renamo base. Vehicles were either allowed to proceed or set alight, especially if they were government-owned. Renamo says it resorted to ambushing road traffic when government soldiers, traveling in civilian vehicles, began shooting at the guerrillas. Renamo did try to discourage civilians from traveling together with FAM personnel. Regular warnings to this end were broadcast by the Voz da África Livre, but achieved little. As the war dragged on, horrific accounts of ambushes on the highway targeted by Renamo began to emerge. A total of 262 people were reportedly killed in two separate ambushes on the north–south highway in October 1987.

Renamo's swift movement to the south was to an extent prompted by the type of opposition it encountered on the ground. As FAM was far better organized in southern Mozambique, it forced Renamo to be constantly on the move, staying in the same base for no more than a week. The pattern changed in the final years of the war when FAM revealed more laxity due primarily to combat fatigue and inadequate logistical support.

5
The Invasion that Never Was

The month before Mário Franque left Chicarre to open the Gaza front, another battalion headed from the Renamo central base to northern Mozambique. Led by Calisto Meque, the battalion included Magurende John, the commander of the Renamo base at Grudja, about 60 km south of the Beira corridor in Sofala. John had gone to Chicarre for a briefing on Renamo's planned return to the north.

Having reached Jambe, a Renamo base near the Revué River (see Map 3), the battalion replenished its stocks with ammunition that had recently been air dropped by South African C-130 Air Force planes. Meque continued his march north, crossing the Beira corridor in the Gondola region at night. Still moving at an average of 50 km a day with the Chimoio–Tete road on their left, Meque's column arrived in the Mungári region of northern Manica by Christmas. During the march northwards, there were reports of Renamo ambushes on the Chimoio–Tete road near Guro, and an attack on the town of Mungári on 12 December.

Bases were established further north near the south bank of the Zambeze River. In August 1982, Meque's forces entered Tete Province, after crossing the Zambeze River, west of Tambara. They began operating along the Mutarara–Kambulatsisi and the Moatize–Zóbuè roads, and on the Mutarara–Moatize railway line. Traffic to and from Malawi was disrupted. Coal from the Moatize open cast mine began to pile up as the route to the port of Beira was no longer safe. Meque's arrival in Tete, which marked the opening of Renamo's Military Region 7, was later than had been expected. His march had to be interrupted on several occasions as most rivers were in flood. By November 1984, his forces moved deeper into Tete, and in subsequent years Renamo spread its operations to virtually the entire province.[33]

From Jambe, having separated from Meque's column, Magurende John returned to his Grudja base. Here he assembled a contingent of 300 men and began marching to Gorongosa early in December 1981. They crossed the Beira corridor on the 10th, and a week later raided Chitengo in the Gorongosa national park. John Burlison, a British ecologist employed by the Mozambique government, and Roberto Carillo, a Chilean, were taken prisoner at Chitengo.

The taking of foreigners during Renamo raids became a regular practice. The movement justified this on the grounds that if left behind they could be killed by government forces and then Renamo blamed for it. Eastern Europeans, however, Renamo treated as hostages, their release often attached to conditions, such as the release of Mozambican political prisoners.

Magurende John established the main Renamo base in Chief Sadjunjira's area, east of the Gorongosa mountain. The return of Renamo to its original stronghold, where it remained until the end of the war, had strong emotional overtones for the guerrillas. They pledged to the villagers never to leave the Gorongosa area again. 'At stake', the guerrillas noted, 'was our credibility among the rural population. If we did not stay put, we would never regain the trust and respect of the local residents.'[34]

A second Renamo contingent of 300 men, mainly recruits, moved from Grudja to Gorongosa in April 1982. A third one, led by John Kupenga, left Jambe for Gorongosa in June. Kupenga's 154-strong group was equipped with heavy weaponry, including a B-10 recoilless gun, mostly captured from FAM during the government's 1980 offensive in Manica province.

Dhlakama and his presidential guard were supposed to leave Chicarre for Gorongosa once Renamo had consolidated its positions around the mountain. Their plan was temporarily disrupted when FAM launched a major attack on Chicarre in December 1981. Renamo had known that an offensive was in the offing since August. Intercepts of FAM's radio communications and monitoring of troop movements revealed a build up around Chicarre from that month onwards.

FAM had established a forward command post at Machaze, northeast of Chicarre, from where Major General Tomé Eduardo would command the attack. From Inhambane, Colonel Domingos Fondo's forces would cross the Save River at Massangena and raid Chicarre from the south. The Zimbabwe National Army sealed off the eastern border with Mozambique between Mávuè and Espungabera, where they would deal with Renamo guerrillas attempting to flee into Zimbabwe.

Renamo was confident that it could not only remain in Chicarre, but also stave off the offensive. They reasoned that in view of the recent departure of Renamo contingents from the base to the south and north of the country, FAM ceased to regard the base as an important target. There were 520 Renamo guerrillas at Chicarre, the majority being Female Detachment personnel.

Early in the morning of 4 December, two MiG-17s bombed the Chicarre base, and over the next two days FAM's artillery shelled it continuously. Renamo forces split into various groups and began vacating the base on the same day. A group moved northwesterly toward the Mabudo mountain, and another to the Chidoco region in the east. Heading a motorized force from Machaze, Maj. Gen. Tomé Eduardo gained control of the base three days later. Fondo's unit failed to crossed the Save River, becoming stranded on the south bank.

By FAM's own admission, only six guerrillas were killed during the course of 'Operation Punishment'. The most resounding success of the operation was perhaps its propaganda value. Found at the base were Renamo documents detailing meetings held in South Africa between the guerrilla leader and senior SADF officials. The documents provided the Mozambique government with hard evidence of South African involvement with Renamo.[35]

From Mabudo, the fleeing Renamo guerrillas moved further north, eventually camping at Jambe. Those at the Chidoco base, led by Ossufo Momade, opted to cross the Save River, joining Vareia Manje's men in Inhambane Province on 17 December. This was prompted by unsuitable terrain conditions north of the river, and in particular the shortage of potable water. By March 1982, Momade's forces began marching to the Gorongosa mountain, stopping at Jambe for reinforcements. They arrived in Gorongosa in late April.

In Gorongosa itself, Magurende John's forces spread in all directions after consolidating their central base. Bases were established near Inhaminga, to the northeast, and along the south bank of the Zambeze River in Vila Fontes and Chemba. The Beira–Zimbabwe railway line was sabotaged in the Amatongas region on 20 January 1982. Nine days later, Renamo attacked the town of Marínguè. The following day, Inhaminga was raided with Renamo claiming to have seized 310 weapons, which were ferried to the Gorongosa central base in two captured trucks. In March, Renamo attacked Macossa and, in a second raid in August, it took the town. In April, the Beira–Zimbabwe railway line was sabotaged twice. In an attack on a People's Militia barracks near Gondola on 17 April, Renamo claimed to have captured 26 armed militiamen.

Marínguè fell to the guerrillas in September. In the same month, the Beira–Zimbabwe railway line was once again sabotaged.

To prevent further sabotage of the railway line, Renamo claimed that FAM planted antipersonnel land mines on both sides of the line. The Sena–Beira railway line and the rail stretch from Inhamitanga to the Marromeu sugar estates were also attacked in September. At around this time, there were reports of Renamo being present in Manga, just 10 km from Beira, Mozambique's second largest city. In December, Renamo sabotaged the fuel tanks within the city's perimeter.[36]

In August 1982, Renamo entered Zambézia, its Military Region 8. Preparations to this end began after Renamo strengthened its positions in and around the Gorongosa mountain. A Renamo unit drawn from Calisto Meque's forces was deployed on the north bank of the Zambeze River in the Ancuaze region of Tete Province. Its mission was to reconnoitre the area which Renamo guerrillas based in Sadjunjira would use as a crossing point into Zambézia. On 11 August, a contingent of 485 men led by Abel Tsequete left Sadjunjira for Vila Fontes. The crossing of the Zambeze River was made in rubber boats fitted with outboard engines, which had been air dropped in Sadjunjira by South African Air Force planes. Once on the north bank of the river, Tsequete linked up with Calisto's men who guided the contingent towards Pinda on the east bank of Chire River in Zambézia. In the same month, a base was established in the Muandiua region of Mureremba, northeast of Pinda. Mureremba became known as Zambézia's First Sector, the second being established weeks later in the Guru region. The Renamo central base in the province was established on the Namuli Mountains where Gimo Phiri's Partido Revolucionário de Moçambique (PRM) had one of its camps. It was here that the two guerrilla movements formally merged, bringing to an end negotiations that had been going on for a few months. Zambézia became Renamo's Co-ordinating General Staff for the provinces north of the Zambeze River, with headquarters at Muadia and afterwards Muaquia. Raúl Luís Dique was put in charge of the Co-ordinating General Staff.

Renamo had first contacted the PRM with a view to a merger in mid-1978. Acting on Cristina's behalf, Khembo dos Santos met Gimo Phiri in Malawi. Joaquim Madeira, the unofficial Renamo representative in that country, organized the meeting. The talks were inconclusive. The PRM doubted Cristina's willingness to merge, considering that for more than a year appeals for assistance had fallen on deaf ears. The PRM questioned the reason for the Voz da África Livre not broadcasting its military communiqués. In fact, the PRM wondered whether Cristina had any say in view of information it had received from Voz da África Livre members in Salisbury to the effect that he had been ousted.[37]

Not known to either the PRM or Khembo dos Santos was Cristina's inability to provide any form of assistance, as well as his decision not to publicize the PRM's activities over the radio station so as not to obscure the then incipient Renamo. It was not a question of helping the PRM, but what Cristina could gain from it in terms of funding for Renamo. Once other channels were opened for Renamo, Cristina's interest in the PRM diminished. The situation changed in view of Renamo's intention to enter Zambézia. The two movements resumed negotiations in mid-1982 through Gilberto Fernandes, a friend of Phiri. Fernandes, who traveled extensively between Malawi and Zimbabwe, contacted Cristina through his acquaintances in Harare.

In terms of the Renamo–PRM merger agreement,[38] Gimo Phiri's forces were distributed among the three Renamo bases in Zambézia. The unification was more to the advantage of the PRM than Renamo proper. Gimo Phiri's resources were scarce, which explained the PRM's low intensity guerrilla activity. From what Renamo learned afterwards, the PRM operated in a most rudimentary manner. According to a former Renamo intelligence officer in Zambézia, the PRM was known as the 'stone people' because of their practice of placing heavy stones on roads to force Frelimo military vehicles to stop. PRM guerrillas would fire at the drivers, while others hurled stones at the Frelimo soldiers, hoping that in the confusion the government soldiers would abandon one or two rifles and some ammunition. Stones were also used to defend PRM bases, normally situated on mountains. PRM guerrillas rolled down stones from mountaintops to try to stop advancing FAM forces.[39]

As in other areas of the country, Renamo made it a policy to liaise first with the traditional leaders of Zambézia. This could explain the widespread support Renamo claims it enjoyed from the outset among the local population. The villagers, says Renamo, 'gave us abundant food, and were quite keen in meeting us after being warned by Meque's men of our imminent arrival'.[40]

Joint Renamo–PRM guerrilla activity in Zambézia spread fast. In the first month of Renamo's presence in the province, it initiated 12 military incidents. These included an attack on the town of Megaza on 25 August 1982, and an ambush on the Morrumbala–Mocuba road on the same day, during which six Bulgarians were captured. Further north, the towns of Luciro and Tacuane were attacked on 30 August. Renamo activity continued unabated in the following month. On 8 September, the bridge over Mussulude River on the Mocuba–Tacuane road was sabotaged, disrupting the ferrying of tea from the Tacuane estates. Two days later, the Mocuba–Quelimane railway line was sabotaged, indicating that Renamo was now operating closer to the coast. The town of Milange was raided on 27 September, and incidents reportedly took place even further north, in the Errego area.

Amid these developments, the Frelimo government embarked on a disinformation campaign, portraying the military situation in Zambézia as being the result, not of Renamo's thrust from central Mozambique, but of an invasion from neighbouring Malawi. Maputo-based foreign correspondents were used as conduits in the propaganda exercise. Citing government officials, the BBC correspondent in the Mozambican capital reported at the time that 'several hundred Resistance men have been involved in an invasion since August across the Malawi border'[41] (see Map 3).

6
The Frelimo Government Counter-attacks

Guerrilla activity, far from having been disrupted as a result of FAM's storming of the Renamo headquarters at Chicarre in December 1981, was spreading fast to new areas. In the south, after having entered Inhambane and Gaza in the second half of 1981, Renamo took its activity closer to the north bank of the Limpopo River. The Mozambican capital lay just over 200 km away. In the north, notably in Zambézia, Renamo was gaining the upper hand.

It was clear from the pattern of Renamo operations that its primary goal was to isolate the government from the rural areas and deprive it of stable inland communications, eventually stifling its economic power base. Ultimately, so Renamo reasoned, the government would be confined to the main cities with no territory to administer. The collapse of the government would then follow.

In fact, the government could ensure neither safe road and rail communications domestically, nor between the landlocked countries and Mozambique's ports. The south–north highway came under constant attack and traveling was in most cases only possible with military escort. Worried that the guerrillas could soon threaten the capital, President Machel announced in June 1982 that a curfew would be imposed in the Mozambican capital. The aim was to control not only the situation within the city, but also the movements of people from the outlying provinces of Inhambane and Gaza into Maputo. Machel said that weapons would be issued to the People's Militia and Frelimo's activist groups. According to the Mozambican leader, 'we must heighten our class repressive measures to fight the bourgeoisie, vagrancy and banditry'.[42]

The disruption of road and railway communications, particularly between the Beira and Maputo ports and Zimbabwe, led to renewed

Zimbabwean military intervention in Mozambique. By November 1982, ZNA forces were reportedly patrolling the Beira corridor, providing escorts along the road, as well as protecting Zimbabwean technicians repairing sections of the oil pipeline sabotaged by Renamo. In December, Renamo claimed that a ZNA armoured personnel carrier had been destroyed in an ambush near Amatongas on the Beira–Zimbabwe road.[43]

Quick and swift action was needed if the Mozambique government were to reverse the situation. A major offensive against Renamo, the largest since the start of the war in 1976, began to be planned in the second quarter of 1982. Its outcome would be decisive in determining what course the war would take afterwards and whether Renamo could be defeated militarily.

Known as Operação Cabana (Operation Shack), the offensive was to be carried out in three phases in southern and central Mozambique. A team of Soviet military advisers led by General Nikolay Zotov assisted FAM in the planning of the operation. Soviet Army officers were seconded to FAM's forward command posts. For the operation, the USSR committed most of the resources of its military co-operation program with Mozambique until 1985, notably ammunitions and logistical equipment.

FAM's personnel strength for Operação Cabana was, according to Renamo estimates, in the region of 10 000 men. Operação Cabana was a semi-conventional operation because of its use of pseudo-guerrilla units. Their mission was to reconnoitre Renamo positions and report them to conventional units stationed at FAM's forward command posts. Wearing civilian clothes and posing as Renamo guerrillas when approaching villagers for information, the Spetsnaz-trained pseudo units occasionally attacked Renamo bases.

The first phase of the operation was supposed to have started simultaneously from the Limpopo valley in the south to the Save River, and from the Beira corridor to the north bank of that river. Sweeping attacks would be carried out against Renamo's main bases in Gaza, Inhambane, Manica and Sofala. Prior to that, the TGF, forming the first defensive line, sealed off the southern and southwestern border areas with South Africa. The 2nd TGF Brigade, based in Massingire, was deployed along the South African border from Ressano Garcia in the south to Pafúri in the north. The 5th TGF Brigade, based in Namaacha, was deployed on Mozambique's southern border with South Africa, and on the west along the Swaziland border, linking up with units of TGF's 2nd Brigade to the south of Ressano Garcia. Conventional units drawn from FAM's 1st Mechanized Brigade, the 2nd and 8th Motorized Brigades, and the 6th Tank Brigade formed the second line of defense. They were deployed along the south–north highway running through Inhambane and Gaza, and on the north bank of the Limpopo River.

The 1st ZNA Brigade moved from its Masvingo Headquarters and the 4th ZNA Brigade from Gonarezhou to seal off the Mozambican border between Pafúri and Espungabera. The North Korean-trained 5th ZNA Brigade, notorious for its recent scorched earth role in Zimbabwe's Matabeleland region, entered Mozambique via Machipanda to join FAM forces involved in sweeping operations towards the north bank of the Save River. Other ZNA units were deployed in the southern region of Gaza.

In addition to the deployment of these forces, FAM began, in the last quarter of 1982, a huge relocation of villagers from northwestern Gaza and southwestern Manica. The 1st and 2nd TGF Brigades were supposed to clear of any living soul a vast area running along the Zimbabwean border on both banks of the Save River. FAM earmarked the area as the 'killing zone' for the second and third phases of Operação Cabana.

The prevailing drought in southern Mozambique played in favour of FAM in that the terrain was more accessible for its forces and Renamo's bases easy to detect. As a result of the offensive, Renamo's food supplies were disrupted, putting FAM forces at an advantage in that their logistics had been assured for the duration of the operation.

The second phase of the operation consisted of herding Renamo guerrillas on the run into the killing zone. And lastly, the third phase would deal a final blow to the guerrillas expected to be entrapped in that zone.

As FAM forces advanced through Inhambane from the east, a number of Renamo bases were either overrun or vacated. The movement's provincial base at Mambyili, east of Chigubo, was taken on 23 August. In Manica, FAM units assisted by ZNA forces began an offensive on Jambe in September 1982, moving from Dombe, Chibabava and Chitaússe.

For Renamo, FAM's intentions were obvious. To ease FAM pressure on its bases in Inhambane and Manica, and subsequently in Gaza, Renamo launched additional attacks in Tete and Zambézia in an attempt to force the government to re-deploy its troops. Reinforcements were sent from Gorongosa to assist Renamo forces that had meanwhile vacated Jambe. Soon, however, Renamo decided that it would be better to disperse and regroup beyond FAM lines, rather than clash with FAM and in the event be pushed into the killing zone. As a Renamo communiqué admitted, its forces had 'opted for a strategic withdrawal from the occupied areas, following instructions from the Chief of General Staff'.[44]

Nonetheless, FAM forces went ahead with Operação Cabana. But a different set of rules applied in Gaza where FAM field commanders were instructed to refrain from using heavy artillery against suspected Renamo areas for fear of killing civilians. In contrast, to the north of the Save River, particularly in Manica, a different approach had long been followed: artillery fire was used indiscriminately against suspected Renamo bases with no consideration shown to civilians. The discriminatory measure shocked FAM officers from provinces other than Gaza. 'This clearly indicated that ethnic-regional considerations prevailed in the conduct of the war', noted a senior FAM officer from one of Mozambique's northern provinces. According to him,

> Samora Machel personally issued the warning during the planning stage of Operação Cabana. He regarded the Renamo issue merely as an ethnic dispute between Ndaus and Senas on the one hand, and the Shangaan on the other over which tribe ruled the country. This approach by the Frelimo leadership came to light as the war escalated. The scorched earth operations conducted in Zambézia, especially under the command of Lagos Lidimo – who was no soldier, but a security man – highlighted that ethnic-regional aspect.[45]

Anything that moved, including civilians, was shot on sight. President Samora Machel allowed a glimpse of this feature of the operation when he inspected FAM forces in Gaza. Speaking during a rally in Chibuto, 'the former capital of the Gaza Empire', as he made a point in stressing it, Machel noted that:

> The Army has come here with a threefold mission. First, to encircle the armed bandits while it assembled the whole might of its weaponry. Then to bombard the enemy for a specific period of time. And while in combat, our forces ensured that the one who took information and food to the bandits, or had anything to do with the bandits should die with the bandits. In other words, while in the battlefield the idea was to kill. Our mission was not to wound, but to kill.[46]

By making such remarks in Gaza, Machel, it appears, might have wanted to pour oil over troubled waters in view of the degree of resentment among FAM officers, who were not native to his home Province of Gaza, to the orders he had issued during the planning stage of Operação Cabana. Orders of such a nature, according to government soldiers, are said to have been discontinued, at least in some areas, after Machel's demise in 1986.

In addition to what President Machel spelt out, FAM's strategy included the mining of tracks leading to areas where Renamo guerrillas usually got their water supplies. Water wells were poisoned and manual water pumps had their handles removed so as to render them useless.

The Operation certainly put the guerrillas on the run, but not in the direction Operação Cabana's strategists had envisaged. As the operation went into full swing, there was a sharp decline in guerrilla activity in Gaza and Inhambane, notably from January to June 1983, an indication that the guerrillas were avoiding direct confrontation during the offensive. Scores of villagers from the two provinces were displaced as a result of the operation, and began to gather around towns or along the country's north–south highway, disrupting not only their lives, but the guerrillas' reliance on them for food and other assistance. Ultimately, the guerrillas moved to where their means of survival could be assured, thus making their presence felt in new parts of the country.

As a whole, Operação Cabana failed to achieve the goals that had been set. Contrary to what the Frelimo Party had predicted, in a major publicity campaign launched during the planning stages of Operação Cabana, the operation had failed to 'defeat the armed bandits'.[47] Renamo's network of bases had been dealt a blow, but its army was intact. Although Machel would claim that from late 1982 until October 1983, FAM 'had captured 3500 bandits and thousands more killed or wounded',[48] this did not appear to have had a significant impact on the military situation in the field. He was either exaggerating the outcome of Operação Cabana or most probably had been led to believe that the goals of the operation had been accomplished. The way Renamo forces responded to the offensive fitted, after all, within the parameters of standard guerrilla warfare tactics.

The fact that Renamo was able to survive an offensive of such magnitude, in which foreign forces and advisers bolstered FAM's effort, was in itself a turning point in the Mozambique civil war. The government could not end the conflict militarily, or diplomatically, as subsequent developments demonstrated. The solution had to be political, but it would take nearly ten years more of war for the Frelimo government to come to that conclusion.

An irony of Operação Cabana was that it resulted in the war spreading further to the south, putting even more pressure on the Mozambican capital. This precipitated Renamo's movement across the Limpopo River and then into Maputo Province by virtue of having opted to move beyond FAM lines to escape the wrath of the offensive. In September 1982, a Renamo reconnaissance team left Inhambane for Maputo Province to prepare for the start of military operations there. Two months later, a Renamo contingent left southern Inhambane and joined forces with other units in Gaza. The joint force then proceeded to the south, crossing the Limpopo River and then the Mazimechopes River, finally establishing a base in the northern region of Maputo Province. The first reports of Renamo activity in the province came when the guerrillas attacked FAM positions near Mapulanguene on 6 and 7 December. Ambushes were mounted on the Mapulanguene–Magude road on 12, 13 and 17 December. The Magude–Chókwè railway line was sabotaged on 25 December. Gradually, the guerrillas extended their activity up to the north bank of the Incomáti River. Maputo lay less than 100 km away.[49]

These developments rang alarm bells in the Frelimo camp. The government contemplated even more drastic measures in an attempt to halt the spread of the insurgency further south. Renouncing its amnesty pledge, in January 1983 Frelimo dispatched two of its most senior members – Sebastião Mabote and Joaquim Chissano – to Macia and Magude in Maputo Province to preside over the public execution of prisoners of war. In Macia on 11 January, captured Renamo guerrillas were put on display before a huge crowd. After a brief speech, Mabote ordered a firing squad to machine-gun the prisoners to death. Five days later in Magude, it was the turn of Joaquim Chissano to officiate at a similar event.

Part V
Rumours of Peace

1

A Different Kind of Operation

Given that the armed conflict was spreading to all parts of the country, it would seem logical for Frelimo, in tandem with its military effort to reverse the situation, to go out of its way to win the hearts and minds of the people. Instead, it seemed bent on retaining the repressive features that lent notoriety to its government in the early days of independence. It was as if the ruling party erred deliberately to keep in place a tradition of being in conflict with all, and in the process attract more resentment and hatred. Some of the decisions taken during Frelimo's Fourth Congress in April 1983 clearly suggest that.

The Congress decided to evacuate to rural areas 'surplus' and 'unproductive' people. These included Mozambicans who had been flocking to cities owing to the unattractive living conditions in the countryside. The prospect of having to live in communal villages, work in state farms for meager salaries or no pay whatsoever, and the ravages of the war prompted many to seek a better life elsewhere. The security threat posed by the large number of unemployed, particularly in Maputo, is likely to have weighed in the government's decision to clear cities of idle people who could wittingly or otherwise act as a conduit for Renamo. The critical food shortages faced by city dwellers was, according to Mozambican anthropologist Luís Brito, another reason for evacuating the surplus residents.[1]

After the Congress, the government launched Operation Production, in which thousands of people would ostensibly be sent back to where they had originally come from. Armando Guebuza, the interior minister who had the unenviable task of populating the re-education camps after independence, was put in charge of the operation. The Defense and Security Ministries assisted in the execution of the operation, as did the Justice Ministry, but in view of the gross human rights violations that unfolded during the exercise, its was a mere token role.

The excesses reported during the operation and the justification for bringing it about bore a striking resemblance to 'Operation Tanzania', the name given by the Tanzanian government to the resettlement of urban dwellers in Ujamaa villages. Operation Production was in fact just another name for an old Frelimo goal: to develop the underpopulated Province of Niassa at the expense of people forcibly removed from cities, and to use them as cheap labor in either existing plantations or new agricultural schemes that relied on a mammoth work force, like the Romanian-sponsored 400 000-hectare project spanning from Cabo Delgado to Niassa. In 1975, that was attempted under the guise of re-education. Some eight years later, the pretext was the 'unproductive' element.

Acting with military precision, Guebuza executed the operation in two phases. The first was a voluntary one, in which people were given 15 days to register at designated areas prior to being evacuated to their home areas. The second phase, as Guebuza directed,

> would be a compulsory one during which appropriate coercive measures shall be employed to force the obstinate to adhere to the decisions taken by the Fourth Frelimo Party Congress.[2]

During this phase, city dwellers had to produce proof of residence, employment, and personal identification in the form of a passport or identity card. In addition to having to carry such documents, people traveling within the country had to produce a *guia de marcha*. Failure to produce one or more of these documents would mean immediate arrest. State companies and the civil service were prohibited from employing new workers during the operation.

The drama of 1975 repeated itself during Operation Production. People with regular jobs were caught in the net for not producing other forms of identification in addition to their employment cards. In Beira, as if to comply with Marcelino dos Santos' order that 'the unemployed [had] no freedom of choice during the second phase of Operation Production',[3] people who were unemployed for health reasons were also rounded up. Housewives, who had never been required to carry proof of employment, were detained as prostitutes. As a government weekly admitted, alleged prostitution was the motive for arresting minors, mainly girls.[4] FAM personnel serving on the various fronts learned of their wives being taken in the wake of Operation Production, a situation that could hardly augur well for the government's own stability.

Despite pledges that the law would be upheld, the privacy of one's home was disregarded at random by Vigilance Groups and heads of residential blocs. Accompanied by armed policemen, they forcibly entered apartments and houses to check whether tenants had the prescribed identity documents. Family integrity, which the government had said would be protected, was ignored. Children and even babies were left unattended at home when Operation Production teams roaming the streets detained their mothers. Teodato Hunguana, the vice minister of the interior, acknowledged that in Nacala there were cases of husbands and wives evacuated to different places, their children left to their own devices.[5]

Nacala was not the only place where such incidents took place. In the city of Inhambane, a widow with two minor children to support was rounded up for not being formally 'productive'. She was in fact self-employed, buying produce from nearby farms and selling it on the Inhambane market. Also in the same city and detained for being 'unproductive' was a divorcee with five children to look after. In this case, their father, who worked as a nurse in Inhambane, took the children.[6]

With the operation's second phase completed and people beginning to be shipped out of cities, no screening was done to decide whether a person from Manica living in Maputo, for instance, would be returned to his or her home town. All those arrested were sent to northern Mozambique regardless of their place of origin. It was estimated that about 15 000 people were forcibly evacuated from Maputo to Niassa.

The operation had come unexpectedly to Mozambique's centralized economy planners whose fuel import quota for 1983 did not take it into account. In a matter of two months, the country's fuel aviation reserves for that year were almost depleted in view of the extra flights needed to meet the operation's requirements. The national carrier suspended most of its domestic flights due to fuel shortages. The ferrying of people by road, in particular from the capitals of Niassa and Cabo Delgado to labor camps, resulted also in an abnormal consumption of commercial fuel. As a result, petrol and diesel rationing was introduced in October.

The state-owned media painted a bright picture of life at the various labor camps, with the evacuees happily building their new homes and eager to work in the fields. A government-commissioned pop singer extolled the whole concept of Operation Production, his tune played repeatedly on the national radio.

'Compared to what Mozambicans experienced when they were sent for re-education', observed a Catholic nun from Maputo, 'Operation Production was in a far larger scale and even worse.'[7] As when re-education camps began to be populated in 1975, those evacuated under Operation Production had to start a living from scratch. No accommodation was available to them on arrival, let alone facilities like running water or medical care. In the first months of their stay in Niassa, the evacuees had to sleep in the open. Their arrival coinciding with the bitter coldest months of the year, many of the evacuees died of exposure. Health care was unavailable for those who fell ill.

An independent correspondent, who visited Niassa a year after the launching of Operation Production, reported that the provincial authorities 'were seriously unprepared for the enormous influx' of people from the cities. Provincial plans, the correspondent noted, had not taken 'into account the extra food that would be needed in reserve until the 1984 harvest'. She noted that:

> Patients recovering from lung ailments, for example, are sleeping on the ground and getting one meal a day. Niassa officials have admitted that great errors committed earlier on in the year did result in dozens of deaths. Many of those placed in state farms complain that they are living in poor accommodation and without blankets or enough food.[8]

Niassa's food shortages, explains Brito, himself an evacuee from Maputo, were of the making of Operation Production planners. Aeroplanes, he says,

> arrived in Niassa loaded with people and then returned to Maputo loaded with bags of maize and beans. The increase in population followed by the outflow of food reserves resulted in an unprecedented famine in the province.[9]

Relatives of the evacuees were kept in the dark as to their whereabouts. A group of 13 women from Maputo arranged to be sent to Niassa with the intention of joining their husbands. They returned home because there was no record of their husbands in the province.[10] Some five years after the operation was launched, there were cases of people still trying to trace relatives evacuated from Maputo. Advertisements appealing for information on the whereabouts of evacuees were regularly inserted in the Mozambique press.[11]

Nampula's Catholic bishop Vieira Pinto, outspoken in his criticism of human rights violations before and after independence, wrote to President Machel, warning him that Mozambicans were questioning the operation 'and could hardly understand what its objective' was.[12] For Pinto, it was difficult to persuade a president who believed that as a whole the operation had 'achieved the envisaged goals' and that it 'was lively hailed' by Mozambicans.[13]

Five years after Operation Production was launched, the government announced that it was officially over. Increased food production, the operation's ultimate goal, never materialized. The evacuees were literally abandoned, destitute and with no jobs. 'Those who decided to remain in Niassa', reported a Maputo daily, 'are still suffering, having resorted to liquor and drugs.' Said a group of evacuees in the province, 'we drink to forget our problems. We have relatives in Maputo, but know nothing about them.'[14]

For Guebuza, the problem with Operation Production lay neither with the goals that had been envisaged at the outset, nor with methods that he meticulously prescribed. For him it was a question of a lack of 'groundwork'. 'A great many errors were committed', he said, 'but as I see it we did not do sufficiently profound groundwork.'[15]

2
The Nkomati Accord

FAM's Operação Cabana failed to turn the military situation in the government's favour in central and southern Mozambique. In the north, Renamo activity continued unabated and spread in other directions.

From the Namúli Mountains, leading a 346-strong Renamo contingent, Ossufo Momade entered Nampula in April 1983. He established Renamo's provincial base near Metaveia on the north bank of the Ligonha River. From there, the guerrillas moved eastwards along the Cuamba–Nacala railway (see Map 4). By July, guerrilla activity was felt some 50 km from the provincial capital. For the rest of the year, Renamo reported road ambushes, sabotage of the Nacala railway line, attacks on FAM garrisons, and the storming of communal villages. Several foreign workers were taken prisoner by the guerrillas.[16]

In August, a year after it had entered Zambézia, Renamo moved from that province into Niassa. With 150 men under his command, Rocha Paulino left the Renamo base in the former domains of chief Corromana in Milange and after crossing the Lúrio River in the Molumbo region (see Map 4), he established a base near Muacanha. The base was situated south of Mecanhelas, an area traditionally hostile to Frelimo. The government's curbing of traditional chiefs played into Renamo's hands as its forces advanced through Niassa. Chief Manuel Catur's area of influence in the province was fertile ground to the guerrillas. Not much earlier, Catur had perished in one of Niassa's re-education camps. Road and railway traffic was disrupted soon after Renamo entered Niassa. The Cuamba–Lichinga railway line was sabotaged on 23 August, and an FAM vehicle ambushed on the Cuamba–Mandimba road. The town of Etatara was raided on Christmas Day.

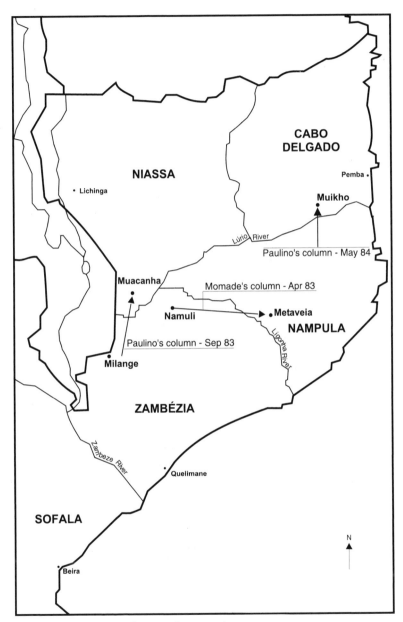

Map 4 — Renamo expands to northern provinces
Designed by Haider-Soft

In December, Paulino's contingent was beefed up with 230 men sent from Gorongosa and Zambézia, led by Ricardo José, a nephew of the Renamo leader. Renamo's strength in Niassa until the end of the war was about 1 300 men. Unlike in other provinces, in Niassa Renamo operated in smaller units because of the difficulty in obtaining food in the country's most sparsely populated area. Operations had to be co-ordinated among the various Renamo military sectors with guerrillas being drawn from several units before an attack could be launched. Nonetheless, guerrilla activity was reported up to the south bank of the Rovuma River. Except for the provincial capital, and the Metangula Navy Base, Renamo attacked all district capitals, temporarily occupying some of them. The town of Mavago remained in Renamo hands until the end of the war. Several re-education camps were attacked between 1984 and 1987, their inmates either set free or joining Renamo.[17]

In central and southern Mozambique the picture looked equally bleak to the government. Renamo consolidated its positions around the Gorongosa Mountain. Road and railway traffic between the port of Beira and Malawi was disrupted, and safety along the Beira corridor undermined. Regular sabotage of power lines deprived Beira of energy. The town of Marínguè fell for the second time into Renamo hands in September 1983. As the Chimoio–Tete road became unsafe, it was necessary to travel through Zimbabwe to reach Tete. FAM could only reach certain areas of Manica through Zimbabwe.

Guerrilla activity resumed in Gaza and Inhambane after pressure from Operação Cabana eased off. In May, Renamo claimed to have overrun FAM's barracks at Chigubo, and clashed with government forces in the coastal town of Jangamo in June. Ambushes were reported in Gaza's Nalazi–Dindiza road in June and August. The army barracks at Massangena and Macháíla were reportedly attacked in early August. The stretch of the Maputo–Zimbabwe railway line running through Gaza came under renewed sabotage. In August, there were reports of ambushes on roads in the northern area of Maputo Province.[18]

The government was being denied access to the hinterland. Primary health and educational services gradually ground to a halt in the rural areas. The economy, adversely affected by the government's own policies, worsened by the war. Exports dropped from 9.9 million contos in 1991 to 4 million contos in 1984. In February 1984, the government was forced to ask its creditors to reschedule Mozambique's foreign debt, estimated then to be in the region of US$1.5 billion.

Frelimo's economic goals envisioned in its ten-year plan had to be abandoned. The disruption of essential services that occurred right after independence, the lack of a cadre of skilled personnel to man the projects contemplated in the plan, in addition to the war burden, noted a former Economic Planning Ministry official, were the factors behind the plan's failure. According to him, the 1978–86 Iran–Iraq war 'impacted negatively on us in that fuel imports that had been negotiated with the Iraqis for the execution of the plan could no longer be supplied in favourable terms'.[19]

Against a backdrop of virtual economic collapse, the government decided to reverse the situation by non-military means. Ideology had to be pushed aside, at least temporarily, and a pragmatic attitude adopted, more so in view of the disenchantment noticeable in government circles towards the Eastern Bloc. By 1983, acknowledged a senior Mozambican official, the country saw a decline in Bloc assistance, notably in technical aid, and in the supply of spare parts for equipment imported from Eastern Europe, as well as other commodities.[20] The USSR's reluctance to have Mozambique as a Comecon member prompted Frelimo to seek greener pastures elsewhere.

Mozambique, which had refused to sign the Berlin Clause as a precondition to benefiting from European Union economic aid, revised its position. In 1984, the government began negotiations with the World Bank and the IMF to obtain full membership status with the two institutions. Mozambique was admitted to the IMF in September, following which the Paris Club of western creditor countries agreed to reschedule payment of about $350 million of Mozambique's debt.

Those were, indeed, trying moments for President Machel. He had to balance between those willing to endorse his overtures to the West and those who remained committed to the Eastern Bloc. Marcelino dos Santos in particular continued to state publicly Mozambique's commitment to the Soviet camp. He told a Comecon meeting in Berlin in October 1983 that

> the only way of overcoming the complicated international situation [in which Mozambique finds itself] rests with the strengthening of the socialist community's unity of purpose.[21]

There were signs of unrest within Frelimo ranks over Machel's willingness to shift alliances, the most obvious occurring in August 1982. Aquino de Bragança, Machel's confidant and adviser, who was perceived to have influenced the Mozambican president in reviewing his foreign policy, miraculously escaped death when he opened a letter-bomb addressed to him. Ruth First, his assistant at the African Studies Centre in Maputo, was killed when Bragança instinctively let the letter-bomb fall on his desk, at which First was sitting.

In early 1983, Frelimo Political Bureau members conspired against Machel. Joaquim Chissano, ranking third in the Frelimo hierarchy, enlisted the support of Armando Guebuza and Mariano Matsinhe in his stand against Machel. The Mozambican president was said to have been alerted by his security minister, Jacinto Veloso, who had since left for France.

Machel tried to resolve the dispute during a Political Bureau session, proposing the expulsion of Guebuza and Matsinhe. Chissano objected to this, walking out on Machel after threatening resignation. Alberto Chipande, the number four in the Political Bureau, sided with Chissano although his relationship with Guebuza had long been tense. Machel could not count on Marcelino dos Santos, though he was not part of the plot.

It was to a large extent due to the shaky ground on which Machel moved, notes a Frelimo official, that he was spurred to finding a diplomatic solution to the war. At least he would lift the pressure off the Armed Forces and in the process strengthen his power base.[22]

The Frelimo government followed two avenues to reach a diplomatic settlement of the war. In May 1983, Veloso met the South African foreign minister, Roelof Botha, to discuss ways of ending Pretoria's support for Renamo. The following month, envoys were sent to Johannesburg to sound out the possibility of a meeting with the Renamo leader through Álvaro Récio. In line with its perception of the Portuguese element in South Africa as being one of the main instigators of the war, Frelimo viewed Récio, a Portuguese businessman who had close links with Jardim before Mozambique's independence, as influential within Renamo. In fact, to that day, Récio had never met the Renamo leader or any of his immediate senior or junior officials. His loose association with Renamo had been through Cristina. The relations between the two at the time of Cristina's death in April 1983 could at best be described as cordial.

João Leitão, one of the envoys, approached Récio on behalf of the Sociedade Comercial e Industrial Moçambicana (Socimo), a Snasp front company. The other, Fernando Honwana, was one of Machel's personal assistants. They enticed Récio and his Roio company with the offer of a joint venture in which Roio would hold 45 per cent of the capital stock. The rationale was to co-opt Récio so as to ultimately manipulate Renamo.[23]

In addition to this, Veloso approached João Quental, a former Portuguese Air Force pilot. They had known each other since the days when both served in the Portuguese Armed Forces in Mozambique. Quental was one of Cristina's trusted friends, and had, until Cristina's death, been flying the Renamo leader in and out of Gorongosa. Veloso openly told Quental that the Mozambican government wanted him to arrange a meeting with Dhlakama. Most probably, Frelimo intended to renew offers that it had informally made to the Renamo leader in the past to accommodate him within the regime.[24]

Aware of these moves, the South African Foreign Ministry maneuvered to engage the Frelimo government in direct negotiations. The South Africans pushed Quental aside, and even had him temporarily detained on spurious charges. He had to be discouraged from trying to arrange the meeting Frelimo wanted. After all, the Frelimo initiative signaled the successful outcome of South Africa's support for Renamo. As Pretoria saw it, the movement's mission was about to draw to a close. South African interests could best be served if an agreement were to be struck with the Mozambican government – not between the latter and Renamo. An agreement to which South Africa was not a signatory would leave Frelimo free to assist the ANC in its struggle against apartheid.

That the South African political establishment was prepared to use Renamo as a bargaining chip was clearly reflected in a commentary broadcast by Radio South Africa, a tool of the Foreign Ministry. Despite the absurdity of the argument, the station could not have put it more bluntly: '...the ideological preoccupations that led Frelimo to support the ANC resulted in other areas in the popular disillusionment from which Renamo was born'.[25]

The South Africans succeeded in having Frelimo negotiating directly with them. For that, they had the support of the United States, in particular its assistant secretary for African affairs, Chester Crocker. What made things even more pleasant for Pretoria was that Washington and Maputo shared its view that Renamo should not be part of a deal.

For the United States and most Western countries, Renamo always had limited political value. In the minds of Western policymakers, Renamo had fulfilled what they privately saw as its mission – to help with the mellowing of the Frelimo government, making it more receptive to the West rather than being too committed to the USSR idea of challenging its interests in southern Africa. A bargain, considering that none in the West had come forward to assist Renamo in any significant form.

Help from the United States had a price that Frelimo was prepared to pay: assist Crocker in making his ambiguous 'constructive engagement' policy work. Crocker viewed the Frelimo regime as 'partners' who 'delivered exactly what we needed': direct access to the core of the Angolan government which, in due course, would put negotiations on the Cuban withdrawal from the long-coveted former Portuguese colony on track. Crocker conceded that Maputo's motive in helping him was that the Frelimo leaders 'hoped that we would assist them in coping with their South African problem',[26] that is, Renamo.

After a series of meetings between Mozambican and South African officials, the two countries signed 'a non-aggression and good neighbourliness accord' in March 1984. It became known as the Nkomati Accord. In essence the two countries agreed not to assist in any way forces opposed to the respective governments in carrying out military operations. Although not mentioned by name in the accord, Renamo and the ANC were the forces in question.

The South Africans were divided over the Nkomati Accord. The DMI tried to discourage the Pretoria government from signing the accord, arguing that it was devoid of any strategic perspective. In view of the evolving military situation in Mozambique, in which the Frelimo government would on a medium-term collapse, DMI reasoned, there was no justification for discontinuing support for Renamo. DMI pointed out to the South African cabinet that there was nothing to prevent Frelimo from resuming support for the ANC once it no longer felt threatened domestically. In the long run, said the DMI, South Africa would have no leverage to use against the Frelimo government.[27]

As its views did not prevail over the South African Foreign Ministry, the DMI ensured that Renamo would receive additional logistical assistance before the accord was signed. DMI contacts with Renamo were not totally severed after the signing of the accord, though logistical assistance to the Mozambican guerrillas never reached the scale of pre-accord years and is believed to have had no impact on Renamo's ability to survive militarily.

By entering into a deal with apartheid-ruled South Africa, Frelimo lost prestige, particularly among its most fervent admirers. It also antagonized the ANC, which felt that the pact could not 'but help perpetuate the illegitimate rule of the South African white settler minority'.[28]

Concerned about his regime's image, Machel was at pains to explain that the accord 'had not been signed by the Frelimo Party, but by the government of Mozambique',[29] suggesting that he could at any given time separate one from the other, even though Frelimo continued to state proudly that it was the 'leading force of state of society'.

More than its prestige, other important considerations prevailed in the Frelimo government's decision to sign the accord. Frelimo believed, that, without South African support, all that was left for Renamo was either to surrender or to succumb to FAM's might. Machel personally told a rally in Maputo that the accord had left the Renamo guerrillas in the lurch and that they would not survive on their own for much longer. The government media helped create the impression of an imminent defeat of the Renamo forces, reporting that 'armed bandits' were either deserting or turning themselves over to the authorities in droves.

Judging by what the Mozambican media put out from March onwards, peace was just around the corner. The opposite was in fact the case. Instead of de-escalating, the war expanded further afield. Neither the Frelimo government nor the South African Foreign Ministry, nor the Western diplomats who encouraged Machel to sign the Nkomati Accord, seemed to have realized that Renamo had acquired a momentum of its own and would be able to sustain its activities into the future even if it were to be deprived of outside logistical assistance.

Renamo did not feel threatened by the accord. Encouraged by the military successes in central and northern provinces, and their ability to withstand FAM's onslaught in the south, the Renamo leaders believed that Frelimo would soon capitulate. The accord was, after all, a sign of weakness. The guerrillas even went to the extent of claiming that with the stigma of a South African alliance no longer in place, the world would finally be able to measure the extent to which they could operate on their own. What Renamo failed to take into account was that Frelimo would go to any lengths to ensure its survival, including increased foreign intervention.

In the interim, Machel took steps to have the dissidents in the Political Bureau removed from Maputo. He designated Guebuza and Matsinhe 'resident ministers' for Nampula and Niassa in June 1984, the title being just another name for that of provincial governor. Matsinhe took up his post, handing over the security portfolio to Sérgio Vieira, who continued as Chipande's deputy in the Defense Ministry, and chief of Frelimo's Security Department. Guebuza did not accept the post, but gave way to Óscar Monteiro, who became the new interior minister. Machel compromised, appointing Guebuza minister of state in the office of the President of the Republic in September. Instead of the Ponta Vermelha Palace, from where Machel worked, Guebuza was given an office at the Central Committee headquarters, several blocks away.

3
The Pretoria Talks

In May 1984, some two months after the signing of the Nkomati Accord, Renamo took the war to Cabo Delgado. The guerrillas entered the province from Nampula (see Map 4). Rocha Paulino, who had opened the Niassa front the previous year, led the guerrilla contingent across the Lúrio River. FAM put up strong resistance to Renamo's attempts to establish a base in Chief Muikho's area to the south of Cabo Delgado. To lessen FAM pressure, Renamo launched diversionary attacks close to the port of Nacala. Eventually the guerrillas succeeded in establishing a presence in Cabo Delgado. The government media acknowledged that it had been possible 'due to the work of former chiefs, notably Muikho'.[30] Chief Muikho and his string of associates, according to Renamo, did mobilize the local population to guide the guerrillas and give them food and shelter, though the course of events was ultimately decided in the battlefield. Renewed FAM pressure forced Renamo to vacate the base in 1985, its guerrillas moving to Namecala, west of the provincial capital, Pemba.

Renamo's entry into Cabo Delgado came in the wake of government reports of subversive activity in the Mueda highlands in January 1984. The provincial governor, Alberto Chipande, suggested that former MANU members with a history of opposition to Frelimo had been behind a series of incidents.[31]

As Renamo's campaign in the province gained momentum, Chipande resorted to tactics similar to the ones recently employed by his fellow Political Bureau members in Maputo Province. In July 1985, Chipande warned villagers in the Montepuez area that every captured guerrilla should be subject to 'popular justice', Frelimo's euphemism for executing someone summarily. With irony, he admonished them: 'I wouldn't want you to send me any armed bandit to Pemba because I have no food for them'.[32] Chipande's utterances highlighted the government's lack of a clear-cut policy to win the hearts and minds of the insurgents. As the war intensified, FAM and its foreign allies simply executed captured guerrillas as well as villagers suspected of collaborating with them. 'No effort was made to convert former guerillas to work for us. We killed them, instead', admitted a former security officer.[33]

Over the years, Renamo expanded its presence in Cabo Delgado from Muikho to Namuno in the west, and to Meluco and Muidumbe in the north. The guerrillas secured the support of the Makonde after a period of indecisiveness, fearing that Renamo was a Makua movement. In Cabo Delgado, Renamo guerrillas operated jointly with forces drawn from Niassa whenever major attacks, such as the ones on Chíure and Meluco, were launched. They could not count on assistance from Renamo forces in Nampula because the Lúrio River, in flood for most of the year, made crossing between the two provinces difficult.[34] Renamo claimed to have raided Namuno and Montepuez in mid-1986, and overran the FAM garrison at Meluco in January the following year. Chiúre was reportedly occupied in September 1987 and again in January 1988. Also in early 1988, Renamo said its forces raided Mueda.

Elsewhere in the country, there was no let up in guerrilla activity. In central Mozambique, Renamo raided the town of Inhaminga in April 1984. In mid-June, it claimed to have killed 79 FAM soldiers in an attack on the garrison guarding the Pungué bridge, 60 km from Beira.

In the southern provinces there continued to be reports of guerrilla attacks on government positions and communications routes. In July, the East German Embassy in Maputo ordered the withdrawal of its nationals working in Inhambane's gas fields, following a land mine incident in Macovane in which two Germans were killed.

Further to the south, pressure continued to be exerted even closer to the Mozambican capital. Towards the end of January 1984, a 60-strong Renamo group, led by Pedro Muchanga, crossed the Incómati River only days before the cyclone Domoina had ravaged the area, making the flooded river an impassable obstacle. The group split into three units of 20 men each, the first operating south of Ressano Garcia, the second north-east of the city of Maputo, and the third on the south bank of the Incómati River near the Moamba area. In March, Muchanga's group raided the town of Moamba, using a 14.5-mm machine-gun captured from an FAM position outside the town. The rebels ransacked more than 30 houses and destroyed installations. Traveling outside the capital became hazardous, with frequent ambushes on both military and civilian traffic. On 29 April, a passenger bus traveling from Gaza to Maputo, was ambushed in the Ricalta area, north of the Mozambican capital. Two passengers were killed and ten others wounded. Trains on the Maputo railway also came under attack. In one such incident on 3 May, 31 people were wounded when a passenger train was ambushed about 29 km north of the city. Electricity supplies to Maputo became erratic due to sabotage of power lines.

In May, the government took steps to thwart Renamo attempts to infiltrate the capital. Vigilance groups active in the city of Maputo's 2600 residential blocks were revamped. Maputo residents were urged to organize patrols to detect possible attacks.[35] In June, several foreign diplomatic missions in Maputo instructed their nationals not to venture beyond the city's boundaries.

The Nkomati Accord had not met the expectations of the Mozambican government. The Catholic Church seized the opportunity to once again come to the fore to stress the need for peace in Mozambique. In a pastoral letter entitled 'The Urgency of Peace', the Church, while hailing the signing of the Nkomati Accord as a decisive step that showed insight and courage, noted that other measures were needed. Specifically, the Catholic bishops called for reconciliation, dialogue, understanding and clemency.[36] A similar appeal was made by Bishop Vieira Pinto in a letter to President Machel. Pinto did not believe the Nkomati Accord on its own was sufficient for restoring peace in Mozambique. The bishop stressed that reconciliation was the main key for peace.[37]

The critical military situation the government faced, rather than the Catholic Church's appeals, forced Frelimo to negotiate with Renamo. While publicly the government media insisted that no talks would ever be held with the guerrillas, Fernando Honwana was again sent to meet Récio. The two met in Maputo on 7 June 1984. Two days later Récio left for Lisbon to discuss with Evo Fernandes Frelimo's conditions for peace. Récio returned to Maputo on 11 June with Evo Fernandes' counter-proposals.[38] Fernandes reiterated the proposals when he met Honwana in Europe days later. Honwana described the meeting as a 'disastrous encounter because Fernandes wanted a capitulation of the Mozambican Government'.[39] Specifically, Fernandes wanted a transitional government to be put in place so as to pave the way for the establishment of a democratic regime, the reorganization of the Mozambique Armed Forces, the reinstatement of traditional authority, and permission for Renamo to operate politically in Mozambique with no restrictions. Basically, Renamo was calling for the implementation of its 1981 program of action.

Despite its eagerness to reach a negotiated solution to the civil war, Frelimo's proposals showed that the divide between the two warring factions was still too wide before there could be hope for genuine peace. As Honwana told Récio in Maputo on 20 June, Renamo should first cease hostilities. The Renamo leaders, he said, would in return be given senior posts in the commerce and industry sectors, while other of the movement's officials would be given funds to settle in foreign countries. 'Traitors like the Bomba brothers and [Snasp defector] Jorge Costa would not be allowed to return', stressed Honwana. Costa, however, had never been part of Renamo.

Nonetheless, the Frelimo government privately agreed to meet Renamo in Pretoria on 16 September. By asking the South Africans to act as mediators, Frelimo had at least succeeded in giving the impression that the talks fitted within the framework of the Nkomati Accord and that Renamo was part and parcel of South Africa's delegation. But in public the Frelimo government continued with a façade of intransigence insofar as sitting at the negotiating table with Renamo was concerned. Jacinto Veloso, who headed the government delegation to the tripartite talks, told correspondents that he was not aware of the Renamo delegation being in Pretoria, noting that he had no objection to it being there as long as its presence 'did not contravene the Nkomati Accord'. Thanks to the news blackout imposed by the South Africans around the talks, Veloso was thus able to keep up with the deception.

No tangible progress was made during the initial sessions of the talks as Renamo refused to deviate from its proposals. On 1 October, Honwana conveyed, through Leitão, a message to Récio, telling him that the Mozambican government delegation would call the day off and return home unless Renamo reviewed its position. Honwana urged Récio to impress on Roelof Botha the need for Renamo 'to come to its senses'. Leitão informed Récio that Machel had advanced a five-point proposal, whereby Renamo should recognize him as head of state; the Mozambican president should be given sufficient time to introduce the reforms Renamo was demanding; there should be national reconciliation; a gradual shift from Marxism-Leninism to an African socialism would follow; and, finally, there should be neither losers nor winners.[40]

Two days later, Roelof Botha, appearing in public for the first time with the Mozambican government and Renamo delegations, announced what would become known as the 'Pretoria Declaration'. The four-point document stated that Machel was acknowledged as the president of the People's Republic of Mozambique; that armed activity and conflict within Mozambique from whatever quarter or source should stop; that the South African government was requested to consider playing a role in the implementation of the declaration; and that a commission would be established immediately to work towards an early implementation of the declaration.[41]

But a few hours after Botha's announcement, Fernandes announced that the war would continue, and that there was no undertaking on Renamo's part to maintain Machel in power, but simply acknowledgement of a fact.[42] Botha had not discussed with the Renamo delegation the exact details of the first point of the declaration. According to Fanuel Mahluza, who attended the talks, Botha had merely asked the Renamo delegates whether they agreed that Machel was head of Mozambique. 'We said, yes, and from there he went to read the declaration without our prior knowledge', noted Mahluza.[43]

The commission to which the declaration referred was set up and the tripartite negotiations continued. The commission's first plenary session was held in Pretoria from 8 to 11 October. It adjourned at Renamo's request until 17 October to study a draft cease-fire agreement that the South African delegation had placed on the negotiating table on 11 October. In terms of the document, a cease-fire would take effect 45 days after the signing of the agreement. 'The cessation of armed activities and conflict', Article 5 of the Draft Agreement read, 'shall continue for a period of 3 months and may be extended by the mutual consent of the PRM [People's Republic of Mozambique] Government and Renamo.'

Article 6 bound both the Mozambican government and Renamo to not gaining any military advantage over the other during the period of cessation of armed activities and conflict. To monitor the implementation of the cease-fire agreement, a Monitoring Committee would be immediately established and each party would in its sole discretion appoint four representatives.

At the request of the Mozambican government delegation, the Draft Agreement included in Article 11 the provision that 'the parties shall not publicly disclose any details of this Agreement or of discussions or activities in the Commission or any other information in connection therewith'.[44]

With this, the Frelimo authorities would be able to keep Mozambicans at home ignorant of what was really happening in Pretoria. The official Mozambique media continued to report that the government had not met, and would never meet Renamo, but would fight it until it was defeated. Personally, Veloso also kept up appearances. Speaking in Pemba, where he had gone to brief President Machel on the progress of the talks, Veloso said 'military action would continue to be the main priority in the struggle against armed banditry in Mozambique'.[45] Machel went one step further, saying that

> Mozambique would not negotiate with kidnappers, bandits, criminals and malefactors, wherever they come from. The People's Republic of Mozambique will liquidate them not before long. A coffin has already been arranged for them.[46]

Statements of this nature kept cropping up from all sides of the Frelimo political establishment. Foreign Minister Chissano told correspondents that 'any negotiations with Renamo [were] out of the question'.[47] It was as a result of the Mozambican government's ambiguous position that Renamo refused to return to the negotiating table on 17 October. The guerrillas set as a condition for their return to the talks that the Frelimo government publicly and unequivocally stated that it was engaged in direct negotiations with them. As no statement toward that end was ever made, the war dragged on for another eight years.

Part VI
Foreign Intervention

1
Zimbabwe's Role Expanded

Prospects of a negotiated settlement with Renamo being ruled out due to the failure of the Pretoria peace talks, the Mozambican government opted for an all out military solution to the conflict. Given the country's deteriorating security situation, the government was compelled to seek greater foreign assistance, in terms both of military training and personnel.

The training programs that had been arranged with Tanzania and Great Britain prior to the 1983–84 peace initiative were extended. As relations with the United States improved, the training agreement with Libya was put on hold. The first and only FAM special forces battalion trained in Benghazi and Tripoli returned to Mozambique in the last quarter of 1984. The recruits had been airlifted to Libya via Cotonou in February that year.[1]

To contain the guerrilla threat in the province of Maputo, an independent battalion was established under the command of Valentim de Sousa, a Portuguese exiled in Mozambique because of his association with the FP-25 extreme-left militia in Portugal. Based in Moamba, Sousa's 1700-strong battalion did not face the same operational and logistical constraints of most FAM units. For this reason, Sousa claimed, the battalion was highly motivated and attained a good rate of success against Renamo.[2]

Direct military intervention by Zimbabwe, and later Tanzania, was decisive in containing, and in some instances reversing, the Renamo threat, notably in central and northern Mozambique. FAM Major General Matias Juma, in charge of the Tete Provincial Military Command, conceded 'that had it not been for ZNA's intervention, the whole of Tete could have been taken by Renamo'.[3]

The deployment of a ZNA Special Task Force in Mozambique came in the wake of high level talks in Harare in June 1985 between President

Machel and the Zimbabwean prime minister.[4] It was agreed that the Special Task Force would come under the overall command of Brigadier Philip Sibanda, a graduate of the British Army's Staff College at Camberley. The Task Force would be involved in combat operations and in escort duty. Personnel were drawn from ZNA's 3rd and 6th Brigades, as well as the Parachute Regiment. The Regiment, comprising former Zimbabwe independence guerrillas and Rhodesian forces, had to an extent replaced the SAS after its disbanding in late 1980. Colonel Lionel Dyke, a former member of the Rhodesia African Rifles, was the Regiment's commanding officer. Dyke had been actively involved with the North Korean-trained 5th Brigade in its campaign to wipe out the Zimbabwean dissidents in the Matabeleland and Midlands Provinces, as well as in Botswana.

The ZNA Special Task Force was about 5000-strong, costing 10 million Zimbabwean dollars annually to keep it in Mozambique.[5] The Harare-based Southern African Research and Documentation Centre reported that the ZNA contingent was increased to 10000 troops in 1989 at an annual cost of 12 million Zimbabwean dollars.[6]

In August 1985, the ZNA stormed several Renamo bases in central Mozambique. The guerrillas' Muxamba base, near the Revué power station, was the first to come under attack. Renamo was almost caught by surprise when ZNA raided Muxamba, the movement's Casa Banana headquarters in Gorongosa having warned the base of an imminent attack precisely when Zimbabwe Air Force planes were over their target. By taking Muxamba, the Zimbabweans believed that they would prevent further Renamo attacks on the oil pipeline and railway line due to the base's proximity to the Beira corridor.

In the early hours of 28 August, the ZNA attacked Casa Banana. Acting on information obtained from intercepted FAM's military communications network, Renamo vacated the installations before the attack took place. The ZNA only gained access to the base the next day, thus compromising the element of surprise. Assuming that fleeing guerrillas had regrouped in bases around the Gorongosa Mountain, the ZNA proceeded to attack Renamo positions in Marínguè, Fábrica, Cavalo and Bunga.

For the operation, ZNA committed six Alouette and Bell helicopters, three Dakota and an equal number of Casa aeroplanes, and an Islander. Flying from the Thornhill base in Zimbabwe, Hunter and Hawk fighter-bombers gave air support, but at this range their time over the targets was limited. Mozambican Air Force Mi-25 helicopters were also used in the operation.

The August 1985 raids bore a striking resemblance to those the Rhodesians had launched against Zimbabwe guerrilla camps in Mozambique. This clearly indicated that former Rhodesian military experts had a hand in the planning of the operation. Indeed, the raids signaled a departure from the manner in which counter-insurgency operations had until then been conducted against Renamo.

The ZNA Parachute Regiment made full use of the fireforce method of combat against Renamo. Relying on gunships, as helicopters mounted with 20-mm cannons were called, the fireforce concept consisted of deploying as many troops on the ground in a given area in as short a time as possible. They would act as stop groups to prevent the guerrillas from escaping the barrage of fire from the gunships. Normally, a propeller-driven fixed wing aircraft would initiate the attack while the helicopters hammered away in support. After the initial air strikes, the main sweep line moved forward towards the centre of the contact area, either killing the guerrillas or driving them on to the guns of the stop groups.[7]

Like the Rhodesians in their counter-insurgency war against Zimbabwe nationalists, the ZNA resorted to the use of pseudo-guerrillas modeled on the Selous Scouts. ZNA recruited former Renamo members who had either been captured by or turned themselves over to FAM, and then trained them as pseudos. Their role was to locate guerrilla hideouts and granaries that Renamo had established in its areas of influence. Helicopters would then raid the areas pinpointed by the pseudos. The aim was to drive the civilian population away from Renamo zones and concentrate them in communal villages. There were instances when the pseudos succeeded in convincing villagers to vacate Renamo areas, alleging that a massive government attack was about to be launched. Whenever Renamo bases came under attack, the pseudos would be deployed around the targeted areas, ready to ambush fleeing guerrillas.

The constant harassment of Renamo areas resulted not only in the guerrillas scattering in small groups, but more importantly in the displacement of the rural population, ultimately disrupting agricultural production and depriving the guerrillas of food and shelter. Sofala Province's Emergency Commission reported in the last quarter of 1987 that there were 34 000 displaced persons in the Gorongosa area alone in need of food, medicines and clothing.[8]

Displacement of civilians was also reported in Tete as ZNA counter-insurgency operations began to be launched in the province. In March 1986, about 11 000 refugees fled the Chiuta and Fíngoè areas into Zambia's Eastern Province. The UNHCR reported that in May 1987 the number of refugees in the Zambian province had risen to 27 000.[9]

Despite the marked improvement in counter-insurgency operations, the military situation remained unstable and the government could not function normally in large areas of the country. Parliamentary elections scheduled for 1985 had to be cancelled. Despite being set for a date to be announced in 1986, the polls did not take place until the war was over.

FAM and ZNA ground and air forces could not venture at random into guerrilla territory. In the wake of the raid on Casa Banana, Renamo downed FAM and ZNA helicopters in Sofala. Casa Banana itself was retaken by the guerrillas after ZNA had handed it over to FAM. By the end of the war, Casa Banana had changed hands several times. The ZNA eventually decided to make it its operational headquarters for central Mozambique, making full use of the Renamo airstrip at Cangamitole.

In Zambézia, the guerrillas still had the upper hand, holding most of the province's towns. In July 1986, they seized the district capital of Gilé, and in August the town of Morrumbala.

In Tete in September 1986, Renamo raided the towns of Dona Ana and Vila Nova, forcing about 800 people to seek temporary shelter in Malawi. In the same month, the towns of Mutarara, Caia, Inhaminga, Marromeu and Chuabo fell in rebel hands. In October, the guerrillas overran the towns of Milange, on the border with Malawi, and Zumbo, on the border with Zambia.

In the face of Renamo attacks in Zambézia and Tete, FAM forces fled across the border into Malawi. By early October, about 1700 FAM soldiers, some of them accompanied by their families, had sought shelter in Malawi following guerrilla attacks on Milange and Ulónguè. A Malawian Embassy spokesman in Maputo announced that more than 70 000 Mozambicans had taken refuge in Malawi in the first two weeks of October due to clashes between Renamo and FAM.[10]

2
The Malawian Connection

As the military situation in Zambézia and Tete worsened, Mozambique accused the Malawian government of allowing its territory to be used as a launching pad for Renamo attacks on Mozambique. Both Malawi and Renamo consistently denied the claim. There is, however, evidence that a connection existed between the two, but not at the level that the claim suggested.

Renamo officials, foreign correspondents and an array of other individuals enjoyed transit facilities in Malawi whenever they wanted to visit the guerrillas' territory in Mozambique. They did this either on foot from the border area or by air. South African Air Force planes are known to have flown from Malawi to drop logistical supplies over Renamo bases in northern Mozambique, before and, to a lesser extent, after the Nkomati Accord.

Using Malawi as a sanctuary for military training and for infiltrating Mozambique would have amounted to a departure from Renamo's *modus operandi*, particularly from September 1979 onwards when the guerrilla command structure became permanently based inside Mozambique. Had there been Renamo bases in Malawi, it would not have been necessary for South African planes to overfly the Mozambican territory and drop supplies for the guerrillas in the northern provinces. It would have been less risky and not as obvious if the supplies were to be carried by porters across the border.

Liaison between Renamo and Malawi was through that country's police force, not the Armed Forces, which attests to the type and level of cooperation between the guerrillas and the Malawians. After all, raids on Renamo installations, including its headquarters, were always carried out within Mozambique's boundaries for the duration of the conflict.

Nonetheless, for the Frelimo government, the Malawi-Renamo con-nection explained the inability of FAM and its allies to contain the guerrillas' inroads, particularly in central and northern Mozambique. In an attempt to end such a connection, the Maputo authorities tried first to impress on Malawi the need to become more actively involved in the then Southern African Development Co-ordination Conference, SADCC. The rationale was that, if Malawi made full use of the ports of Nacala and Beira, it would reconsider its support for Renamo. The Front-line states met in Luanda in August 1986 and urged Malawi to endorse that policy. The message was personally conveyed to the Malawian government by Machel and his Zimbabwean and Zambia counterparts in Blantyre the following month.

The Blantyre meeting appeared to have been a fiasco, judging from Machel's remarks on his return to Maputo. He threatened to shut down traffic from Malawi to South Africa and Zimbabwe, and place missiles on the border with that country in case 'the Malawian authorities did not stop their support for armed banditry in Mozambique'.[11] A few days later, Machel, accompanied by Soviet and Cuban military advisers, went to Tete to 'study where best to place defensive equipment along the Malawian border'.[12]

For their part, the Malawians continued to deny the charges. A Mala-wian official said his country had 'presented her side of the story based on what is actually happening and there is nothing more to discuss'.[13] That was a reference to the flight of FAM soldiers into Malawi, after coming under Renamo attack inside Mozambique. For Malawi, this clearly showed that there were no Renamo bases in its territory, other-wise FAM soldiers would not have risked seeking shelter in the guerrillas' own sanctuary.

In fact, FAM not only used the Malawian territory for temporary shelter, but also to mount operations against the guerrillas whenever they could not reach their targets from within Mozambique itself. According to the guerrillas, the FAM raid on their Alfazema base in Milange District in 1983, to rescue the six Bulgarians taken prisoner by Renamo, was launched from Malawi. In 1986, FAM once again made use of the Malawian territory to attack the Renamo base at Nhandandanda in the Mutarara region of Tete Province.[14]

But the government in Maputo thought differently, and from the threats publicly made by Machel, plans to take decisive action against the Banda regime began to be worked out by the Mozambican and Zimbabwean governments. On 16 October 1986, a meeting was held in Maputo between Machel and a high-level Zimbabwean defense and security delegation. Machel proposed what he termed a double approach to effectively remove Banda from power. On the one hand, Zimbabwean diplomats would seek Banda's concurrence to allow ZNA and FAM to enter Malawi from Zambézia and Tete, on the pretext of wanting to reach Renamo guerrilla bases through the Malawian territory. Once inside Malawi, FAM and ZNA would work closely with Banda's opponents in the Army to oust his regime. Machel also suggested that Mozambique and Zimbabwe could 'organize a Malawi liberation front, and equip and infiltrate it into Malawi to liquidate the bandits there'.[15]

The Mozambican border with Malawi would, in accordance with the plan, be sealed off. In the event of the Malawi government attempting to use Tanzanian and Zambian routes to the sea, FAM and ZNA would sabotage road and rail bridges in these two countries. 'Yes, that can be done', said Ernest Kadangure, Zimbabwe's minister of state for defense. And the Zimbabwean Army commander, General Rex Nhongo, concurred: 'We are ready for that'.

Machel told the Zimbabwean delegation that on 8 October he had a meeting with Mozambican, Cuban and Soviet military personnel and that it had been decided that they should at once go to Zambézia to prepare for the arrival of 1500 FAM soldiers. MiG-21s would be transferred to the Beira Air Force Base, and MiG-17s would be deployed in Zambézia itself.[16]

A further meeting between Machel and the Zimbabweans was scheduled for 22 October during which final preparations of the plan to overthrow Banda would be discussed. The meeting never took place. On 19 October, Machel died in a plane crash *en route* from Zambia where he had gone to meet Kenneth Kaunda and the Zairian president for talks on the Mozambican military situation.

To date the plane crash remains shrouded in controversy. Days after the crash, with no formal investigations into its causes even started, the Mozambican government blamed South Africa for it. Specifically, the South Africans were accused of having erected a decoy navigational radio aid (VOR) near the scene of the crash inside South Africa. The intention was to divert the presidential plane from its intended path, eventually forcing it to crash. According to Mozambique, the decoy VOR had the same frequency as the one installed at the Maputo airport, but it was a more powerful one.

An inquiry into the accident of President Machel's Tupolev 134A-3 gave as the most probable cause for the change in the flight path the crew's inadvertent selection of the Swaziland airport's VOR instead of

Maputo's. The recently installed Swaziland airport VOR's frequency, 112.3 MHz, was very close to Maputo's 112.7 MHz. Mbuzini, the hilly region of South Africa where the aircraft crashed, in fact lies in the direction of the Swazi airport. Although the Swazi department of civil aviation had issued a Notice to Airmen (Notam), informing regional airports of the new VOR, Mozambique denied knowledge of it and had, accordingly, not briefed the Tupolev 134A-3 crew about the development.

The Board of Inquiry, which included a retired British Lord Justice of Appeal, a former American chief test pilot, astronaut and aeronautical engineer, and a former chief inspector of the accidents branch of Britain's Ministry of Transport, stressed that the sole function of a VOR is to indicate azimuth, that is, direction in the horizontal plane – it is not a guide to descent and it would not cause an aircraft to descend. In dealing further with the alleged decoy VOR, the Board of Inquiry pointed out that the Maputo VOR operated normally immediately before and after the plane crash, and that the presence of a more powerful VOR using the same frequency would have been registered by the aircraft's digital flight data recorder, which was not the case.

The report pointed out that the aircraft was not following any VOR after it changed its flight path, but was being navigated on the Doppler. Admitting the possibility of a spurious VOR, the Board's report stated that it would not be located inside South Africa, as the Mozambican authorities continued to insist, but in Mozambique itself.

The Soviet crew was blamed for the accident. The Board of Inquiry concluded that the crew had

> failed to follow procedural requirements for an instrument let-down approach, but continued to descend under visual flight rules in darkness and some cloud, i.e. without having visual contact with the ground, below minimum safe altitude and minimum assigned altitude, and in addition ignored the GPWS [Ground Proximity Warning System] alarm.[17]

The Soviet Union and Mozambique, as manufacturer and owner of the aircraft respectively, refused to take part in the investigations and declined requests from the investigators to allow survivors of the crash, notably the flight engineer, to appear before the Board of Inquiry.

3
Changing of the Guard

In the wake of Samora Machel's death, the Frelimo Political Bureau designated Joaquim Chissano as the new party leader. He took precedence over Marcelino dos Santos, who was at a disadvantage due to his ethnic background. In terms of the Mozambican Constitution, Chissano automatically became head of state.

The new Mozambican leader introduced discreet but sweeping changes. High on his agenda was the need to build his own power base. Addressing the aspirations of those whom Machel had neglected since independence was a way of achieving that.

More concerned with the non-racial image of his regime, which he wanted to project internationally, Machel made a point of surrounding himself with a great many non-black Mozambicans. He appointed them to party and government posts as well as to state enterprises and institutions. The façade of racial and ethnic harmony maintained during Machel's tenure cracked after his demise. The grievances among black Frelimo members came into the open even before the Political Bureau had time to choose a new leader. In a manifesto issued on behalf of the independence war veterans, they complained that

> The bitter experience that we have had in extending political power to each and every citizen has created us problems due to the dishonesty and lack of patriotism of citizens also regarded as Mozambicans, though irremediably compromised with the outside world.

Addressed to Chissano, Chipande, Guebuza and Matsinhe – the same people who had conspired against Machel in 1983 – the manifesto demanded 'the total exclusion of non-indigenous Mozambicans from political, economic and military power'. Indicative of the ethnic disputes still plaguing Frelimo, the manifesto added:

> We believe that at the central government (Council of Ministers), the representativity of each province is fundamental and a source of stability. At the central government, we should avoid a disproportionate concentration of members of a single province, which could cause tribal and regional problems. We believe that if we adopt this measure we would be able to end the South–North dispute.

The manifesto called for a negotiated settlement with Renamo, but demanded that the movement should not include 'non-indigenous' Mozambicans in the peace talks. Having acknowledged that the Renamo–Frelimo dispute was in fact a civil war, the veterans' manifesto urged the next Mozambican government 'not to internationalize the conflict as a means of solving it – that would only protract the problem and waste time. Our people want peace.'

The war veterans proposed Guebuza for prime minister. As for the new Mozambican president, they wanted someone who used 'a language that is in keeping with the standing of a head of state [...], a language that is free of insults'. The reference to Machel could not be more obvious: the late Frelimo leader often used abusive language when talking to Mozambicans in general, including the independence war veterans whom he once called 'warthogs'. Machel's habit of humiliating senior FAM officers, including physically assaulting them in the presence of others, had certainly been in the minds of those who drafted the manifesto.

For the signatories to the manifesto, Chissano was the right candidate because he 'was, after all, a true diplomat'. They wanted Chipande and Matsinhe to become vice president of the Republic and security minister, respectively. The 22-member cabinet as proposed in the manifesto did not include a single 'non-indigenous' Mozambican.[18]

Marcelino dos Santos was the first 'non-indigenous' Mozambican to react to the manifesto. In an emotionally charged eulogy to Machel drafted jointly with Fernando Ganhão, the principal of the Eduardo Mondlane University, Santos lashed out at those behind the manifesto, as he hailed the late Frelimo leader's qualities:

> You taught us that behind racism, tribalism and regionalism is always hidden the mean face of ambition which so often leads to crime and treason. Such views were reflected not only in your political

positions, but also in the overwhelmingly unprejudiced manner in which you related to people of all tribes and races, the friendships you chose, and in all your private life. You saw in each man solely their concrete qualities and universal dimension. You used to say during the struggle: we do not fight to change the colour of the exploiters nor to replace foreign with domestic oppression.[19]

Despite the apprehensions that the manifesto had aroused amongst non-black Political Bureau members, Chissano departed from his predecessor's stand on the racial composition of his cabinet. Credited as being in fact the instigator of the manifesto, or at least connected in some way with those who drafted it, Chissano effectively removed most non-black Mozambicans from senior positions. Guebuza and Matsinhe, who had been demoted by Machel in the wake of the 1983 plot, were restored to full ministerial titles. Guebuza became the new transport and communications minister, replacing Alcântara Santos, the white Mozambican who had died in the plane crash. Chissano designated Matsinhe as the new security minister, firing Sérgio Vieira from the post Machel had given him in 1983. It was a case of killing two birds with one stone: Chissano wanted also to settle an old score with Vieira, who had had him under house arrest on suspicion of conspiring against Machel. Black Mozambicans eventually replaced the ministers of agriculture, industry, and commerce. José Luís Cabaço, the former information minister, famous for putting on a black Mozambican accent at public functions and influential in designing Frelimo's propaganda strategy, which portrayed opposition to government as representing the views and interests of former white settlers, had to give way to an 'indigenous' Mozambican.

The white-dominated news media also felt the impact of Chissano's measures. The white editors of state-owned media outlets were gradually replaced with black Mozambicans. As the long-delayed blackening of the regime was in full swing, leading journalists, who had made a name under Machel, began complaining of racial prejudice under Chissano's tenure.

Four years after Chissano's rise to power, Frelimo continued to be plagued by racial bias. In the People's Assembly there were heated debates over birthright, with independence war veterans like António Hama Thai resurrecting the 'non-indigenous'[20] ghost. Once again, Marcelino dos Santos came to the fore, lecturing his peers about 'nationhood [being] a historic process – not something that runs in the blood or comes about automatically'.[21]

Regarding the civil war, Chissano pursued the military solution adopted by his predecessor, disregarding the manifesto's call for negotiations with Renamo. The FAM General Staff, encouraged by the results achieved since ZNA's intervention, assured Chissano that a Renamo defeat was possible. As if to deter the veterans from their commitment to a negotiated settlement, the media renewed its portrayal of Renamo as a Portuguese settler outfit, manipulated by powerful interests in Lisbon, Pretoria, Washington and Bonn, that is, an organization as 'irremediably compromised with the outside world' as the 'non-indigenous' Mozambicans referred to in the manifesto. The message was also applicable to the Mozambican Catholic Church in view of its insistent appeals for dialogue with Renamo.

Chissano's military option was also reflected in external operations conducted by the Mozambican security services. The assassinations of Renamo officials João Ataíde and Mateus Lopes while in transit through Malawi in November 1987, and of former Renamo secretary general Evo Fernandes in Portugal in April 1988 were examples of that.

The informal amnesty offers of the past were made into law in December 1987. As no significant numbers of guerrillas had answered the amnesty call, the government had to recall some of its agents who had infiltrated Renamo abroad, as were the cases of Paulo Oliveira, alias Alcino, and Chanjunje João. The two 'defected' in 1988, ostensibly in response to the government's amnesty program.

As for Malawi, the plan devised with Zimbabwe was brushed aside. Claims of Renamo sanctuaries in Malawi, or of the Malawian territory being used as a launching pad for attacks on Mozambique, ceased to be made. Instead, a defense and security pact was signed with Malawi barely a month after Chissano's inauguration. The pact gave a role for the Malawi Army to play against Renamo, but not inside Malawi. As noted in a joint statement issued at the end of talks between Chissano and Banda in Blantyre in mid-1988, the Mozambican and Malawian leaders

> expressed their satisfaction with the continual and successful co-operation efforts between the two countries against the armed bandits as seen in the joint endeavour to ensure the functioning of the Nacala corridor through the involvement of Mozambican and Malawian troops.[22]

Afterwards, fingers were pointed at Kenya for allegedly training and infiltrating Renamo guerrillas into Zambézia. Renamo refuted the allegation, claiming that it was made either out of sheer ignorance or as a deliberate attempt to implicate the Kenyan government in the conflict. According to Renamo, one should go back to the 1950s, when floods ravaged Zambézia, to find a plausible explanation for the alleged Kenyan involvement. Britain sent in relief aid, including yellow maize flour from Kenya. The commodity, not usually produced or even consumed by Mozambicans, became known by residents of the flood-stricken areas as 'Kenya flour' because of the markings on the bags. When Renamo raided Gilé in June 1992, the guerrillas took yellow maize flour from the town, which they then cooked for themselves. Because of that, the residents began referring to the guerrillas as the 'Kenya people' or the 'Kenya group', hence the apparent Kenyan connection.[23]

4
Britain and Tanzania Assist FAM

By the end of 1984, a year after it had entered the Province of Maputo, Renamo made its presence felt in the southern region, establishing bases in Ponta d'Ouro, Bela Vista and Salamanga. Also in 1984 there were reports of Renamo guerrillas having been captured on the outskirts of the Maputo.

In 1985, the government tightened its security around the Mozambican capital. Additional checkpoints were introduced to prevent what the Maputo Military Command viewed as the 'possibility of the armed bandits infiltrating the city while mingling with the residents of Matola and Machava'.[24]

In the first quarter of 1986, Renamo established its Maputo Provincial Base at Ngungue, and in August its regional base near Manhiça. By the end of 1986 there were reports of guerrillas active in the Mozambican capital's Liberdade Ward. In a show of force, the government publicly executed captured Renamo guerrillas in the presence of the ward's residents.

Despite these and other measures, the security situation deteriorated further, forcing the government to seek additional foreign military assistance. In 1987, the Tanzania People's Defence Force (TPDF) joined in to beef up both ZNA and FAM forces. The TPDF's mission was to regain much of the territory lost to Renamo in Zambézia.

The 3000-strong TPDF contingent established its forward command post at Mocuba, Zambézia. Better organized and more effective than FAM, emphasizing the use of the air force and reconnaissance missions, the TPDF contingent did not, however, pose to the guerrillas the same threat that they faced from ZNA. Using primarily conventional tactics, the TPDF succeeded in regaining areas like Namanjavira, Alto Benfica, Megaza, Chire, Pinda, Milange, Tengua, Luabo, Marromeu and others.

Like the Zimbabweans, the TPDF subsequently placed recaptured territory under FAM control. But once deployed elsewhere, the Tanzanians could not prevent Renamo from returning to positions from which they had withdrawn.

As part of its efforts to restore control in Zambézia, in June 1987 the government assigned Snasp's counter-intelligence chief Lagos Lidimo as the province's military commander. Lidimo employed in Zambézia the same ruthless methods that had characterized his role in the security service. He was feared even among his own men, and was referred to by former government and Renamo members as having personally executed FAM officers who failed to comply with his orders in the province.

Military assistance came also from Britain. The British Conservative government, through Defense Systems Limited (DSL), expanded its training program for FAM's special forces. Initiated in 1983, the program had met veiled opposition from various FAM quarters, particularly the old and ill-trained members of the Mozambican military establishment. Committed to a conventional approach to the Renamo problem, some of them felt threatened by the likelihood of a new elite emerging in the country. Others, for whom the war had become a profitable venture, feared that their schemes would be undermined with the introduction of new blood. This prompted the British to set up their training camp at Cuamba, in the far north. Eventually, Britain decided that its interests would be best served with the transfer of the entire training program to Zimbabwe.[25] By operating the program from outside Mozambique, the United Kingdom was able to play a more prominent role in the Mozambican conflict without being actually accused of direct involvement.

Run by the British Military Advisory and Training Team (BMATT), the program started in February 1986 with the opening of the first camp in Nyanga, eastern Zimbabwe. In October that year, the British government awarded a £1.6 million contract to Defence Sales Limited for the supply of military hardware to FAM, including training.[26] Additional training facilities for FAM personnel were set up in Nyanga in April 1987 and in July 1990. At Nyanga, said Tom King, Britain's secretary of state for defense, 'BMATT would give the Mozambicans the best training in the world in counter-insurgency'.[27] Senior FAM officers were trained at the Sandhurst military academy in Britain.

Under Chissano, Mozambique renewed efforts to enlist US military assistance in the war against Renamo, despite the so-called Reagan Doctrine, which pledged support for resistance movements fighting pro-Soviet regimes. Under pressure from the State Department, the

Reagan administration was asked to drop Renamo from the list of such movements, and to assist the Frelimo government militarily. Attempts to provide US non-lethal aid to FAM were thwarted by the pro-Renamo lobby in the US Congress. Despite the setback, Mozambique remained the United States' largest recipient of economic aid in the whole of sub-Saharan Africa during both the Reagan and the Bush administrations.

Though on a lesser scale, the Zambian Army intervened in the conflict as well, by temporarily deploying units over the border with Tete Province. This led to Renamo taking retaliatory action inside Zambia.

Portugal too became indirectly involved in the Mozambican conflict, assisting both factions. Portugal's token hardware and training assistance to Renamo stemmed from the Frelimo government's decision to fund FP-25 activities.

In 1987, Spain announced that it would expand bilateral co-operation into the defense field. FAM officers received training at a Guardia Civil academy outside Madrid in early 1988. In October 1989, 160 FAM members completed training in Spain for the Mozambican Army's first 'anti-terrorist' unit, supposedly for the protection of a Spanish funded agricultural and livestock project north of Maputo.[28]

In mid-1987, Zimbabwean military instructors gave training to FAM's counter-insurgency units in Nhamatanda, central Mozambique. Zimbabwe expected to train 4500 FAM soldiers by 1988.[29]

In an unprecedented move, the official media began portraying the civil war as an ethnic dispute between northerners and southerners. Renamo activity in southern Mozambique was described as being spearheaded by either Ndau or Sena ethnic groups. It appears that the intention was to revive the old dispute with the Ndau in the minds of southerners, and in doing so hinder Renamo's attempts to establish itself among local villagers.

In a departure from Frelimo's stand on the so-called sequels of the traditional-feudal society, the government enlisted the support of Manuel António, a man claiming to have supernatural powers. António said he was immune to bullets thanks to a potion, or *naparama*, given to him by Jesus Christ. The government armed António and his militiamen (who also drank the potion and became known as Naparama), airlifting them to war zones in Nampula and Zambézia. Renamo acknowledged that the government's paramilitary force posed a 'temporary problem' to its guerrillas, and that it had to assign 'more experienced commanders' to areas where the Naparama were active so that they could handle the situation.[30] In mid-1991, Manuel António and 16 of his men were killed in a clash with Renamo in Nampula.

The Catholic Church in northern Mozambique regarded António's claims as sheer superstition and viewed him as being part of the government's psychological war effort. But Frelimo, in the eyes of its Nampula governor, saw the Naparama as 'a phenomenon that should be the subject of a profound analysis'.[31]

5
Renamo's Response

Zimbabwe's military intervention in the Mozambican civil war posed perhaps the biggest threat Renamo faced throughout the conflict. ZNA's counterinsurgency measures represented not only an unprecedented military challenge, but also undermined the power base that the guerrillas had built amongst the rural population. The displacement of villagers as a result of ZNA tactics caused food shortages, particularly in and around the Gorongosa Mountain, which had initially been marked by the Zimbabweans as their main target area. Subsequent FAM/ZNA/TPDF operations along the Zambeze valley worsened Renamo's situation in Sofala since the guerrillas' food supply lines from the agriculturally rich province of Zambézia were also disrupted. Hermínio Morais, a senior Renamo commander, conceded that had it not been for the partial cease-fire agreement of 1991, whereby ZNA forces were supposed to be confined to areas along the Beira and Limpopo corridors, Renamo would in the long run have found it extremely difficult to cope with the Zimbabweans' constant harassment of its positions.[32] Nonetheless, Renamo had to adapt to the new situation and try to make the best of it.

To deal with ZNA-operated pseudo guerrillas, Renamo commanders, through the traditional chiefs, impressed on villagers the need to be alert whenever approached by someone claiming to represent the guerrilla movement. Invariably, the chiefs or village headmen would engage the pseudos in protracted conversations to give time for the network of informers (the *mujiba*) to warn the next Renamo post.

After initial setbacks in the face of ZNA's fireforce raids, the guerrillas eventually succeeded in sustaining fewer casualties. 'Instead of retreating in the direction of the stop groups, as the enemy intended us to do', recalls Morais, we scattered sideways and even towards the advancing ground forces, trying to break through their lines. There were instances where the enemy ended up firing at each other since none of us were in the middle as they had expected.[33]

Adriano Faustino, a former Renamo chief of staff, noted that whenever the first air strike was launched, the guerrillas would remain static on the ground, against a tree or a rock, hoping that the air force gunships would not recognize them. 'This worked perfectly, especially where the terrain was of a more barren type', said Faustino.[34]

In yet another attempt to forestall ZNA's plans, Renamo increased the number of bases around already existing ones. Its military structure was reorganized with companies split into more platoons and platoons into newly created units of five men. Known as the *equipa*, or team, these units set up small camps over a vast area with the intention of easily identifying advancing forces, and also of not providing them with an easy target. At the crack of dawn, the guerrillas, with small portions of dried meat and mealie meal in their rucksacks, would leave their camps and mount ambushes on tracks leading to the main bases. After sunset, the groups returned to their camps, leaving the tracks booby-trapped during the night and warning the local population not to venture into designated areas. This led to a reduction in attacks on Renamo bases. At night, according to Morais, the guerrillas

shelled enemy positions to force them to respond and waste ammunition and live under a permanent state of tension. We also used to set up decoy guerrilla camps, starting small fires near known enemy positions. Often, the enemy would respond with mortar attacks.[35]

To ease ZNA pressure on its forces, Renamo decided in May 1987 to retaliate inside Zimbabwe. Operating in groups of between five and ten men, Renamo initially launched attacks from Tete, and subsequently from Manica, along Zimbabwe's northeastern and eastern border with Mozambique. Afterwards, attacks were reportedly carried out deeper inside Zimbabwe, with the guerrillas claiming to have set up 'operational military bases' in that country. Police stations and government vehicles were said to have come under attack. Economic and civilian targets appeared also to have been hit by Renamo, judging from government sources in both Zimbabwe and Mozambique. The Mozambique News Agency (AIM) reported that on 28 July Renamo had crossed the border from Manica to attack the Katiyo Tea Estates. A Harare-based correspondent reported in August that Renamo had hacked to death three elderly Zimbabwean men, abducted eight women and set a village ablaze in northeastern Zimbabwe near the border post of Nyamapanda. The report said the incident had occurred some 50 km from the area where Renamo had killed 12 Zimbabwean villagers in June.[36] In September, Renamo claimed to have killed 17 ZNA soldiers in the Mount Darwin area, some 125 km northeast of Harare.[37]

In the wake of renewed incidents inside Zimbabwe, the country's agriculture and land affairs minister, Moven Mahachi, accused workers employed in farms in the Middle Sabi region of eastern Zimbabwe of collaborating with Renamo.[38] Renamo attacks continued in the following year. In January 1988, Renamo said it had attacked Marondera, east of Harare, as well as Chipinge and Dangabvuro, near the Zimbabwean eastern border, resulting in the death of 32 ZNA soldiers.[39]

Towards the end of the year, Zimbabwean Vice President Simon Muzenda announced in Parliament that 'Renamo was no longer active as before, and the number of atrocities against Zimbabwe's civilian population had decreased' as a result of intensified ZNA operations along the border with Mozambique. Muzenda, however, pointed out that ZNA 'was having some problems with the bandits because they were fighting a guerrilla war and it is difficult to assess the MNR tactics'.[40]

In late 1989, SARDC reported that between September and November, Renamo had carried out 33 attacks across Zimbabwe's eastern border, resulting in the death of 43 Zimbabweans. The report noted that Renamo continued to attack Zimbabwe's communication and fuel lines to the port of Beira, and that seven attempts had been made to sabotage the Beira–Feruka oil pipeline in October and November, bringing Zimbabwe's petrol, diesel and jet fuel losses to almost 2 million litres in 1989.[41]

The possibility of an alliance between Renamo and some of Zimbabwe's opposition forces, though plausible, never materialized. Claims by the Reverend Ndabaningi Sithole, a veteran Zimbabwean nationalist belonging to the same ethnic group as the Renamo leader, that his newly formed Zimbabwe Freedom Army, Zifa, had struck an accord with the Mozambican guerrillas, appeared to have been nothing more than wishful thinking. Morais, who had first hand knowledge of Renamo's operations inside Zimbabwe, stresses that no Zimbabwean known to be opposed to Robert Mugabe's government ever operated with Renamo inside that country right up to the end of the war.

The intervention of foreign forces in the Mozambican civil war gave rise to claims and counterclaims of wholesale atrocities against the civilian population. In the case of the ZNA, in particular members of its 5th Brigade, Renamo often accused it of indiscriminately bombing villages perceived to harbor or provide assistance to anti-government guerrillas.[42] 'The pattern of atrocities by the Zimbabwean military within Mozambique', noted the London-based Renamo lobby group, Mozambique Institute, 'mirrors their behaviour within their own country throughout the early 1980s.'[43]

When the 5th Brigade was deployed in Matabeleland in early 1983, says Welshman Ncube, a professor in the Faculty of Law at the University of Zimbabwe, 'it subjected the people of that region to severe brutalities'. Prof. Ncube cites Ndebele villagers as giving accounts of

> harrowing and hair-raising tales of massacres, cold-blooded murders, torture, rapings and destruction of houses and other property. Hundreds and hundreds of civilians were massacred.[44]

In a report published in March 1997, the Catholic Commission for Justice and Peace in Zimbabwe stated that the 5th Brigade had been responsible for 'thousands of atrocities, including murders, mass physical torture and the burning of property'. As a result of 5th Brigade action, said the report, 'many communities lost huts and granaries, and village members who had been killed or abducted'.[45]

The use of defoliants in conjunction with the relocation of villagers came to light after ZNA's intervention in the Mozambique civil war. According to Renamo, in late 1986, light aircraft, equipped with crop spraying devices, released chemicals over trees along the Guro–Changara stretch of the Tete road.[46] The claim was subsequently corroborated by independent sources. Richard English, a tourist who traveled from Zimbabwe to the city of Tete in early 1987, told the BBC that 'the roadside had been defoliated and the population moved, the villages were empty, the trees were dead'. English, who was travelling with his companion in a convoy escorted by ZNA, added:

> It's mostly chemical defoliation in order that Renamo can't be lurking in the bushes ready to ambush the convoy that does come through. And until we got to Tete we didn't see a soul, not a soul.[47]

In December 1986, Renamo accused FAM and ZNA of using chemicals during raids in the Marínguè and Gorongosa areas. Renamo claimed that at least 557 civilians were killed in the raids.[48]

As part of its counterinsurgency operations, the human rights organization, Africa Watch, reported that ZNA had been 'deliberately depopulating a wide swathe of territory down the Mozambican side of the border'. The practice of clearing roadsides so as to prevent guerrilla ambushes became evident in other of Mozambique's highways. An area of 500 metres to each side of the Nhamatanda–Chimoio stretch of the Beira corridor was cleared of any vegetation by ZNA's engineering corps. The Amatongas forest, through which the highway runs, was literally wiped out.[49] Villagers in the Maluana region north of Maputo were forcibly evicted from their homes next to the great north–south highway, and their homes flattened to the ground.

Poisoning of water wells in traditional Renamo areas was said to be a common practice by government forces. Dhlakama's nephew, Francisco Girmoio, and some of his men died in 1983 after drinking poisoned water from a well in Inhambane. Poisoned bags of flour were deliberately abandoned by government forces in Renamo areas, as if they were spoils of an attack.[50] In the same province, the Mozambican government embarked on a program to contaminate Renamo bases with Neisseria gonorrhoeae. Women infected with the bacterium were instructed to live in villages near known Renamo bases and befriend guerrillas at random.[51]

6
Recruits and Collaborators

Both factions in the Mozambican civil war resorted to the press-ganging of recruits, including youths. Renamo was singled out for having enlisted children to serve both as soldiers and informers. Given UNICEF's definition of a child as someone up to the age of 17, it can be conceded that FAM too had children in its ranks.

As is normally the case with unconventional military forces, those in the Renamo ranks had no defined length of service to complete. The same could be applied to FAM although regulations clearly stated that conscripts would be demobilized after completing the standard period of military service. Organizational constraints, coupled with the need to increase the size of the armed forces, resulted in a large number of FAM soldiers serving longer than expected.

In line with the government's Compulsory Military Service (SMO) plan, recruitment at the height of the war was conducted in a most unorthodox fashion. The 'take off shirt' campaign was how the routine practice of arbitrarily rounding up youngsters perceived to be eligible for military service became known. Once stopped on streets or picked up in public places, including schools, youngsters had their shirts taken off so that they could be easily identified if attempting to escape. They would normally be tied with a rope around the waist and taken to waiting military trucks. An effort was made to have recruits trained at camps far from their homes so as to avoid desertion.

Under SMO's arbitrary methods of recruitment, children as young as 13 were drafted for military service. The chairman of the Mozambican Association of Demobilized Soldiers (Amodeg), himself a former FAM officer, commented that

It was only a question of unfolding a rifle's butt. If it reached one's shoulders then he was eligible for military service and drafted. I think there were hundreds upon hundreds of such cases.[52]

Confidential Mozambican government statistics show that out of a group of 15 682 FAM soldiers earmarked for demobilization in 1992, 12.4 per cent had been enlisted when they were 16 or 17; 4.38 per cent when they were 14 or 15, and 2.16 per cent when they were 13.[53]

In the rural areas, Renamo's recruiting methods relied also on the use of force, though on a lesser scale because its army was smaller than FAM's.

Despite FAM's effort to beef up its ranks, the disorganized state of its logistics, the inefficient administration and command structures, the meager remuneration of military personnel, coupled with combat fatigue and rampant corruption, thwarted the prospects of an effective campaign against Renamo. Attempts to improve FAM's standards with assistance from foreign quarters proved fruitless. Regardless of the standard attained in training programs outside Mozambique, ultimately the new intakes had to operate under the existing FAM command structure and adhere to the old conventional approach to guerrilla warfare. Moreover, they were subject to the same logistical constraints that slowly but surely were wearing through the fabric of the Mozambican military establishment.

What caused resentment amongst those trained outside the country was that, upon their return home, the government lowered the grades that they had reached on completion of training. The Mozambican authorities feared that there would be friction among other FAM members who had the same or even longer time of service, but would be junior to them. The last thing the government wanted was a 1974 Portuguese-type of military coup stirred by promotion disputes, and thus it failed to address the problem head on. In the end, there were many desertions among those trained by the Libyans and the British, some of them fleeing to South Africa.

Rather than having boosted their morale, the intervention of foreign forces created dissent among FAM's rank and file. With more resources and better training, ZNA forces, for instance, tended to look down on the ill-equipped and unfit Mozambican Army. The last straw came when ZNA personnel began preying on cash-strapped Mozambique womenfolk. Residents of Chimoio, the forward headquarters of the ZNA Special Task Force, complained that the Zimbabwean contingent promoted prostitution in the city. They also blamed the ZNA personnel for the flourishing of Chimoio's black market.[54] In exchange for essential commodities smuggled from Zimbabwe, ZNA officers traded in ivory and rhino horns. Evidence of ZNA personnel being involved in poaching of elephants and rhinos in Mozambique came from within the ranks of the Zimbabwean contingent itself. ZNA Captain Edwin Nleya, who served in Mozambique until December 1988, threatened to disclose the names of those involved in the racket. Detained by CIO members, Nleya was subsequently found murdered.[55] Some two years later, ZNA Lieutenant Shepherd Chisango met the same fate when he tried to prevent ZNA military vehicles crossing the Mutare border with a consignment of what he believed to be ivory and rhino horns as well as narcotics.[56]

At senior level, the animosity between the two armies was also self-evident. Senior ZNA officers in Mozambique felt that there would be no end to the war unless the calibre of FAM forces was reviewed. According to the CIO:

> The war will be protracted as there are no signs of it getting anywhere near to a solution and in this context the need to reorganize the legitimate defence force of the country should remain ZNA's priority as demonstrated by those already trained.[57]

A similar view of FAM forces was held by the TPDF command in Mozambique, who 'was not happy to operate under someone considered junior in rank and pompous in professional approach . . . '.[58]

It was from around this time, Renamo claims, that FAM began collaborating with the guerrillas. Government soldiers are said to have given information to Renamo through the latter's network of informers, the *mujiba*. These were usually youngsters who lived in villages, towns or even cities and had relatives in the guerrilla ranks. They mingled with the population and commuted between their homes and Renamo forward posts without arousing suspicion.

Renamo has also claimed that FAM units failed to carry through their operations, deliberately abandoning war materiel, which they knew would end up in rebel hands, or actually making it reach guerrilla bases. After the war, the official Mozambique news agency (AIM) reported that FAM had regularly supplied military equipment to a Renamo base in Sofala. According to AIM, 'Mozambican air force helicopters often landed at Renamo bases in Gorongosa, apparently to unload supplies'.[59]

Still according to Renamo, government soldiers radioed Renamo to warn the guerrillas of military plans or of attacks in the offing. Renamo says it was kept informed of changes in FAM's telecommunications codebooks. Air traffic controllers at the Beira Air Force Base are said to have informed the Renamo headquarters at Maríngue of pending air raids.

Vareia Manje, who was at the head of Renamo's provincial base in Maputo from 1986 until the end of the war, says he was often warned in advance by FAM elements of air force or artillery attacks on his Ngungue base. Ngungue could be reached by air from the Maputo Air Force Base in a matter of minutes, and it was on several occasions evacuated prior to air or major ground strikes. And even during air attacks, Vareia points out, it was obvious that the visible targets were deliberately missed. 'The pilots simply did not wish to bomb their brothers', he claimed.[60] Or feared being hit by Renamo's anti-aircraft weapons, one could argue.

For families whose sons happened to be serving different factions of the conflict, the time to define allegiances would eventually arise. 'It was a question of who could best convince the other about the justness of their cause, and start collaborating from then on', noted a Renamo member.[61]

7
The Washington Lobby

Renamo's early association with the rural population of Mozambique influenced the manner in which the movement evolved in the following years. Its rank and file was primarily of peasant extract, their views reflecting the environment in which they lived. If, on the one hand, the lack of a viable sanctuary in any of Mozambique's neighbouring countries from which Renamo could promote its cause internationally served to strengthen the symbiotic relationship between the guerrilla movement and the peasants at home, on the other hand, it resulted in the widening of the divide between Renamo and the outside world. The death of Cristina in 1983 and the signing of the Nkomati Accord in the following year contributed to the further isolation of the guerrillas. Evo Fernandes' brief role as Renamo's secretary general went virtually unnoticed. Unlike Cristina, who at least realized the importance of working with the Mozambican exiles to further Renamo's cause, Fernandes merely kept them in the cold, antagonizing most of them.

The effect that the international community could have on the outcome of Renamo's campaign to oust the Frelimo government was never really appreciated by the guerrillas. After all, as Renamo saw it, a victory or defeat in the war would be decided domestically, not in foreign capitals.

It was, therefore, not surprising that a serious initiative to promote Renamo internationally would be taken not by the organization or any of its foreign missions, but by outsiders. Despite the perception that Renamo was merely a warmongering organization with no ideology or coherent political program, there were quarters in the West that felt otherwise and were prepared to give a hand to the guerrilla movement.

The Freedom Research Foundation was instrumental in introducing Renamo to influential circles in the United States. Jack Wheeler, an academic from California and a personal friend of President Reagan, led the Foundation. Seizing on Reagan's policy of supporting guerrilla movements opposed to pro-Soviet regimes throughout the world as a counter measure to the Brezhnev Doctrine, in 1983 Wheeler traveled to all guerrilla hot spots, from Nicaragua to Afghanistan, Eritrea and Angola. His ultimate goal was to bring all the guerrilla movements under the umbrella of Resistance International, a loose group around which gathered Western European intellectuals of the likes of Raymond Aron and Simone Veil, as well as dissidents from the Soviet bloc.

Wheeler's effort to band Renamo together with the other movements came up against strong opposition from the US State Department's Bureau of African Affairs. His initiative coincided with a warming of American–Mozambican relations. In tandem with Bureau's policy, Chester Crocker had already decided to scrap Renamo from his agenda. Renamo had become a spanner in his 'constructive engagement' policy, a nonentity that warranted neither assistance nor sympathy for the very government that the Mozambican guerrillas wanted to oust was the same that was proving useful to the Department's assistant secretary for African affairs.

When Resistance International was about to be launched at the UNITA headquarters in May 1985, Renamo was not invited to the founding ceremony. More important issues had prevailed in UNITA leader Savimbi's evaluation of what was at stake, and which required him to be attuned to Bureau of African Affairs thinking. Savimbi eagerly awaited the repeal of the Clark Amendment in mid-1985, which would put an end to the ban on American assistance to Angolan political forces. Any public display of UNITA sympathy for Renamo would be counter-productive, especially in the light of an earlier announcement by the American ambassador to Maputo that his country would provide military assistance to the Frelimo government, and of the assertion by Crocker's deputy, Frank Wisner, that Renamo 'had its days numbered' since its leaders 'were climbing up the walls'.[62] And in view of the US–Mozambican *démarche* on the Cuban presence in Angola, Savimbi felt that his political ambitions would be closer to fruition once the Angolan government was deprived of Cuba's military support. Indicative of Savimbi's rationale were the remarks by his Washington representative, who believed that 'President Samora Machel had shown an understanding of the conflict in Angola and that is the kind of understanding which we find much appreciative'.[63]

Savimbi went out of his way to underline his position, not only by publicly dissociating UNITA from Renamo, but also by adding his voice to the campaign to discredit the Mozambican movement. In common with Frelimo as well as Crocker and his deputies, Savimbi felt that Renamo lacked a foundation that could legitimize its struggle.[64] For them, Renamo had no right to exist since it had not fought for Mozambique's self-determination, despite the fact that the movement stemmed from conditions that only emerged after independence.

The Frelimo government would later on reward the UNITA leader for his stand on Renamo. A Mozambican band was flown from Maputo to Jamba to perform at one of the many public relations exercises that Savimbi regularly organized at his headquarters. The occasion this time was the UNITA leader's 55th birthday celebrations.

Nonetheless, Wheeler continued campaigning on behalf of Renamo in the United States. Conservative groups, including the World Anti-Communist League, the Heritage Foundation, the Conservative Caucus, the American African Public Affairs Council, joined in. In May 1986, Renamo opened the Mozambique Information Office in Washington. Its executive director, Thomas Schaaf, an American reared in Zimbabwe, operated from the same building where The Heritage Foundation was located. Renamo had in Schaaf, as well as in the Mozambique Institute's David Hoile, the most articulate public promoters of its cause abroad.

Congressmen from both floors of the US legislature rallied behind Renamo, keeping in check the Reagan administration's policy on Mozambique. In March 1985, Howard Wolpe, chairman of the Democrat-controlled House of Representatives Africa Subcommittee, opposed a motion placed by the administration, seeking approval for an $18 million aid package for the Frelimo government, including $3.2 million for military training and non-lethal equipment. In the Senate, Robert Kasten, chairman of the Appropriations Foreign Operations Subcommittee, followed suit. Wisner's plea on behalf of the administration left the legislators unperturbed, despite his claim that President Machel was ready to change allegiances, that is, from being pro-Soviet to become Western oriented, but was unable to do so because of Renamo. 'The Mozambique government's turn away from heavy reliance on the Soviet Union', Wisner argued, 'is being called into question by continued anti-government violence committed by Renamo...'[65]

It was clear that in US government circles, the question of Mozambique's foreign allegiance was taking precedence over the domestic causes that had led to the outbreak of the civil war. Regardless of whether Machel was pro-Soviet or would suddenly become a Western ally, the fact remained that Mozambique was still under totalitarian rule with the Frelimo leaders showing no signs of embracing what they dismissively

called the 'bourgeois concept' of parliamentary democracy, one of Renamo's key demands. Renamo had indeed been a contributing factor to
the Mozambique government's apparent change of heart. If Frelimo
faced no domestic opposition it would be highly unlikely that Samora
Machel would be predisposed to consider a reversal of allegiances merely
to address the economic dire straits engulfing the country. For Frelimo,
after all, 1981 had been a successful economic year, and had it not been
for the war the country would have been on the way to fulfilling the
tenets reiterated at the party's 1977 Congress, when Frelimo formally
became a self-styled Marxist–Leninist Vanguard Party. In any event,
Frelimo, and, after independence, its government had been staunch
'natural allies' of the Soviet bloc long before Renamo came into being.

The March 1985 bill was subsequently voted through by both Houses
of Congress, but with strings attached. Specifically, before it could get
American aid, the Frelimo government had to improve the human
rights situation at home; restore free enterprise and property rights;
reduce the estimated 1600 Eastern Bloc military advisers to 55; commit
itself to free elections by September 1986; and hold discussions with all
major political groups in the country.[66]

In view of the setback it suffered in Congress, the US government
assured Frelimo that all was not lost. Ambassador Jon de Vos pledged
that the Reagan administration would be 'working very, very forcibly to
eliminate these amendments and to restore funds for assistance to
Mozambique in 1986'.[67] On the question of free elections, Machel
cited the former American ambassador to Harare, David Miller, as having told him in 1985 to 'accept the formation of a puppet party so that
they could say in the United States that there is democracy in Mozambique because there is more than one party'.[68] Frelimo, however, was
unwilling to abrogate its claim of being 'the leading force of state and
society', which made no provision for any other political grouping,
puppet or otherwise.

When Machel visited the United States in September, Senator Mal-
colm Wallop and Dan Burton, vice chairman of the House of Representatives Africa Subcommittee, introduced legislation in Congress to end
US economic aid to the Frelimo government. Moreover, the two congressmen called for financial assistance to Renamo during the 1986
fiscal year, totaling $5 million.[69] In December, Wallop and Burton
invited Dhlakama to visit the United States and address the Congress.
The State Department declined to issue visas to a Renamo delegation.

Following Machel's death in October 1986, Burton urged President
Reagan to endorse Renamo's call for a cease-fire and free elections.

Burton told the president that 'it was time that the State Department should take its head out of the sand' and realize that Renamo presented 'an opportunity for a new, truly nationalist, pro-Western government in Mozambique'. As for Crocker, Burton wanted him 'summarily fired'.

The administration told Burton that it still believed the Mozambican government was leaning towards the West, and that US aid to Mozambique would continue as planned.[70]

The administration's repeated claim that Mozambique was gradually shifting its Soviet allegiance, and that this and other moves constituted what Secretary of State George Shultz once referred to as 'major desirable changes in its orientation',[71] eventually prompted the Mozambican government to put the record straight. Statements of this nature could certainly go down well in Washington circles, but embarrassed the Frelimo leadership who felt they were being publicly treated as mere puppets, keen on abandoning one master for another. Information Minister Teodato Hunguana denied that Mozambique was shifting from one side to another, stressing that the Soviet Union had been 'an historic ally'.[72] Earlier, Chissano said Mozambique was not relinquishing its 'socialist option' because it had chosen this path 'as a result of our experiences with the scientific teachings of Marxism-Leninism'.[73]

The Renamo lobby in Washington continued to exert pressure on the Reagan administration to change its policy on Mozambique. In April 1987, Burton wrote to the president to say that there was an urgent need to change US policy of 'supporting and courting the communist government of Mozambique'. Touching on a sore point, Burton said:

> We are distressed about the possibility that on such a critical issue our policy might be determined by the State Department alone without reasonable debate within the administration and a final decision by you.[74]

In the wake of Burton's missive, Senator Bob Dole urged the administration not to restrict its assistance to the Frelimo government, but to also deal with Renamo in view of the famine afflicting the drought-stricken areas of southern Mozambique. Recently, USAID had claimed it had difficulty in contacting Renamo to include its areas in the delivery of relief aid. Dole called 'on the State Department and AID to get off their duffs, pick up the telephone, call the local Renamo office here in Washington – and start the food flowing to people who do not have much time left'.[75]

Dole also wrote to Schultz and the USAID administrator, Peter McPherson, proposing that the US government undertook a three-part program. Specifically, he wanted the administration to urge a temporary cease-fire by both Frelimo and Renamo forces for the sole purpose of permitting delivery of food to people in war-torn areas; to establish contacts with Renamo to explore the possibility of facilitating the provision of food assistance through its organization or through some other vehicle, to all needy people in Mozambique; and to offer to establish communications between the Mozambican government and Renamo for the sole and non-political purpose of facilitating the delivery of relief supplies.[76]

Given the State Department's reluctance to distribute relief aid to Renamo areas, Congressmen continued to apply pressure on the administration. In the Senate Committee on Foreign Relations, Jesse Helms blocked the confirmation of Melissa Wells as ambassador-designate to Mozambique. Backed by 27 Senators, Helms submitted an unprecedented list of 247 questions for Wells to answer. 'Until the State Department backs up and agrees to treat freedom fighters in all countries the same way, then you are going to have a problem with me', Helms told a Senate hearing seeking Wells' confirmation. The senator took issue with Wells for echoing the Frelimo government's description of Renamo as 'armed bandits'. Senator Helms made it a condition of Wells' confirmation that there should be a simple 'yes' from the State Department in response to his demand for talks between Renamo and the administration.[77] The State Department stuck to its guns and withdrew the nomination for the time being.

Meanwhile, a group of 28 members of the House of Representatives, led by Jack Kemp and Burton, invited Dhlakama for a visit to the United States so that the Renamo leader 'could present his cause before American Congressmen and the citizens of our country'.[78] The State Department once again refused to grant Dhlakama an entry visa.

In November 1987, Frank Carlucci, the US president's national security adviser, received a group of six Renamo lobbyists, including Thomas Schaaf and Grover Norquist, foreign policy adviser to Pierre S du Pont, a former presidential candidate. According to Norquist, Carlucci assured them that if Chissano did not move soon towards opening negotiations with Renamo, the administration's attitude towards him would change.[79]

Prior to the November meeting, Renamo's foreign relations secretary, Artur da Fonseca, had been granted an audience at the White House. Patrick Buchanan, the White House director of communications, was reported to have organized the meeting.

The Renamo lobby in Washington proved that it was able to obstruct US government policy on Mozambique, and keep the Mozambican authorities in check.

The Mozambican authorities saw these developments as the nullification of all that they had laboriously done to isolate Renamo internationally. They feared that eventually Renamo could achieve, if not the same, at least a similar status to that which UNITA enjoyed in the United States. Thus Renamo could be in a position to challenge efforts to destroy it domestically.

The Bureau of African Affairs felt embarrassed given the Frelimo government's willingness to develop closer ties with the United States. Crocker, in particular, saw that rewarding the Frelimo government for creating conditions for talks on the withdrawal of Cuban forces from Angola and finding accommodation with South Africa, was being systematically thwarted in Congress by people who simply did not want to let Renamo vanish into the wilderness.

A new strategy had to be devised. Ultimately, it would be one that would not only destroy Renamo's already dwindling credibility in foreign circles, but also force its sympathizers to reconsider their public show of support for the Mozambican guerrillas. The aim was to prove that the guerrillas were not 'freedom fighters' nor was the movement's leadership 'truly nationalist' as US congressmen claimed them to be.

Frelimo made use of an incident of FAM's making in which 424 civilians were reportedly massacred at Homoíne, and Renamo was blamed for it.[80] For its part, the State Department engaged Robert Gersony, a refugee consultant, to write a report in which he portrayed Renamo as being primarily to blame for an increase of 300 per cent in the number of Mozambican refugees in southern Africa.[81] In his report, Gersony endorsed the official Mozambican estimate that Renamo had murdered more than 100 000 civilians.[82]

After raiding Homoíne and putting government forces to flight, Renamo faced a concerted counter-attack. Combat vehicles from Maxixe fired upon the town from a nearby road, while the Air Force strafed suspected guerrilla positions, eventually evicting Renamo from Homoíne. The Homoíne carnage occurred when the Libyan-trained FAM unit based at Panda went on to Homoíne and took the government forces that had just regained control of the town for Renamo guerrillas, and acted accordingly. The government, noted a Snasp operative, 'had to wash its hands of the incident, and to blame Renamo was the most convenient way of doing it'.[83]

Gersony's report overlooked the fact that the flow of refugees – the bulk of which fled to Malawi, as he acknowledged it – had coincided with the intervention of the Zimbabwean and Tanzanian armies in the Mozambican civil war. The introduction of unprecedented counter-insurgency measures, as discussed above, was designed to deprive Renamo, if not of the support, at least of the contact with the rural population. That such measures led to the displacement of persons was corroborated by the Mozambique government's own relief agency, the DPCCN. The agency attributed the displacement of persons in Zambézia Province, which borders Malawi, to military operations against 'armed bandit hideouts', that is, Renamo bases. A DPCCN report revealed that in Zambézia's Pebane area the number of displaced persons rose from 64 000 in February 1988 to 151 000 in August 1999. The trend continued in the following years. By June 1990, said the report, Zambézia had a total of 1.2 million needy people. Of these, 909 598 had been displaced and 205 735 affected by the war. The report noted that:

> The influx of people stems from military operations by the Mozam-bican Army against armed bandit hideouts in that province, which permitted the freeing of a large number of people who lived in captivity.[84]

Epilog

In mid-1989, the Frelimo government finally agreed to a political settlement of the civil war. But it took nearly a year before the peace talks could be firmly put on track. Initially, the government was as ambivalent as at the time of the tentative 1984 peace talks. It saw the need for peace, and yet it had difficulty in accepting that this implied not only negotiating with its opponents on an equal footing, but above all acknowledging that there was opposition in Mozambique.

The government's 12-point settlement agenda – which the Mozambican president saw as neither a peace plan nor an official document, but a 'non-paper' – stated that what Mozambique had been witnessing since 1976 was not a civil war, but a destabilizing operation with no political goals in mind. Renamo, said Chissano in his first public acknowledgement of the peace initiative, 'should not be considered a political movement, let alone a party – they are none of those'. As a precondition for direct talks, Renamo not only had to accept this, thus effectively negating the very essence of its campaign, but also unconditionally cease fire – 'to stop all terrorist and banditry actions', in Chissano's words – and then seek to be reintegrated into the existing political order. Afterwards, the government would create conditions for all Mozambicans, including Renamo, to participate in discussions on how the country's political, economic, social and cultural affairs should be dealt with. Acceptance of the Constitution, which Renamo had long rejected for not having been drafted and approved by an elected Parliament, was another prerequisite.[1]

Nonetheless, Chissano's announcement would set in motion an irreversible process: one that would be full of ironies.

The Catholic Church, whom the government media had consistently vilified for calling for dialogue with Renamo, became the mediating party. As the first session of exploratory talks was scheduled to start in Nairobi on 12 June 1989, the Renamo delegation failed to arrive in the Kenyan capital. About a week before, FAM and ZNA forces mounted a concerted attack on the movement's stronghold in Sofala. The Renamo-controlled Massala area, particularly the landing strip from where the delegation was due to fly out of Mozambique, came under ground and air attacks.[2]

Once in Nairobi, the Renamo delegation stated its commitment to peace and reconciliation in Mozambique, and that in the end there should be neither losers nor winners. To accomplish that, Renamo reiterated its long-standing principle of establishing a democratic form of government in Mozambique, while upholding the values of traditional society. Renamo saw its armed campaign not as an end in itself, but as a last resort to uphold the rights denied to Mozambicans. In its 16-point proposal, Renamo called for the cessation of propaganda directed against the movement, as this would not change the political and military reality in Mozambique nor would it be conducive to national reconciliation. As for the presence of foreign forces, Renamo saw it as an obstacle to peace and an affront to the dignity of Mozambicans, and an infringement of their sovereignty and independence.[3]

269

Although Chissano saw Renamo's proposals as 'meaningless', the Frelimo government eventually dropped all preconditions for a negotiated settlement of the conflict. Frelimo's room to maneuver was in fact quite limited. The country's deteriorating economic and military situation, the doubts that had begun to be raised in Zimbabwe as to the viability of its intervention in the Mozambican dispute, as well as the international community's second thoughts about financially supporting a government with an unstable country to rule, were the main reasons that made Chissano opt for negotiations. Even Britain reviewed its policy of assisting the Frelimo government in resolving the conflict militarily. Instead, the British would discreetly assist and advise Renamo at the negotiating table.[4]

As Nairobi and then Blantyre were no longer acceptable venues for both the government and Renamo, the two sides agreed to meet in Rome, under the auspices of the Roman Catholic St Egidio Community. The first meeting was held on 8 July 1990, at the end of which both sides committed themselves 'to end the war and to create political, economic and social conditions for a lasting peace'. They pledged to concentrate on what united rather than what divided them.[5]

As the second round of direct peace talks was under way, Frelimo announced in Maputo that it would introduce a multiparty system in Mozambique, despite, as Chissano claimed, the objections from the overwhelming majority of Mozambicans to a democratic form of government. This and a number of political reforms announced unilaterally, but which Renamo had long been advocating, were clearly aimed at cutting the ground from under the movement's feet and depriving it of an agenda at the negotiating table. Renamo had also been calling for the disbanding of the political police, Snasp, but the government renamed it SISE, leaving more or less intact the draconian powers that the former had always enjoyed.

The same happened to Parliament, which ceased to be called the People's Assembly and became known as the Assembly of the Republic, but with the same unelected Frelimo Party deputies as its sole members. Even the country's name, which Renamo's program of action stated would be Republic of Mozambique, was adopted by Frelimo when it introduced a new Constitution while the peace talks continued in Rome. The Frelimo government's changes fell short of addressing other issues like an independent judiciary and a nonpartisan news media.

Despite the political reforms, the talks dragged on for more than two years until agreement was reached on a number of issues raised by Renamo. These included the confinement of foreign troops to positions far from Renamo zones, and their withdrawal from the Mozambican territory before elections could be held; the formation of a single, non-partisan national army with members drawn from both warring factions; the reorganization of the police force whose activities, in addition to being monitored by a National Commission for Police Affairs at which Renamo was represented, had to conform with fundamental human rights and freedoms; the disbanding of private armies like the Naparama; and the curtailing of SISE's powers, which was placed under the control of a 21-member National Intelligence Commission at which Renamo was also represented.

The United Nations was accorded special supervisory and controlling powers during the transition to the envisaged multiparty democracy, which, to all intents and purposes, signified that the Frelimo government would temporarily surrender its sovereignty to the world body. Accordingly, the United Nations was to chair a Supervisory and Monitoring Commission established within the framework of the peace accord, and act as guarantor of the first free elections in the country. Also during the transition to democracy, Renamo was accorded full jurisdictional powers over areas under its control, and the government pledged not to offer any hostility towards the movement's administration structures as well as the traditional authorities in place in such areas. Furthermore, President Chissano undertook that his government would not enact any laws that were contrary to the terms of the protocols that had been signed since the start of the Rome peace talks.[6]

As part of a World Bank-sponsored Economic Recovery Program introduced in early 1987, the Frelimo government gradually abandoned its centrally planned economy. Those staunchly opposed to matters entrepreneurial resurfaced as fervently pro-capitalist as they had been pro-Marxist. They would in due course use their positions in government and the influence that they commanded within the ruling circles to further their business ventures in the banking, transport, communications, investment and industrial sectors. As the government reinstated private ownership of housing, law chambers and health clinics, Frelimo members, who had equated it with 'exploitation, oppression and humiliation of the people', were amongst the first to take advantage of the new situation.

To date, land remains state property. But since the economic liberalization, government officials and ordinary Mozambicans have been investing heavily in land. The new landowners have neither the capacity nor the resources to develop the huge tracts of land registered in their names. Their only hope appears to be to use their newly acquired assets as a stake in business ventures likely to be proposed by leading foreign companies.

The privatization of state enterprises, as recommended by the World Bank, is generally seen as a means of serving a privileged minority closely associated with the establishment. People in key positions have seized the opportunity to benefit from an economy that is subsidized by over 60 per cent from abroad. Contracts for externally funded projects and the importation of merchandise are normally awarded to those who control tender boards or are able to influence their decisions.

Multiparty elections have been held since the signing of the 1992 peace accord. Mozambique's experiment with multiparty politics suggests that the consolidation of democracy in the country will be an uphill battle. Elections at central and local levels have been dogged by controversy.

In the 1994 elections, there were claims of fraud, with the UN mission privately conceding that the government had been responsible for a number of irregularities. Frelimo retained power despite scoring less than half of the overall number of ballots. The combined 55.7 per cent of the votes won by the opposition parties did not alter the status quo owing to the d'Hondt system of distribution of seats in Parliament. Advised by the international community, Renamo accepted the results. With no governing experience, the former guerrilla movement would in a short period of time have worn out its credibility if faced with the mammoth task of steering the country away from the chaotic social and economic situation in which it found itself after the war.

In 1998, the opposition parties boycotted the local government elections in protest against the ruling Frelimo Party's decision to organize the polls only in specific areas of the country. The move was interpreted as an indication that Frelimo feared losing power if it agreed to hold elections in all of the country's constituencies. Less than 15 per cent of the electorate turned out on polling day. The Supreme Court validated the election results as reflecting the will of the people.

In the December 1999 polls, the Frelimo-dominated National Elections Commission (CNE) delayed the release of funds donated by the international community to assist competing parties in their campaign. Unaffected by this, Frelimo and its presidential candidate campaigned throughout the country while the other parties waited for funding. The CNE further delayed the announcement of the election results after ordering that information fed into its database should no longer be checked against result sheets certified by polling station officers representing the various political parties. Accredited independent observers were prevented from monitoring the counting of ballots.

Three days behind schedule, the CNE declared the Frelimo Party and its presidential candidate as winners. Second came the Renamo-Electoral Union, which won in six of the most densely populated of the country's 11 provinces.

The coalition opposed the results, alleging that over 1 000 result sheets had not been entered into the CNE database. This and several other alleged irregularities were referred to the Supreme Court, forming the basis of an appeal for a recount of the ballots, using the existing certified result sheets. The Supreme Court rejected most of the opposition's allegations, while declining legal responsibility over others, even though it was acting on behalf of the country's Constitutional Council. Although it saw no need for a recount, the Supreme Court conceded that there had been discrepancies in the counting of ballots, but argued that they were insignificant and could not weigh in the outcome of the elections.

Mozambican society in general felt that a recount would have been justified, especially in view of the narrow margin by which the presidential candidate and the parliamentary list had been declared the winners.

Beyond the scope of the 1999 elections, the Supreme Court's verdict set a legal precedent by concluding that what matters in a constitutional dispute is not an offense as such, but whether its outcome would be significant enough to warrant further action. In addition to leaving a question mark hanging in the air as to whether the election results reflected the true will of the voters, the verdict also contributed to the heightening of the north–south divide, with the northerners believing that the coalition and its presidential candidate had been deprived of their rightful claim to power. As a legacy of the former one-party state, the Supreme Court could not escape being viewed as having sided with a party in continual conflict with those it seeks to rule.

Notes

PART I   A TRADITION OF CONFLICT

1:   Marriage of Convenience

1   Diogo Freitas do Amaral, *Uma Solução para Portugal* (Lisbon: Publicações Europa-América, 1985), p. 37.
2   António de Spínola, *País Sem Rumo – Contributo para a História de uma Revolução* (Lisbon: Editorial SCIRE, 1978), pp. 41–2.
3   'Mozambique Parties Answer Osagyefo's "Close Ranks Call"', *Evening News*, Accra, 6 June 1962, pp. 1,2.
4   'Memorandum of Conversation' between William L. Wight, Jr, deputy director, Office of East African Affairs, and Eduardo Mondlane at the State Department, Washington, DC on 16 May 1961. This and other State Department documents released at author's request under the Freedom of Information Act, Request No. 9101351 (hereinafter FOIA:).
5   Eduardo Mondlane, 'Present Conditions in Mozambique', 1 May 1961, pp. 10a, 12 from the Immanuel Wallerstein Collection of Political Ephemera, Reel Number 4, Sterling Memorial Library, Yale University.
6   FOIA: Under Secretary of State Chester Bowles to National Security Adviser McGeorge Bundy, 23 May 1961.
7   FOIA: 'Memorandum of Conversation', 16 May 1961, op. cit.
8   FOIA: 'Memorandum of Conversation' at the State Department on 8 February 1962. Participants: Robert Stephens, Office of Cultural Affairs; Charles W. Grover, Office of East African Affairs; and Eduardo Mondlane.
9   Televisão de Moçambique, 20 September 1997.
10   Francisco Ferreira, interview with author in Lisbon, 23–24 November 1988. Ferreira was an exiled Portuguese Communist Party member during Santos' visit to Moscow in 1957.
11   Udenamo and MANU statement, Dar es Salaam, 25 May 1962.
12   *Evening News*, op. cit.
13   FOIA: 'Memorandum of Conversation', 8 February 1962, op. cit.
14   FOIA: Foreign Service Dispatch, American Embassy, Dar es Salaam, 19 June 1962.
15   Ibid.
16   FOIA: Confidential Telegram, American Embassy, Dar es Salaam, 26 June 1962.
17   FOIA: Confidential Telegram, American Embassy, Dar es Salaam, 29 June 1962.
18   FOIA: Confidential Airgram, American Embassy, Dar es Salaam, 10 July 1962.
19   Ibid.

2: Profile of a Leader

20 André-Daniel Clerc, 'Eduardo Mondlane: Dados Biográficos pelo seu Tutor', *Datas e Documentos da História da Frelimo*, Lourenço Marques 1975, pp. 361–369.

21 Eduardo Mondlane, 'Mozambique' in Ronald H. Chilcote, *'Emerging Nationalism in Portuguese Africa – Documents'*, pp. 410–411, Stanford, California: Hoover Institution Press, 1972.

22 Professor Adriano Moreira, interview with author, Lisbon 9 December 1988.

23 *Notícias*, 23 February 1961, pp. 1, 15; 26 March 1961, pp. 1, 4; and 30 March 1961, pp. 18–19.

24 Prof. Adriano Moreira, op. cit.

25 Prof. Adriano Moreira, ibid.

26 Nadja Manghezi's *'O meu coração está nas mãos de um negro'* (Maputo: Centro de Estudos Africanos, 1999) pp. 221–222.

27 FOIA: Confidential Telegram, American Embassy, Dar es Salaam, 15 August 1962.

28 FOIA: Confidential Telegram, American Embassy, Dar es Salaam, 18 September 1962.

29 Hlomulo Chitofo Gwambe, letter written from Cairo, 5 September 1962, pp. 1,2.

30 FOIA: Official Use Only Airgram, American Embassy, Dar es Salaam, 6 September 1962.

31 FOIA: Confidential Airgram, American Embassy, Dar es Salaam, 22 October 1962.

32 Fanuel Mahluza, interview with author, Nairobi, 29 March 1982.

33 FOIA: Confidential Airgram, American Embassy, Dar es Salaam, 13 October 1963.

34 'Mozambique' in Ronald H. Chilcote, *'Emerging Nationalism in Portuguese Africa – Documents'*, op. cit.

35 'Evolução Histórica do Pan-africanismo e Desenvolvimento dos Partidos de Libertação em Moçambique (Confidencial)', General Staff of the Portuguese Armed Forces, March 1967, p. 119.

36 Ronald H. Chilcote, op. cit.

37 Mennen Williams, recorded interview, p. 63, John F. Kennedy Library Oral History Program.

38 Robert Kennedy, letter to Mennen Williams, 25 February 1963, John F. Kennedy Library, Boston.

39 Mennen Williams, letter to Robert Kennedy, Washington, 16 April 1963, John F. Kennedy Library, Boston.

40 James W. Symington, letter to Robert Kennedy, 11 April 1963, John F. Kennedy Library, Boston.

41 Nadja Manghezi, op. cit., pp. 221, 233, 237.

42 FOIA: Confidential Airgram, American Embassy, Dar es Salaam, 20 June 1963.

43 FOIA: Confidential Airgram, American Embassy, Dar es Salaam, 27 June 1963.

44 CIA Special Memorandum No. 28–65: 'A New Look at the Prospects for the African Nationalist Movements in Angola and Mozambique', 17 November 1965, p. 10.

45 FOIA: Confidential Airgram, American Embassy, Dar es Salaam, 13 October 1963.
46 'Evolução Histórica do Pan-africanismo e Desenvolvimento dos Partidos de Libertação em Moçambique (Confidencial)', op. cit.

3: Southerners and Those from Afar

47 Mazisi Kunene, *Emperor Shaka The Great: A Zulu Epic*, (London: Heinemann, 1979).
48 Michael Westcott and Carolyn Hamilton, *A Historical Tour of the Ngwane and Ndwandwe Kingdom* (Manzini: Macmillan Boleswa, 1992).
49 A. Rita Ferreira, *Povos de Moçambique: História e Cultura* (Porto: Afrontamento, 1975).

4: Mondlane's Dilemmas

50 FOIA: Confidential Telegram, Dar es Salaam, 15 October 1964.
51 Richard Mahoney, *JFK: Ordeal in Africa* (New York: Oxford University Press, 1983), pp. 187, 192–193, 204–205, 209–222.
52 Franco Nogueira, *Salazar: A Resistência (1958–1964)*, Vol. V (Porto: Livraria Civilização Editora, 1984) pp. 514–519.
53 FOIA: Confidential Airgram, American Embassy, Dar es Salaam, 12 October 1963.
54 FOIA: Confidential Telegram, American Embassy, Dar es Salaam, 13 October 1963.
55 Franco Nogueira, op. cit., pp. 530–536.
56 FOIA: Confidential Memorandum, 4 November 1963.
57 Nadja Manghezi, op. cit. pp. 244–245, 250.
58 FOIA: Confidential Memorandum, 4 November 1963, op. cit.
59 FOIA: Secret Telegram, American Embassy, Dar es Salaam, 25 January 1964.
60 Author's interview with Frelimo official.
61 FOIA: Secret Telegram, American Embassy, Dar es Salaam, 21 May 1964.
62 Ludovick Mwijage, interview with author, Mbabane, 31 March 1992.
63 FOIA: Secret Telegram, American Embassy, Dar es Salaam, 10 May 1964.
64 Seifulaziz Leo Milás, 'What Is Wrong With the Mozambique Liberation Front', 19 September 1964, p. 3.

5: Independence War

65 FOIA: Confidential Telegram, American Embassy, Dar es Salaam, 19 October 1964.
66 Bonifácio Gruveta Massamba, interview in *Notícias*, 13 September 1988, p. 8.
67 Portuguese Army General Staff: O Caso de Moçambique, *Cadernos Militares*, No. 7 August 1969; and *Resenha Histórico-Militar das Campanhas de África (1961–1974)*, Estado-Maior do Exército, Comissão para o Estudo das Campanhas de África, 1° Volume (Lisboa: Beira Douro, 1988).

68 João Paulo Borges Coelho, *O Início da Luta Armada em Tete, 1968–1969: A Primeira Fase da Guerra e a Reacção Colonial* (Maputo: Arquivo Histórico de Moçambique, 1989), p. 62.

69 PIDE – Polícia Internacional e de Defesa do Estado. Communiqué issued on 26 December 1964, '*Datas e Documentos da História da Frelimo*', João Reis and Armando Pedro Muiuane (eds) (Lourenço Marques: Imprensa Nacional, 1975).

70 PIDE – Polícia Internacional e de Defesa do Estado. Communiqué issued on 30 May 1965, '*Datas e Documentos da História da Frelimo*', op. cit.

71 FOIA: Confidential Telegram, American Consulate, Lourenço Marques, 8 September 1965.

72 FOIA: Airgram, American Embassy, Dar es Salaam, 30 July 1964.

73 Portuguese Army General Staff: 'O Caso de Moçambique', op. cit.

74 FOIA: Secret Research Memorandum, 'Mozambique: The Status of the Rebellion', 9 August 1968, by Thomas L Hughes, State Department's director of intelligence and research.

75 Augusto dos Santos, Tirar a Água ao Peixe in José Freire Antunes, *A Guerra de África 1961–1974*, Vol. I (Lisbon: Círculo dos Leitores, 1995), p. 288.

76 Kaúlza de Arriaga, *Guerra e Política. Em Nome da Verdade dos Anos Decisivos* (Lisbon: Edições Referendo, 1987), pp. 305–307; 311–315.

77 Costa Gomes, General Paradoxo, in José Freire Antunes, op. cit. p. 121.

78 *O Processo Revolucionário da Guerra Popular de Libertação* (Maputo: 1977) pp. 109, 112, 182–183.

79 Eduardo Mondlane, *Lutar por Moçambique* (Lisbon: Sá da Costa, 1977) pp. 153–157.

80 Eduardo Mondlane, speech at The Royal Institute of International Affairs, London, 7 March 1968, p. 6.

6: Zambia Backs Frelimo Dissidents

81 José Baltazar da Costa Chagonga, letter to Dr Eduardo Mondlane, Zambia, 4 November 1964. Original kept at the Museu da Revolução, Maputo.

82 Eduardo Mondlane, letter to José Baltazar da Costa Chagonga, Dar es Salaam, 10 December 1964. Original kept at the Museu da Revolução, Maputo.

83 Paulo José Gumane, Failure of Unity Talks, 15 February 1965, in Ronald H. Chilcote, op. cit., pp. 479–481.

84 Fanuel Gideon Mahluza, interviews with author, Nairobi, 29 March 1982 and 13 November 1988.

85 FOIA: Limited Official Use Telegram, American Embassy, Lusaka, 8 April 1965.

86 A. J. K. Kangwa, Conclusions of the Committee Set Up Yesterday 24th March 1965 To Consider Some Common Basis For Unity, from the Immanuel Wallerstein Collection of Political Ephemera, op. cit.

87 FOIA: Limited Official Use Airgram, American Embassy, Blantyre, 7 February 1965.

88 Eduardo Mondlane, letter to Janet Mondlane, Monrovia, 24 October 1965 in *Domingo*, 25 June 1995, p. 5.

89 CIA Special Memorandum No. 28–65, op. cit. pp. 11, 12.

90 Coelho, op. cit., pp. 62, 63.
91 Richard Gibson, *African Liberation Movements* (London: Oxford University Press, 1972) p. 289.
92 Coremo, Memorandum Submitted to the 3rd Assembly of the Heads of State and Government of the OAU, Lusaka, (1966), pp. 2, 3 in Ronald H. Chilcote, op. cit. pp. 481–483; and *O Combatente*, Órgão Oficial do Coremo, 2 March 1972, pp. 1–6.
93 *Times of Zambia*, 4 March 1972.
94 José da Silva Ramalho, interview with author, Johannesburg, 28 October 1980. Ramalho served as an interpreter during interrogations of captured PAC guerrillas.

7: Mondlane and Che Guevara

95 FOIA: Confidential Telegram, American Embassy, in Dar es Salaam, 17 March 1965.
96 Secret memorandum from Mennen Williams, 23 June 1965. W. Averell Harriman Papers, Container No. 495, Library of Congress, Manuscript Division.
97 FOIA: Secret telegram from American Embassy, Dar es Salaam, 29 July 1965.
98 Secret Memorandum of Conversation between Ambassador Anderson and Prime Minister Oliveira Salazar, 22 October 1965. W. Averell Harriman Papers, op. cit.
99 Ahmed Ben Bella, Che as I knew him, *Le Monde Diplomatique* (English edition) October 1997. http://www.monde-diplomatique.fr/md/en/
100 Juan F. Benemelis, *Castro – Subversão e Terrorismo em África* (Odivelas: 1986).
101 Che Guevara: Pasajes de la guerra revolucionaria. Congo, in William Gálvez, *Che in Africa* (Melbourne: Ocean Press, 1999), p. 40.
102 Paco Ignacio Taibo II, Froilán Escobar and Félix Guerra, *O Ano em que Estivemos em Parte Nenhuma* (Porto: Campo das Letras, 1995), p. 137.
103 Eduardo Mondlane, interview with *Liberation News Service*, Washington, 6 March 1968.
104 Teofilo Acosta, Desenmascarado el President del Frelimo, *Juventud Rebelde*, 21 May 1968, p. 3.

8: The Rise of Samora Machel

105 Frelimo Central Committee report to the Second Congress, in *Documentos Base da Frelimo 1* (Lourenço Marques: Tempográfica), p. 65.
106 Manuel António Nasinho da Maia, interview with author, Maputo, 10 May 1995.
107 FOIA: Confidential Telegram, American Consulate, Lourenço Marques, 8 September 1965, op. cit.
108 CIA Special Memorandum No. 28–65, op. cit., p. 11.
109 Manuel Lisboa Tristão, interviews with author, Nairobi, 27 March 1982 and 14 November 1988; correspondence with author (May 1983–March 1989).
110 Emília Magaia, as told to Barnabé Ngauze Lucas, Maputo, 20 April 1998.

111 Armando Khembo dos Santos, interview with author, Mbabane, 2 October 1995.
112 Manuel Lisboa Tristão, interviews with author, op. cit.
113 Frelimo Central Committee resolution, October 1966, in *Documentos Base da Frelimo 1*, op. cit. p. 41.
114 Zacarias Mwaluma Mwanjahane, interview with author, Matsapha, 20 August 1994.
115 Uria Timóteo Simango, Gloomy Situation in Frelimo, Dar es Salaam, 3 November 1969, pp. 2, 3.

9: Student Unrest

116 Author's interviews with former IM students Francisco Nota Moisés, Mbabane, 14 May 1984; João Baptista Truzão, Mbabane, 23 October 1988; and Joaquim Njanje, Nairobi, 13 November 1988.
117 Eduardo Mondlane, Frelimo. A Brief Account of the Situation of the Mozambican Students Abroad and of Their Participation in the Struggle for National Liberation, Dar es Salaam, December 1967, in *African Historical Studies*, II, 2 (1969), pp. 319–333.
118 Eduardo Mondlane, ibid.
119 Unemo, União Nacional dos Estudantes Moçambicanos, The Mozambican Revolution Betrayed, May 1968, in *African Historical Studies*, III, 1 (1970), pp. 169–180.
120 Stanley Meisler, Rebel Unit Split Over Africa Goals, *Los Angeles Times*, 30 June 1968.
121 Author's interviews with Armando Khembo dos Santos, Nairobi, 12 November 1988, and Joaquim Njanje, Nairobi, 13 November 1988.

10: Crisis within Frelimo Mounts

122 Mateus Pinho Gwenjere, mimeographed autobiographical notes, 16 November 1972, p. 5.
123 *Notícias da Beira*, 24 August 1974, p. 6.
124 *Notícias*, 30 November 1969, pp. 1, 4.
125 FOIA: Secret Telegram, American Embassy, Dar es Salaam, 13 February 1969.
126 FOIA: Secret Research Memorandum by Thomas L. Hughes, op. cit.

11: Mondlane Assassinated

127 FOIA: Confidential Telegram, American Embassy, Addis Ababa, 24 February 1969.
128 FOIA: Secret Telegram, America Embassy, Dar es Salaam, 6 February 1969.
129 FOIA: Secret Telegram, 13 February 1969, op. cit.
130 FOIA: Limited Official Use Telegram, Department of State, Washington, DC, 4 February 1969.
131 *Notícias*, 5 November 1969, p. 1.
132 Lídia Viana, interview with author, Lagos, Portugal, 7 August 1990.

133 O Ressuscitar dos Fantasmas. PIDE Matou Mondlane, *Expresso*, 21 February 1998, www.expresso.pt.
134 Manuel Garcia and Lourdes Maurício, *O Caso Delgado – autópsia da Operação Outono* (Lisbon: Edições Jornal Expresso, 1977).
135 David Martin, Interpol solves a guerrilla whodunit, *The Observer*, 6 February 1972, p. 4.
136 FOIA: Confidential Memorandum of Conversation between American Consul John G. Gossett and Governor General Rebello de Souza, Lourenço Marques, 4 February 1969.
137 FOIA: Secret Memorandum of Conversation between Thomas R. Pickering, Deputy Chief of Mission, American Embassy, and unidentified senior Tanzania CID officer, Dar es Salaam, 24 March 1969.
138 Ibid.
139 Ibid.
140 FOIA: Secret Telegram, American Embassy, Dar es Salaam, 21 April 1969.
141 FOIA: Secret Telegram, American Embassy, Dar es Salaam, 25 March 1969.
142 Ludovick Simon Mwijage, interview with author, Mbabane, 31 March 1992.

12: Frelimo after Mondlane

143 Uria Timóteo Simango, Gloomy Situation in Frelimo, op. cit.
144 Wehia Ripua, as told to Barnabé Ngauze Lucas, Maputo, 15 April 1998.
145 Uria Timóteo Simango, op. cit.
146 Frelimo Executive Committee communiqué, 8 November 1969, *A Voz da Revolução*, Dar es Salaam, January 1970.
147 Josefate Muhlanga, interview with author, Nairobi, 13 November 1988.
148 Final communiqué, 4th Frelimo Central Committee session, May 1970, *Documentos Base da Frelimo 1*, op. cit., pp. 148–159.
149 Uria Timóteo Simango, Memorandum for the OAU African Liberation Committee (Annex), 17 January 1970, p. 5.
150 União Nacional dos Estudantes Moçambicanos, petition to the president and secretary general of the OAU, Washington DC, 8 June 1970, seeking protection for Samuel Dhlakama, Gabriel Simbine, Eduardo Mbateya, Eli Ndimeni and Miguel Murupa.
151 Miguel Murupa, Eu Fui da Frelimo, *Notícias*, 28 January 1971, pp. 1, 4.
152 Interview with Wills Symes Kadewell by Luísa Ribeiro, *Notícias*, 7 May 1972, p. 4.
153 João José Craveirinha Voltou Desiludido, *Notícias*, 15 July 1972, pp. 1, 2.
154 José Freire Antunes, op. cit., p. 331.
155 Marcelino dos Santos in interview with Rádio Moçambique, 1100 GMT 21 and 22 June 1988.

PART II INDEPENDENCE

1: Portugal Transfers Power to Frelimo

1 António de Spínola, *Portugal e o Futuro* (Lisbon: Arcádia, 1974) pp. 234, 240.

2   Bernardino G. Oliveira, *Aqui Portugal Moçambique* (Famalicão: Empresa Distribuidora de Livros e Discos, nd).
3   António de Spínola, *País sem Rumo*, op. cit., pp. 294–296.
4   Fanuel Mahluza, interview with author, Nairobi, 29 March 1982.
5   Máximo Dias, interview with author, Johannesburg, 31 December 1980.
6   Joana Semião, Declaração à Imprensa, 19 January 1974.
7   Máximo Dias, communiqué issued on behalf of Gumo's Central Committee, Inhambane, 14 May 1974.
8   Comunicado No. 4 da Frecomo, in *Notícias da Beira*, 2 July 1974, p. 2.
9   Comunicado No. 5 da Frecomo, in *Notícias da Beira*, 6 July 1974, p. 3.
10 *Notícias da Beira*, 24 August 1974, p. 6.
11 Comunicado do Partido de Coligação Nacional, *Notícias da Beira*, 24 August 1974, p. 8.
12 António de Spínola, *País Sem Rumo*, op. cit.

2:   Jorge Jardim – Myth and Reality

13 Franco Nogueira, op. cit., and Jorge Jardim, *Para Servir Moçambique* (Lisbon: Silvas, Lda. 1959).
14 Orlando Cristina, interview with author, Salisbury, 24 August 1976.
15 Jorge Jardim, *Moçambique Terra Queimada* (Lisbon: Intervenção, 1976) p. 417.
16 Augusto de Carvalho, A Zâmbia Rompe Finalmente o Silêncio sobre o Polémico Livro de Jorge Jardim, *Expresso Revista*, Lisbon, 3 December 1976.
17 José Freire Antunes, *Jorge Jardim Agente Secreto* (Venda Nova: Bertrand Editora, 1996), p. 513.
18 Antunes, ibid., p. 546.
19 Antunes, ibid., p. 493.
20 Joaquim Veríssimo Serrão, *Marcello Caetano: Confidências no Exílio* (Lisbon: Verbo, 1985) p. 190.
21 Augusto de Carvalho, op. cit.

3:   The Long Arm of Frelimo

22 Eschel Rhoodie, *The Real Information Scandal* (Pretoria: Orbis SA (Pty) Ltd., 1983).
23 José Freire Antunes, *Champalimaud* (Lisbon: Círculo de Leitores, 1997).
24 Manuel Lisboa Tristão, interview with author, Nairobi, 14 November 1988.
25 CIO 'Secret' report, Salisbury, 6 October 1974, p. 5.
26 CIO 'Secret' report, op. cit.
27 Lutero Simango, interview by Bento Balói in *Domingo*, Maputo, 12 December 1993, p. 3.
28 Manuel Lisboa Tristão, interview, op. cit.
29 *Notícias*, 18 April 1975, p. 3.
30 Priscilla Gumane, letter to author, Cologne, 12 February 1990.
31 Samuel Brito Simango, interview with author, Maputo, 16 April 1995.
32 A Confissão de Uria Simango, *A Tribuna*, 14 May 1975, pp. 1, 12, 21–23.
33 Manuel Njanje and Armando Khembo dos Santos, interviews with author, op. cit.

4: Totalitarian State

34 Janet Rae Mondlane, The Echo of Your Voice, unpublished manuscript, Fundação Eduardo Mondlane, Maputo.
35 Samora Machel, speech in Sofia in *Voz da Revolução*, No. 70, Maputo, January 1980, pp. 21–24.
36 Lúcia Maximiano, interview, in *Notícias*, Maputo, 28 December 1984, p. 3.
37 Dirce Costa, interview with author, Maputo, 29 June 1998.
38 Samora Machel, Colecção Palavras de Ordem, No. 25, Maputo, November 1983, p. 29.
39 Jorge Rebelo, Rádio Moçambique, 17OO GMT 17 April 1986.
40 *Documentos da Conferência Nacional do Departamento de Informação e Propaganda da Frelimo*, Macomia, 26–30 November 1975, p. 30.
41 Raúl Honwana, interview, Rádio Moçambique, 1030 GMT 7 May 1995.
42 David Aloni, interview with author, Maputo, 15 August 1999.
43 Nadja Manghezi, op. cit. pp. 345–346.
44 Jorge Rebelo, address to second national information seminar, Rádio Moçambique, 1800 GMT 8 January 1980.
45 Samora Machel, *Documentos do 1° Seminário Nacional da Informação*, Maputo, 12–15 September 1977, p. 22. Ministério da Informação, nd.
46 Jorge Rebelo, *Documentos do 17° Seminário Nacional da Informação*, Maputo 12–15 September 1977, pp. 29, 30. Ministério da Informação, nd.
47 Pedro Pires, *Domingo*, Maputo, 28 July 1991, p. 13.

5: Political Police

48 João Trindade, É necessário rever as leis em Moçambique, *Notícias, 1* March 1991, p. 1.
49 Decree-Law No. 21/75 of 11 October in *Boletim da República*, I Série, No. 46, 11 October 1975, pp. 193, 194.
50 Jacinto Veloso, interview in *Notícias*, 11 October 1980, p. 3.
51 Samora Machel, speech in *Notícias*, Maputo, 23 June 1984, p. 3.
52 Frelimo Standing Political Committee report to the Central Committee's 4th session, *Voz da Revolução* No. 61, September 1978, p. 11.
53 Jacinto Veloso, interview in *Notícias*, 11 October 1980, p. 3.
54 Tomás Carolina Bomba, interview with author, Mbabane, 12 April 1991. Bomba was a former SIIP (Frelimo) member.
55 Ministry of the Interior communiqué, *Notícias*, 1 November 1975, p. 1.
56 Samora Machel, speech, Rádio Moçambique, 1100 GMT 19 March 1977.

6: Re-education

57 The Da Costa File in *Scope*, 25 February 1983, p. 34.
58 *Notícias*, Maputo, 27 November 1976, p. 3.
59 Samora Machel, speech in Colecção Palavras de Ordem No. 22, 1981, p. 38.
60 Mário Mangaze, interview by António Souto, *Notícias*, 4 January 1985, p. 3.
61 Cassamo Issufo Tava, interview with author, 10 April 1981.

62 José Capela and Eduardo Medeiros, *O Tráfico de Escravos de Moçambique para as Ilhas do Índico, 1720–1902* (Maputo: Departamento de História da Universidade Eduardo Mondlane, 1987).
63 Samora Machel, speech, Colecção Palavras de Ordem No. 14, December 1979, p. 22.
64 *Notícias*, Maputo, 13 August 1976, p. 3.
65 Ibid.
66 Jorge Costa, op. cit., p. 35.
67 Fanuel Mahluza, interview with author, Nairobi, 12 November 1988.
68 Atanásio Afonso Kantelu, interview with author, Nairobi, 28 March 1982, and written statement dated 8 August 1983.
69 António Isaac Maria, interview with author, Salisbury, 6 June 1977.

7: M'telela–The Last Goodbye

70 Maria Flora Casal Ribeiro, interview with author, Maputo, 8 February 1997.
71 Jorge Costa, written statement to author, citing Abel Assikala's remarks.
72 Ministry of Security. Order of Action No.5/80 signed by Jacinto Veloso, Maputo, 29 July 1980 in *Scope*, 11 February 1983, pp. 34, 35.
73 Ministry of Security, op. cit.
74 Samora Machel, speech, *Notícias*, Maputo, 3 October 1981 (supplement).
75 Samora Machel, speech, Rádio Moçambique, 5 November 1981.
76 Resolution 7/82 adopted by the Standing Commission of the People's Assembly, *Notícias*, 26 June 1982, p. 1.
77 Manuel José Pereira, interview with author, Maputo, 16 April 1995. Pereira was a former M'telela inmate.
78 Judite Casal Ribeiro, letter to Lutero Simango (the Simangos' eldest son), Metangula, 19 June 1984.
79 Letter to author from Gillian Nevins, Amnesty International, Africa Research Department, London, 30 March 1989.
80 Priscilla Gumane, letter to President Joaquim Chissano, Cologne, 10 February 1988.
81 José Marangue, 'Trip to Mozambique, 1993 – Reflections', p. 10.
82 Maria Flora Casal Ribeiro, op. cit.
83 Frelimo Central Committee Report to 4th Congress in Colecção 4° Congresso 1983, p. 85.

8: Coup Attempt

84 *Notícias*, 16 October 1975, p. 3 and 17 October 1975, p. 3.
85 Reverend Deacon Daniel José Sithole, 'The Mozambique Tragedy', Nairobi, 23 August 1981, pp. 8, 9. Rev. Sithole was a former inmate of the Ruaura re-education camp.
86 FPLM High Command communiqué 19 December 1975, *Notícias*, 20 December 1975, p. 1.
87 Communiqué, op. cit.
88 Jacob Carlos Chinhara, interview with author, Salisbury, 15 September 1976.
89 Samora Machel, 20 September 1974, speech in Reis et al., op. cit., p. 206.

90 FPLM General Staff communiqué, *Tempo* No. 272, Maputo, pp. 28–36.

9: Destroying the Sequels

91 Frelimo, Programa e Estatutos, *Documentos do 3° Congresso do Partido Frelimo* (Departamento do Trabalho Ideológico da Frelimo, 1977), pp. 8,9.
92 V. I. Lenin, *Collected Works*, Vol. 31, p. 244.
93 Decisões do Conselho de Ministros, in *Boletim da República* No. 15, 29 July 1975.
94 Frelimo 1977 program of action, *Documentos do 3° Congresso do Partido Frelimo*, op. cit., pp. 32–35.
95 Yussuf Adam, Mueda, 1917–1990: Resistência, Colonialismo, Libertação e Desenvolvimento in *Arquivo*, No. 14, October 1993.
96 Carlos Adrião Rodrigues, Letter to the president of the Republic of Mozambique, Lisbon [no date].
97 Report of the Economic and Social Council to the UN Secretary General, A// 32/96, 9 June 1977, pp. 18, 19.
98 Samora Machel, speech, Rádio Moçambique, 11 November 1978.
99 Samora Machel, speech, Rádio Moçambique, 1745 GMT 8 February 1980.
100 Samora Machel, speech, Rádio Moçambique, 1800 GMT 4 December 1979.
101 *Domingo*, Maputo, 14 April 1991 pp. 8,9.
102 Samora Machel, speech, *Diário de Moçambique*, 25 July 1985 p. 16.
103 *Notícias*, 14 December 1991, p. 1.
104 Samora Machel, speech, *Notícias da Beira*, 6 August 1979, p. 4.
105 *Notícias*, Maputo, 10 July 1981, p. 3.
106 *Notícias*, Maputo, 24 November, 1976, p. 2.
107 T M Burley, Mozambique Rice: Is State Farming Working?, *African Business*, September 1982, p. 43.
108 CEA, Memorando Interno N° 11, 31 October 1979, B 7,8.
109 Joanmarie Kalter, The Economics of Desperation in *Africa Report*, New York, May–June 1984, pp. 19–23.
110 Ibid.
111 T. M. Burley, op. cit.
112 Arlindo Lopes, CAIL – O Gigante Desperta, *Tempo*, 13 December 1981, p. 12, 17.
113 T. M. Burley, op. cit.
114 António Souto, Por um novo meio rural (Parte I), *Notícias*, 24 June 1987, p. 3.
115 CEA, Memorando Interno N° 11, 31 October 1979, C 2.
116 Comunicado Final e Recomendações do Primeiro Seminário Nacional de Agricultura, Marrupa, 29 May–4 June 1975, in J. P. Borges Coelho, Protected Villages and Communal Villages in the Mozambican Province of Tete (1968–1982), Ph.D. dissertation, Arquivo Histórico de Moçambique, Maputo.
117 José António Silva, in panel discussion chaired by António Souto, *Notícias*, 25 January 1985, p. 3.
118 Henriques Tomás, interview with author, Mbabane, 3 September 1994.
119 Fernando Manuel, Algodão em Nampula: Organizar o futuro aprendendo do presente, *Tempo*, 29 August 1982, pp. 17–24.

120   Salomão Moyana, Produzir algodão e castanha de cajú não é favor é ordem do Estado, *Tempo*, 19 October 1986, pp. 12–15.

10:   Revolutionaries and Traditionalists

121   Primeira Reunião Nacional das Aldeias Comunais, Gaza, 27 March 1980, p. 12, Centro de Estudos Africanos, Maputo.
122   Borges Coelho, op. cit., p. 431.
123   Fernando Osório, interview with author, Salisbury, 13 October 1981.
124   Borges Coelho, op. cit., pp. 349, 350.
125   Yussuf Adam, op. cit., p. 45.
126   Ibid. p. 46.
127   Primeira Reunião Nacional das Aldeias Comunais, op. cit., p. 3.
128   Frelimo Party Central Committee Confidential Report, 14 December 1982 in Borges Coelho, op. cit., p. 345.
129   Mozambique Government report in Borges Coelho, op. cit., p. 360.
130   Samora Machel, speech, 25 June 1975, *Datas e Documentos da História da Frelimo*, op. cit., p. 494.
131   Bertil Egerö, *Mozambique: A Dream Undone. The Political Economy of Democracy, 1975–84* (Uppsala: Scandinavian Institute of African Studies, 1990) p. 152.
132   Primeira Reunião Nacional das Aldeias Comunais, op. cit., p. 7.

11:   Frelimo and Religion

133   Samora Machel, speech, Rádio Moçambique, 1000 GMT 11 November 1978.
134   Samora Machel, speech, 1 June 1975, in *Datas e Documentos*, op. cit., p. 399.
135   A Igreja Católica em Moçambique, *Tempo* No. 452, Maputo, 10 June 1979 p. 35.
136   O Papel da Igreja Católica em Moçambique, *Tempo* No. 448, 13 May 1979, pp. 37–40.
137   Fé – Às Comunidades Cristãs, pastoral letter issued by the Mozambique Catholic Bishops, June 1976, p. 5.
138   *Notícias*, 3 January 1979, p. 4.
139   Combate Popular Organizado Contra Estandartes do Imperialismo – Circular issued by the Frelimo National Political Commissariat, *Notícias*, 17 October 1975, pp. 2,5.
140   *Washington Post*, 22 April 1976.
141   *Notícias*, 9 June 1978, p. 3.
142   *Tempo* No. 475, 18 November 1979, pp. 21–29.
143   Samora Machel, speech, *Notícias*, 9 October 1975, p. 1.
144   *Awake!*, 8 January 1976, pp. 16–26.
145   *Domingo*, 4 October 1981, p. 3.

PART III   RESISTANCE

1:   The Conflict with Malawi and Rhodesia

1   Samora Machel, speech, *Notícias*, 27 September 1975, p. 2.
2   Samora Machel, speech, *A Voz da Revolução*, 7 August 1978, p. 17.
3   Os Acontecimentos no Kampuchea e o Conflito Entre a China e o Vietnam, statement issued by the Frelimo Central Committee Secretariat, *A Voz da Revolução*, February–March 1979, No. 79, pp. 3–6.
4   Samora Machel, speech, *Notícias*, 22 August 1976, p. 2.
5   Rádio Moçambique, 1800 GMT 9 August 1995.
6   Janet Rae Mondlane, op. cit.
7   Partido Revolucionário de Moçambique, statement, nd.
8   Gimo Phiri, letter to author, Blantyre, 10 August 1983.
9   Communiqué issued by the Revolutionary Military Tribunal, Quelimane, 12 February 1981, *Notícias*, 16 February 1981, pp. 3, 4.
10   Gimo Phiri, op. cit.
11   Communiqué issued by the Revolutionary Military Tribunal on 16 June 1982, *Notícias*, 18 June 1982, p. 7.
12   Ron Reid Daly and Peter Stiff, *Selous Scouts – Top Secret War* (Alberton: Galago Publishing, 1982) p. 108.
13   *Rhodesia Herald*, 5 January 1975.
14   *Rhodesia Herald*, 12 February 1975.
15   Daly and Stiff, op. cit.
16   Ibid.
17   P. K. van der Byl, speech, Parliament of Rhodesia, Salisbury, 1 July 1975.

2:   The *Magaia* Pamphlet

18   João Baptista Barros, interview with author, Lagos, Portugal, 25 August 1992. Barros was Orlando Cristina's stepfather.
19   João Pires Marreiros, interview with author, Lagos, Portugal, 29 August 1992. Marreiros was a MUD member in southern Portugal. Subsequent aspects of Orlando Cristina's life based on author's conversations with Cristina between 1976 and 1982, and on interviews with Manuel Gomes dos Santos in Lisbon and Johannesburg, and with Lucinda Serras Pires Feijão in Pretoria, between 1984 and 1995.
20   Dominic de Roux, O Quinto Império (Lisboa: Edições Roger Delraux, Belfond, 1977) pp. 183–185.

3:   The Voz da África Livre

21   Orlando Cristina, hand-written statement, circa 1979.
22   Frelimo's 1962 program of action, *Documentos do 3° Congresso do Partido Frelimo*, op. cit. pp. 32–35.
23   Voz da África Livre, 1700 GMT 14 March 1980.
24   Voz da África Livre, 1700 GMT 1 March 1983.

25 Rádio Moçambique, 1100 GMT 26 September 1976.
26 Jacob Carlos Chinhara, interview with author, Salisbury, 3 April 1978.

4: Renamo, the Early Days

27 Voz da África Livre, 1800 GMT 30 September 1976.
28 Orlando Cristina, conversation with author, Johannesburg, 17 August 1981.
29 Orlando Cristina, ibid.
30 Luís Garife Matsangaice Dyuwayo, interview with author, Maputo, 31 April 1995.
31 Aires de Oliveira, interview with author, Salisbury, 18 March 1977.
32 Pedro Silva, Francisco Esteves e Valdemar Moreira, com colaboração de Gilberto Santos e Castro, *Angola – Comandos especiais contra os cubanos* (Braga: Braga Editora, 1978) pp. 177–182.
33 Olímpio Cambona, interview with author, Maputo, 2 March 1993.
34 Afonso Dhlakama, interview with author, Lisbon, 29 November 1980.

5: The Quest for Autonomy

35 Voz da África Livre, 1800 GMT 25 September 1978.
36 Orlando Cristina, A Resistência Nacional Moçambicana (RNM), July 1981, unpublished paper, p. 20.
37 Jorge Jardim, letter to Orlando Cristina, Las Palmas, 9 February 1977.
38 Peter Burt, Secret report: Jorge Jardim, August 1976, p. 5.
39 Orlando Cristina, conversation with author, Salisbury, 24 December 1976.
40 Orlando Cristina, conversation with author, Johannesburg, 17 August 1981.
41 Ibid.
42 Ken Flower, op. cit., pp. 300–302.

6: Gorongosa

43 Orlando Cristina, A Resistência Nacional Moçambicana (RNM), op. cit.
44 Orlando Cristina, ibid.
45 Voz da África Livre, 1800 GMT 2 February 1979.
46 Author's interviews with Filipe Augusto, Olímpio Cambona and John Kupenga, 10–15 November 1992, and Vareia Manje, 3 June 1997.
47 John Kupenga, interview with author, 15 May 1993.
48 Raúl Domingos, conversation with author, Pretoria, 21 August 1981.

7: Matsangaice Killed

49 Orlando Cristina, conversation with author, Johannesburg, 17 August 1981.
50 Olímpio Cambona and Filipe Augusto, interviews with author, 10–15 November 1992.
51 FPLM General Staff Communiqué, *Notícias*, 3 November 1979, p. 1.
52 *Domingo*, 25 December 1988, p. 13.

53 Afonso Dhlakama, conversation with author, 27 September 1982.
54 Ibid.
55 Roberto Wayne, conversation with author, Salisbury, 30 May 1978.

8: Cristina Marginalized

56 Zeca Caliate, conversation with author, Salisbury, 25 May 1978.
57 Zeca Caliate, Relatório Sobre a Missão, Salisbury, 22 May 1978, p. 6.
58 Afonso Dhlakama, conversation with author, 4 October 1980.

9: The Renamo Program

59 Author's interviews with Afonso Dhlakama, 27 September 1982, and Olímpio Cambona, 10–15 November 1992.
60 Fumo letter to Rhodesian prime minister, nd.
61 Fumo letter, 28 February 1977.
62 Peter Burt, memorandum for the CIO's Mozambique Desk chief, 17 March 1977, p. 3.
63 Domingos Arouca, letter to Renamo, 28 March 1977.
64 Resistência Nacional Moçambicana, Estatutos, 1979.
65 Ibid.
66 Maria Regina Arouca, letter to Rhodesian Foreign Minister David Mukone, Lisbon, 27 September 1979.
67 Ibid.
68 Olímpio Cambona, op. cit.
69 Marcelino dos Santos, interview by Emílio Manhique, Televisão de Moçambique, 19 September 1997.

10: Renamo Survives the Wind of Change

70 Samora Machel, speech, Rádio Moçambique, 1800 GMT 22 December 1979.
71 Author's interviews with Orlando Cristina in Johannesburg, 17 September 1981, and Afonso Dhlakama, 27 September 1982.
72 BBC This Week and Africa program, 0635 GMT 7 June 1980.
73 *Africa Research Bulletin*, 1–30 May 1980.
74 Author's interviews with Olímpio Cambona, Filipe Augusto and John Kupenga, 10–15 November 1992, and Vareia Manje, 3 June 1997.
75 BBC Summary of World Broadcasts, 22 August 1980.
76 Relatório do Governo sobre as Forças Armadas, Maputo, 25 June 1985, *Notícias*, 29 July 1986, p. 3.
77 Author's interview with former Tanzanian diplomat.

PART IV   THE TURNING POINT

1: South Africa Backs Renamo

1 David Martin and Phyllis Johnson, *The Struggle for Zimbabwe* (London: Faber and Faber, 1981) pp. 125–157, and Ian Smith, op. cit., pp. 159–210.

2   Mário J. Azevedo, A Sober Commitment to Liberation? – Mozambique and South Africa 1974–1979, *African Affairs* Vol. 79, No. 317, pp. 567–584.
3   William Minter, *Apartheid's Contras* (London: Zed Books, 1994) p. 265.
4   Theodorico de Sacadura Botte, *Memórias e Autobiografia*, (Maputo:1985/86) Vol. 3, pp. 209–214.
5   Wenela's statistical information released on 7 February 1997 at author's request.
6   Lewis Carroll and W.S. Gilbert, Why help the enemy?, *To The Point*, 1 July 1977, pp. 6–9.
7   Ibid.
8   Ibid.
9   The Da Costa File, *Scope*, 18 February 1983, pp. 26–37.
10 Vladimir Shubin, *ANC: a View from Moscow* (Belville: Mayibuye Books UWC, 1999), p. 197.
11 Carlos Lacerda, conversation with author, Johannesburg, 30 November 1981. Lacerda was a Fumo delegation member.
12 Domingos Arouca, Message to Mozambicans and friends of Mozambique, *Fumo–Boletim Informativo*, December 1980, p. 3.
13 Orlando Cristina, conversation with author, Johannesburg, 30 July 1981.
14 Author's conversations with Orlando Cristina, Afonso Dhlakama, Manuel Domingos, and Raúl Domingos, Lisbon, 29–30 November 1980.
15 Renamo National Council Members, Chicarre, 13 March 1981. Signed by Raúl Manuel Domingos and Afonso Dhlakama.

2:   Renamo Reviews the 1979 Program

16 Interview with Jorge Jardim by Pedro Correia, *Tempo*, Lisbon, 12 November 1981, pp. 2–4.
17 Orlando Cristina, Relatório de Informação – Viajem à Europa, 29 November 1980, p. 10.
18 Carlos Lacerda, Diligências Efectuadas para a União dos Movimentos Moçambicanos, 10 April 1981, p. 4.
19 Resistência Nacional Moçambicana (RNM), Manifesto e Programa, 1981 – Departamento de Informação da RNM.
20 Remo, Esclarecimento p. 5 nd. This unsigned document released by Remo in late 1981 was drafted by Carlos Lacerda.
21 Resistência Nacional Moçambicana, minutes of the 22–23 May 1982 meeting, p. 2.

3:   Cristina Killed

22 Voz da África Livre, 1700 GMT 24 September 1982.
23 Fanuel Mahluza, conversation with the author, Nairobi, 12 November 1988.
24 Afonso Dhlakama, conversation with author, 27 September 1982.
25 João Quental, conversation with author, Johannesburg, 1983.
26 Paula Serra, *Dinfo–Histórias Secretas do Serviço de Informações Militares* (Lisbon: Publicações Dom Quixote, 1998) p. 220.

27 Author's interview with former DMI officer, London, 31 September 1997.

4: Heading for Maputo

28 *The Herald*, 13 January 1981, p. 4.
29 *The Herald*, 12 June 1981, p. 1.
30 Renamo intercept of radio conversation between Colonel Fondo and Major Manjichi, 24 June 1981.
31 Antónia Edfonso, former Renamo Female Detachment captain. Interview with author, Maputo, 2 September 1996.
32 Author's interviews with Afonso Dhlakama, 27 September 1982, and Vareia Manje, 26 October 1996.

5: The Invasion that Never Was

33 Author's conversation with Afonso Dhlakama, 27 September 1982, and interview with Filipe Augusto and John Kupenga, 10–15 November 1992.
34 Ibid.
35 Details about the fall of Chicarre based on author's conversations with Afonso Dhlakama, 27 September 1982; Raúl Domingos, 12 November 1982; Amade Viajem and Olímpio Cambona, 5–8 November 1992; and on Mozambique media reports.
36 *A Luta Continua!*, No.3, 1 February 1982 and No. 4, 7 May 1982; Voz da África Livre news bulletins December 1981–December 1982.
37 Armando Khembo dos Santos, interview with author, Maputo, 6 June 1996.
38 Acordo Provisório de Unificação – draft unification accord between Renamo and the PRM; and cover letter from Orlando Cristina to Jerónimo Gimo (Gimo Phiri), 28 June 1982.
39 Henrique Damião, interview with author, 15 March 1993.
40 Ibid.
41 BBC Focus on Africa program, 1710 GMT 5 October 1982.

6: The Frelimo Government Counter-Attacks

42 Samora Machel, speech, *Notícias*, 22 June 1982, p. 2.
43 Voz da África Livre, 1700 GMT 9 December 1982.
44 Voz da África Livre, 1700 GMT 2 February 1983.
45 Author's interview with former FAM officer.
46 Samora Machel, speech, Rádio Moçambique, 1800 GMT 19 February 1983.
47 'Quem São os Bandidos Armados e Como Vamos Derrotá-los', *Notícias*, 31 July 1982, pp. 5,6.
48 Samora Machel, speech, Rádio Moçambique, 1413 GMT 17 March 1984.
49 Briefing on the Country's Military Situation by Chief of General Staff Raúl Domingos in Voz da Resistência Nacional Moçambicana, 1700 GMT 22 July 1983.

PART V RUMOURS OF PEACE

1: A Different Kind of Operation

1 Luís de Brito, statement to the BBC, Portuguese Service, 2030 GMT 1 November 1999.
2 Directiva Ministerial Sobre Evacuação das Cidades, *Notícias*, 20 June 1983, p. 3.
3 Marcelino dos Santos, speech, *Diário de Moçambique*, 9 August 1983, pp. 8,9.
4 Francisco Munia, Sofala: Os Passos Que a Operação Produção Deu, *Tempo*, 6 November 1983, pp. 29–35.
5 *Notícias*, 20 August 1983, p. 2.
6 Author's interview with Mozambican Catholic nun, Mbabane, 12 September 1984.
7 Ibid.
8 Louise Brown, report to the BBC's Focus on Africa program, 1515 GMT 3 August 1984.
9 Luís de Brito, op. cit.
10 *Notícias*, 12 July 1984, p. 2.
11 *Tempo*, 21 Feb 1988, p. 41.
12 Manuel Vieira Pinto, letter to President Samora Machel, Nampula, 30 March 1984.
13 Samora Machel, speech, *Notícias*, 30 December 1983, p. 3.
14 *Notícias*, 21 June 1997, p. 6; 28 July 1998, p. 2.
15 Armando Guebuza, interview by Emílio Manhique, Televisão de Moçambique, 25 November 1998.

2: The Nkomati Accord

16 Author's interview with Chinagana Agostinho Celestino, former Renamo chief of Nampula Province's General Staff, Maputo, 20 March 1993.
17 Author's interviews with the following Renamo officials: Henriques Damião, former intelligence chief, Zambézia Province; Manuel Rudolfo; Virgílio Quirole Tomo; and Martins Gamito Wizimane in Maputo, 20–25 March 1993.
18 Voz da Resistência Nacional Moçambicana, 2–23 August 1983 news bulletins.
19 Author's interview with former Mozambican Economic Planning Ministry official.
20 Luísa Diogo, interview by Emílio Manhique, Televisão de Moçambique, 7 August 1998.
21 *Notícias*, 21 October 1983, p. 1.
22 Author's interview with Frelimo official.
23 Álvaro Récio, interview with author, Mbabane, 16 September 1985; Johannesburg, 17 February 1989.
24 João Quental, interview with author, Johannesburg, 4 November 1984.
25 Radio South Africa, 0500 GMT 1 December 1983.
26 Chester A. Crocker, *High Noon in Southern Africa* (New York: W.W. Norton & Company, 1992) p. 238.
27 Author's interview with former DMI officials.

28 Radio Freedom, 1930 GMT 16 March 1984.
29 Samora Machel, speech, Rádio Moçambique, 1413 GMT 17 March 1984.

3: The Pretoria Talks

30 Albano Naroromele, Sobre os Bandidos em Cabo Delgado in *Notícias*, 20 October 1986, p. 3.
31 Rádio Moçambique, 1900 GMT 23 January 1984.
32 *Notícias*, Maputo, 17 July 1985, p. 8.
33 Author's interview with former Snasp operative.
34 Author's interview with Manuel Mussindo, former Renamo intelligence chief for Cabo Delgado Province, Maputo, 19 and 20 March 1993; Renamo communiqués issued by Washington representative.
35 Rádio Moçambique, 1700 GMT 4 May 1984.
36 A Urgência da Paz, Mozambique Catholic Bishops Conference, 7 May 1984.
37 Bishop Manuel Vieira Pinto, op. cit.
38 Álvaro Récio, op. cit.
39 Honwana, as told to Récio.
40 Álvaro Récio, op. cit.
41 Rádio Moçambique, 1420 GMT 3 October 1984.
42 Agence France Press, 1808 GMT 3 October 1984.
43 Fanuel Mahluza, conversation with author, Nairobi, 11 November 1988.
44 Details of discussions in First Plenary Session of the Commission Established in Terms of the Pretoria Declaration of 3 October 1984: 8–11 October 1984, Pretoria (Top Secret), signed by Louis Nel, Jacinto Veloso, Evo Fernandes, Fanuel Guideon Mahluza, Pretoria, 11 October 1984.
45 Rádio Moçambique, 1030 GMT 13 October 1984.
46 *Notícias*, 16 October 1984, p. 1.
47 Rádio Difusão Portuguesa, 1900 GMT 19 October 1984

PART VI FOREIGN INTERVENTION

1: Zimbabwe's Role Expanded

1 Author's interview with former FAM member.
2 Colonel Valentim de Sousa, interview with author, Inhassoro, 15 September 1997.
3 CIO, Top Secret Memorandum – ZNA Operations in Mozambique, June 1987.
4 Rádio Moçambique, 1900 GMT 12 June 1985.
5 Nathan Shamuyarira, interview by Kwabena Mensah, BBC Network Africa program, 0735 GMT 2 March 1987.
6 South African Press Association (SAPA), 1750 GMT 12 Dec 89.
7 Details of the fireforce concept in Chris Cocks, *Fireforce – One Man's War in the Rhodesian Light Infantry* (Alberton: Galago Publishing, 1988) pp. 41–42.
8 *Notícias*, Maputo, 13 October 1987, p. 8.
9 *Zambia Daily Mail*, 31 March 1986, p. 4, and SAPA 1035 GMT 6 May 87.
10 Radio RSA, 0630 GMT 14 October 1986.

2:   The Malawian Connection

11   Rádio Moçambique, 0800 GMT 12 September 1986.
12   AFP in English, 1101 GMT 17 September 1986.
13   Malawi News Agency/Pan-African News Agency, 1035 GMT 13 November 1986.
14   Amade Viajem, op. cit.
15   Minutes of a meeting between 'His Excellency the President of the Republic and a Zimbabwe Military and Security Delegation' held in Maputo from 1545 to 1800 on 16 October 1986.
16   Ibid.
17   Report of the Board of Inquiry into the Accident to Tupolev 134A-3 Aircraft C9–CAA on 19 October 1986 (ISBN 0 621 11239 9).

3:   Changing of the Guard

18   Lettre des Anciens Combattants, *Politique Africaine*, No° 29, March 1988 pp. 115–123.
19   Marcelino dos Santos' eulogy to Samora Machel, in *Notícias*, 29 October 1986, p. 4.
20   *Notícias*, 10 October 1990, p. 8.
21   *Notícias*, 11 October 1990, p. 8.
22   *Notícias*, Maputo, 8 July 1988, p. 1.
23   Author's interview with Manuel António Nasinho da Maia, op. cit.

4:   Britain and Tanzania Assist FAM

24   *Notícias*, 18 November 1985, p. 1.
25   Author's interview with former Mozambican official.
26   *Financial Gazette*, 24 October 1986, p. 11.
27   *The Herald*, 10 and 11 July 1990.
28   *Notícias*, 19 September 1989, p. 1; Radio Maputo, 1800 GMT 23 April 1991.
29   Zimbabwe Broadcasting Corporation, 1600 GMT 24 October 1987.
30   Hermínio Morais, interview with author, Maputo, 9 March 1993.
31   Rádio Moçambique, 1030 GMT 28 June 1991.

5:   Renamo's Response

32   Morais, op. cit.
33   Ibid.
34   Adriano Faustino, interview with author, Maputo, 8 April 1995.
35   Morais, op. cit.
36   Capital Radio, 1500 GMT 20 August 1987.
37   AFP, 0241 GMT 11 September 1987.
38   *Notícias*, 14 September 1987, p. 1.
39   Renamo, *Boletim de Informação Militar* No. 1, January 1988.
40   SAPA, 1538 GMT 31 August 1988.

41 SAPA, 1538 GMT 12 December 1989.
42 Renamo Press Release issued by Luís Serapião, Washington, 14 December 1987.
43 Zimbabwe's Vietnam?, Mozambique Institute, London, p. 3, nd.
44 Welshman Ncube: Horrors of Fifth Brigade cannot be forgiven nor forgotten, *Financial Gazette*, 15 October 1992, p. 3.
45 Catholic Commission for Justice and Peace Report on the 1980s Disturbances in Matabeleland and the Midlands.
   http:/www.mg.co.za/mg/zim/zimtitle.html
46 Morais, op. cit.
47 Richard English, interview by Hilton Fyle, BBC Network Africa Program, 0635 GMT 24 February 1987.
48 *The Washington Post*, 30 December 1986, p. 14.
49 Morais, op. cit.
50 Amade Viajem, op. cit.
51 Author's interview with former FAM member.

6: Recruits and Collaborators

52 *Tempo*, No. 1352, 17 November 1996, pp. 4,9.
53 Confidential report, Ministério das Finanças – Gabinete de Reintegração (Maputo 1992), in Michel Cahen, Dhlakama É Maningue Nice! An Atypical Former Guerrilla in the Mozambican Electoral Campaign, *Transformation* 35 (1998) p. 40.
54 *Domingo*, 18 April 1983, pp. 8,9.
55 *The Star*, 13 March 1990, p. 8.
56 *Africa Analysis*, 23 August 1991, p. 4.
57 CIO Top Secret Memorandum, op. cit., p. 12.
58 Ibid., p. 11.
59 *Mozambiquefile*, September 1993, p. 22.
60 Vareia Manje, interview with author, Maputo, 16 March 1995. Other accounts of alleged collaboration of government forces with Renamo gathered during author's interviews with Olímpio Cambona, head of Renamo's telecommunications department, and his deputy, Amade Viajem, in Maputo between 10 and 15 February 1993.
61 Amade Viajem, op. cit.

7: The Washington Lobby

62 Rádio Moçambique, 1900 GMT 15 January 1985; *Notícias*, 18 February 1985, p. 1.
63 BBC Focus on Africa program, 1709 GMT 25 May 1985.
64 *Expresso*, 8 September 1984, pp. 12–15.
65 *Rand Daily Mail*, 9 March 1985, p. 4.
66 *The Star*, 19 May 1985, p. 10; 12 July 1985, p. 2.
67 Radio Maputo, 1100 GMT 19 July 1985.
68 Meeting between 'His Excellency the President of the Republic and a Zimbabwe military and security delegation', op. cit. pp. 5,6.

69   *International Herald Tribune*, 21–22 September 1985.
70   *Human Events*, 8 November 1986.
71   *Current Documents*, 1986, p. 631.
72   *The Times*, 7 March 1987.
73   Rádio Moçambique, 1800 GMT 3 February 1987.
74   Dan Burton to Ronald Reagan, Washington, 29 April 1987.
75   Congressional Record – Senate. Vol. 133, No. 69, 1 May 1987, p. 5785.
76   Bob Dole to George Schultz and Peter McPherson in Congressional Record–Senate, ibid.
77   Senator Jesse Helms to Luis Serapião, 6 March 1987; Serapião to Helms, 9 March 1987.
78   Jack Kemp to Afonso Dhlakama, 30 September 1987.
79   *International Herald Tribune*, 12 November 1987, p. 5.
80   Frelimo Party Political Bureau communiqué, Rádio Moçambique, 1400 GMT 22 July 1987.
81   Robert Gersony, Summary of Mozambican Refugee Accounts of Principally Conflict-Related Experience in Mozambique, US Department of State, Bureau for Refugee Program, Washington DC, April 1988.
82   *Domingo*, 28 September 1986, p. 1.
83   Author's interview with Alberto Leão Fino, Renamo's former intelligence chief, Inhambane Province, Inhassoro, 8 September 1994; and former Snasp operative; Mário Ferro: Os BA's vieram a Homoíne (3), *Notícias*, Maputo, 27 July 1987 p. 3.
84   *Notícias*, 7 September 1989, p. 8.

EPILOG

1   Joaquim Chissano, news conference, Maputo, Rádio Moçambique, 1800 GMT 17 Jul 1989.
2   Viajem, op. cit.
3   Renamo's 16-point agenda issued in Nairobi on 15 August 1989 in André Thomashausen, War and Peace in Mozambique, unpublished paper, Pretoria, November 1999.
4   André Thomashausen, ibid.
5   Rádio Moçambique, 0700 GMT 11 July 1990.
6   Acordo General de Paz, Rome, 4 October 1992.
7   Joaquim Chissano, news conference, Maputo, Rádio Moçambique, Oct 1989.
8   Acordo General de Paz, op. cit.

Index

.